T5-CVL-615

# OXFORD THEOLOGICAL MONOGRAPHS

# OXFORD THEOLOGICAL MONOGRAPHS

THE PRINCIPLE OF RESERVE IN THE WRITINGS OF JOHN HENRY NEWMAN
R. C. Selby (1975)

THE COSMIC CHRIST IN ORIGEN AND TEILHARD DE CHARDIN
A Comparative Study
J. A. Lyons (1982)

THE HIDDEN GOD
Samuel E. Balentine (1983)

PROTESTANT REFORMERS IN ELIZABETHAN OXFORD
C. M. Dent (1983)

REVELATORY POSITIVISM?
Barth's Earliest Theology and the Marburg School
Simon Fisher (1988)

THE COMMUNION OF SAINTS
Radical Puritan and Separatist Ecclesiology 1570–1625
S. Brachlow (1988)

PROBABILITY AND THEISTIC EXPLANATION
Robert Prevost (1990)

VERBAL ASPECT IN NEW TESTAMENT GREEK
Buist M. Fanning (1990)

'WORKING THE EARTH OF THE HEART'
The Messalian Controversy in History, Texts, and Language to AD 431
Columba Stewart, OSB (1991)

THE LORDSHIP OF CHRIST
Ernst Käsemann's Interpretation of Paul's Theology
David V. Way (1991)

BEAUTY AND REVELATION IN THE THOUGHT OF SAINT AUGUSTINE
Carol Harrison (1992)

# The Muratorian Fragment and the Development of the Canon

GEOFFREY MARK HAHNEMAN

CLARENDON PRESS · OXFORD
1992

*Oxford University Press, Walton Street, Oxford* OX2 6DP
*Oxford New York Toronto*
*Delhi Bombay Calcutta Madras Karachi*
*Petaling Jaya Singapore Hong Kong Tokyo*
*Nairobi Dar es Salaam Cape Town*
*Melbourne Auckland*
*and associated companies in*
*Berlin Ibadan*

*Oxford is a trade mark of Oxford University Press*

*Published in the United States*
*by Oxford University Press, New York*



*British Library Cataloguing in Publication Data*
*Data available*

*Library of Congress Cataloging in Publication Data*
*The Muratorian fragment and the development of the canon*
*Geoffrey Mark Hahneman.*
*(Oxford theological monographs)*
*Includes bibliographical references.*
*1. Muratorian fragment. 2. Bible. N.T.—Canon. I. Title.*
*II. Series.*
*BS2320.H34 1992 225.1′2—dc20 92–4184*
*ISBN 0–19–826341–4*

*Typeset by Joshua Associates Ltd, Oxford*
*Printed in Great Britain by*
*Bookcraft (Bath) Ltd, Midsomer Norton, Avon*

DEDICATED

to my mother

*requiescat in pace*

# ACKNOWLEDGEMENTS

THIS present work owes its existence to studies begun at Virginia Theological Seminary, in Alexandria, Virginia, under the direction of the Revd Canon Reginald Fuller, then Professor of New Testament. After serving as a curate at the Church of the Advent in Boston, I continued these studies at Christ Church, Oxford, under the careful guidance of the Revd Canon Maurice Wiles, Regius Professor of Divinity, whose criticisms and encouragement played a large part in the direction of this study.

My studies at Oxford, however, would not have been possible without the kind benefaction of the Episcopal Church Foundation and more particularly, that of Garrett and Diane Carlson. To them I am indebted for the opportunity to have pursued and completed my work. However, even this would not have been possible without the creative distraction of my children Clare, Nicholas, Catherine and Stephen, and especially without the loving care, support, and many sacrifices of my wonderful wife Kimberly. To them I am far more indebted for the life I enjoy.

The final form of this work exists only after the conscientious editing of my wife and Professor Wiles, but also the careful attention of Len Scott and Leofranc Holford-Strevens. For their assistance, I am most grateful.

GEOFFREY HAHNEMAN

*The Cathedral Church of St Mark*
*Minneapolis, Minnesota*

# CONTENTS

# ABBREVIATIONS

| | |
|---|---|
| *AF* | *The Apostolic Fathers*, ed. J. B. Lightfoot, 2nd edn., 2 pts in 5 vols. (London, 1889–90) |
| *AJT* | *American Journal of Theology* |
| *ANZTR* | *Australian and New Zealand Theological Review* |
| *BJRL* | *Bulletin of the John Rylands Library* |
| *CBQ* | *Catholic Biblical Quarterly* |
| *CQR* | *Church Quarterly Review* |
| *DCB* | *Dictionary of Christian Biography*, ed. W. Smith and H. Wace, 4 vols. (London, 1877–87) |
| *FP* | *Florilegium Patristicum* |
| GCS | Die griechischen christlichen Schriftsteller der ersten drei Jahrhunderte |
| *HeyJ* | *Heythrop Journal* |
| *HTR* | *Harvard Theological Review* |
| *HTSt* | *Harvard Theological Studies* |
| *IDB* | *The Interpreter's Dictionary of the Bible*, ed. G. A. Buttrick *et al.*, 4 vols. (New York, 1962) |
| *JBL* | *Journal of Biblical Literature* |
| *JTS* | *Journal of Theological Studies* |
| KT | Kleine Texte für Vorlesungen und Übungen |
| *LCC* | *Library of Christian Classics* |
| *NKZ* | *Neue kirchliche Zeitschrift* |
| *NTSt* | *New Testament Studies* |
| *PG* | *Patrologiae Cursus Completus*, *Series Graeca*, ed. J. P. Migne, 162 vols. (Paris, 1857–66) |
| *RBén* | *Revue bénédictine* |
| *RBib* | *Revue biblique* |
| *StudBib* | *Studia Biblica* |
| *StudEvan* | *Studia Evangelica* |
| *StudPat* | *Studia Patristica* |
| *TDNT* | *Theological Dictionary of the New Testament*, ed. G. Kittel, trans. G. W. Bromiley, 10 vols. (Grand Rapids, Mich., 1968–78) |
| *TSt* | *Theological Studies* |
| TU | Texte und Untersuchungen |
| TxSt | Texts and Studies |
| *VC* | *Vigiliae Christianae* |
| *WUNT* | *Wissenschaftliche Untersuchungen zum Neuen Testament* |

| | |
|---|---|
| *ZKG* | *Zeitschrift für Kirchengeschichte* |
| *ZNW* | *Zeitschrift für neutestamentliche Wissenschaft* |
| *ZWT* | *Zeitschrift für wissenschaftliche Theologie* |

# INTRODUCTION

In 1964, Albert C. Sundberg, Jr., published a distinguished work on the Old Testament in the early Church.[1] This well-received study refuted the hypothesis of an Alexandrian Jewish canon and radically changed the traditional understanding of the formation of the Christian Old Testament. It is now widely believed that the Christian Church did not receive a closed canon of scripture from Judaism but a looser collection of sacred writings. The Jewish canon appears not to have been established until after the Christians had left the synagogues. It was not until the third century and later that the Christians came to struggle with the problem of establishing their own canon of Jewish writings. This explains why the Old Testament of the early church differs from the Jewish canon.

The year after Sundberg published his monograph, and as a consequence of this earlier work, he argued at the Third International Congress on New Testament Studies (Oxford, 1965) for a revision of the history of the New Testament canon.[2] Sundberg insisted that 'the struggle to determine the Old Testament canon in the church plays a more significant role, at least as paralleling more closely the canonization of the New Testament in point of time and, perhaps, as an influencing factor in the formation of the New Testament canon'.[3] Such a revision, Sundberg acknowledged, would entail moving the decisive period of New Testament canonical history from the end of the second century into the fourth.

The traditional belief that a New Testament canon was established by the end of the second century was based primarily upon the evidence of the Muratorian Fragment in the West and the Peshitta in the East.[4] The tradition was

[1] A. C. Sundberg, Jr., *The Old Testament of the Early Church* (hereafter, *Old Testament*) (London, 1964).

[2] Id., 'Towards a Revised History of the New Testament Canon' (hereafter 'Revised History'), *StudEvan* 4/1 (1968), 452–61.

[3] Ibid., 'Revised History', 461.

[4] B. F. Westcott, *A General Survey of the History of the Canon of the New Testament* (hereafter *Canon of the New Testament*), 4th edn. (London, 1875).

thought to be further supported by the existence in the second century of the Old Latin versions and by the scriptural references of Irenaeus of Lyons, Clement of Alexandria, and Tertullian in North Africa. As Westcott wrote, 'From the close of the second century the history of the Canon is simple, and its proof clear.'[5] This history of the New Testament canon has remained virtually unaltered for the last 130 years.

However, the traditional argument for a New Testament canon at the end of the second century has been weakened by the results of several modern studies. It has now been shown, for instance, that the Peshitta did not originate until at least the late fourth century and is thus not a witness to a second-century New Testament canon. The Old Latin versions are no longer viewed as a unity and therefore do not represent a 'canon', but only scattered translations, much like the Old Syriac versions. As F. Kenyon wrote, 'we are not to suppose that the whole of the New Testament was translated at any one time, but at various times somewhat unliterary versions of different books were made, which were subject to haphazard revision and improvement at different times and in different localities'.[6] Moreover, the demonstration of extensive use of non-canonical writings by Clement of Alexandria, and to a lesser degree by Irenaeus and Tertullian, further weakened the hypothesis. The redating of the so-called Anti-Marcionite and Monarchian prologues to the gospels has also undermined the tradition of a second-century core New Testament. R. P. C. Hanson's conclusion that Clement of Alexandria and Origen had no concept of a New Testament canon in the third century showed yet another serious weakness in the traditional hypothesis.[7]

It is quite possible [he wrote] that the Alexandrian school was unusual in their attitude to the Canon. We have the evidence of the Muratorian Canon to show that in the time of Clement of Alexandria the 'closed canon' was a conception known at Rome . . . But certainly

[5] Westcott, *Canon of the New Testament*, 6.

[6] F. Kenyon, *Our Bible and the Ancient Manuscripts*, rev. A. W. Adams (London, 1958), 239.

[7] R. P. C. Hanson, *Origen's Doctrine of Tradition* (London, 1954), 133, 137, 143–4, 182–3.

in Alexandria in the time of Clement and Origen the conception of a closed 'apostolic canon' is unknown.[8]

Thus the traditional hypothesis of a core New Testament canon at the end of the second century has now become dependent primarily upon the evidence of the Muratorian Fragment.

A significant factor in Sundberg's call for a revised history of the formation of the New Testament was the redating of the Muratorian Fragment, for which he argued at the Oxford Congress in 1965. However, it was not until 1973 that Sundberg published in full his argument for the redating of the Fragment.[9] He questioned the traditional late second-century dating and Western provenance generally assigned to the Fragment since its publication in 1740. Instead he suggested an early fourth-century date and an Eastern (Syrian/Palestinian) provenance. The idea of a later date for the Fragment was known to Westcott, who noted that 'the opinions of those who assign it to the fourth century . . . scarcely deserve mention'.[10] Similarly Sundberg's argument has generally been dismissed by scholars, usually in footnotes, as 'not convincing', 'arbitrary', 'questionable', not persuasive, or raising more problems than it solves.[11] E. Ferguson has published the only substantial rebuttal to Sundberg, but one that is still brief and dismissive.[12] Yet a few scholars have been persuaded by Sundberg's argument.[13] And Norman Perrin and Dennis Duling recognized the

[8] Ibid. 143–4.

[9] Sundberg, 'Canon Muratori: A Fourth-Century List' (hereafter 'Canon Muratori'), *HTR* 66 (1973), 1–41; Sundberg had earlier published an outline of his argument in 'Revised History', 458–9.

[10] Westcott, *Canon of the New Testament*, 210.

[11] e.g. J. D. Quinn, '$P^{46}$—The Pauline Canon?', *CBQ* 36 (1974), 379–85, at 382 n. 21; W. G. Kümmel, *Introduction to the New Testament*, trans. H. C. Kee (London, 1975), 492 n. 69; John A. T. Robinson, *Redating the New Testament* (London, 1976), 319 n. 41; C. F. D. Moule, *The Birth of the New Testament* (London, 1981), 260 n. 1; R. E. Brown, *The Epistles of John* (New York, 1982), 10 n. 14; W. R. Farmer and D. M. Farkasfalvy, *The Formation of the New Testament Canon* (New York, 1983), 60; H. Y. Gamble, *The New Testament Canon: Its Making and Meaning* (Philadelphia, 1985), 32 n. 25; Farkasfalvy, 'The Ecclesial Setting of Pseudepigraphy in Second Peter and Its Role in the Formation of the Canon', *The Second Century* 5 (1985–6), 3–29, at 29 n. 50.

[12] E. Ferguson, 'Canon Muratori: Date and Provenance', *StudPat* 17/2 (1982), 677–83.

[13] e.g. N. A. Dahl, 'The Origin of the Earliest Prologues to the Pauline Letters', *Semeia* 12 (1978), 233–77, at 237; R. Collins, *Introduction to the New Testament* (London, 1983), 35.

importance of the question, noting that 'if he is correct, one of the major turning points in the development of the canon cannot be sustained as is usual'.[14]

Sundberg's hypothesis deserves serious study and consideration because the date of the Muratorian Fragment is so crucial to the common understanding of the history of the New Testament. The present work will confirm Sundberg's argument that the traditional dating for the Fragment cannot be sustained. Based upon a careful analysis of its traditional dating and its place in the history of the canon, it will suggest an Eastern provenance and a fourth-century date for the Fragment. It will also reinforce Sundberg's call for a revised history of the New Testament canon, and will sketch a development of the Christian Bible that is more gradual in its formation and that culminates not at the end of the second century, but in the midst of the fourth.

[14] N. Perrin and D. C. Duling, *The New Testament: An Introduction* (London, 1982), 442 n. 3.

# 1

# BACKGROUND OF THE MURATORIAN FRAGMENT

BETWEEN the years 1738 and 1742, Lodovico Antonio Muratori (1672–1750), archivist and librarian at Modena (1700–50), edited a collection of seventy-five essays in six volumes on different historical themes, entitled *Antiquitates Italicae Medii Aevi*. In the third volume of this collection (Milan, 1740), Muratori included an early list of the books of the New Testament from a codex in the Ambrosian Library at Milan (I. 101 sup.), where he was formerly a librarian (1695–1700). His purpose in publishing this document, the so-called Muratorian Fragment, was to exhibit a striking example from medieval Italy of the barbarism of some scribal transcriptions.[1]

The Muratorian Fragment consists of only 85 lines;[2] the beginning and probably the end are missing, for the Fragment commences in the midst of a sentence and ends abruptly.[3] In the text as printed below, lines in bold type are rubricated in the manuscript; letters in parentheses were erased by corrector(s); those italicized were added by corrector(s) either by substitution or superscription.[4]

[1] The Muratorian Fragment is located within *Dissertatio XLIII* (cols. 807–80), entitled 'De Literarum Statu, neglectu, & cultura in Italia post Barbaros in eam invectos usque ad Anum Christi Millesimum Centesimum', at cols. 851–6.

[2] A facsimile tracing was published in S. P. Tregelles, *Canon Muratorianus* (Oxford, 1867); photographs were first published in S. Ritter, 'Il Fragmento Muratoriano', *Revista di archeologia cristiana*, 3 (1926), 226–31; see also editions in E. S. Buchanan, 'The Codex Muratorianus', *JTS* 9 (1907), 537–45; G. Rauschen, 'Monumenta Minora Saeculi Secundi', *FP* 3 (1914), 24–34; H. Lietzmann, *Das Muratorische Fragment und die monarchianischen Prologe zu den Evangelien* (KT 1; Bonn, 1908); A. Schaefer and M. Meinertz, *Einleitung in das Neue Testament* (Paderborn, 1949), 410–14.

[3] This reading is taken from Tregelles, 17–20, with whom I concur with the following emendations: *proferam* > *proferat* (l. 28); *prodecessuris* > *prodecessoris* (l. 48); *non nisi* > *nonnisi* (l. 49); *efesius* > *efesios* (l. 51); *assian(u)om* > *assianum* (l. 84), where a corrector appears to have made a *u* into an *o*.

[4] Buchanan, 539, 540–2, suggested that two different correctors ($m^1$ and $m^2$) corrected the Fragment, but that neither of them was more than a century removed from m*.

[10r] quibus tamen Interfuit et ita posuit ·
**tertio euangelii librum sec(a)*u*ndo Lucan**
Lucas Iste medicus post a*s*censum xp̃i.
Cum eo Paulus quasi ut iuris studiosum.
Secundum adsumsisset numeni suo
ex opinione concr*ib*set dñm tamen nec Ipse
(d)uidit in carne et idẽ pro*ut* asequi potuit ·
Ita et ad natiuitate Iohannis incipet dicere.
**quarti euangeliorum Iohannis ex decipolis**
cohortantibus condescipulis et ep̃s suis
dixit conieiunate mihi · odie triduo et quid
cuique fuerit reuelatum alterutrum
nobis ennarremus eadem nocte reue
latum andreae ex apostolis ut recognis
centibus cuntis Iohannis suo nomine
cun*c*ta discrib*e*ret et ideo licit uaria sin
culis euangeliorum libris principia
doceantur Nihil tamen differt creden
tium f(e)*i*dei cum uno ac principali s̃pũ de
clarata sint in omnibus omnia de natiui
tate de passione de resurrectione
de conue*r*satione cum decipulis suis
ac de gemino eius aduentu
Primo In humilitate dispectus quod (fo
tu) secundum pote*s*tate regali pre
clarum quod foturum est. quid ergo
mirum si Iohannes tam constanter
sincula etiã In epistulis suis proferat
dicens In semeipsu Quae uidimus oculis
nostris et auribus audiuimus et manus
nostrae palpauerunt haec scripsimus (uobis)
[10v] Sic enim non solum uisurem sed (&) auditorem
sed et scriptorẽ omnium mirabiliũ dñi per ordi
nem profetetur Acta autẽ omniu apostolorum
sub uno libro scribta sunt Lucas obtime theofi
le conprindit quia sub praesentia eius singula
gerebantur sicut(e) et semote passionẽ Petri
euidenter declarat Sed (&) profectionẽ pauli a(d)*b* ur
be(s) ad spaniã proficescentis Epistulae autem
Pauli quae a quo loco uel qua ex causa directe
sint uolen(ta)tibus intellegere Ipse declarant
Primũ omnium corintheis scysmae heresis In
terdicens deIncepsb callae*c*tis circumcisione

Romanis autē or(ni)dine scripturarum sed (et)
principium earum (osd) esse xp̄m Intimans
prolexius scripsit de quibus sincolis Neces
se est ad nobis desputari Cum ipse beatus
apostolus paulus sequens prodecessoris sui
Iohannis ordinē nonnisi (c)*n*omenatī semptaē
eccles(e)*ii*s scribat ordine tali a corenthios
prima.ad efesios seconda ad philippinses ter
tia ad colosensis quarta ad calatas quin
ta ad tensaolenecinsis sexta. ad romanos
septima Uerum cor(e)*i*ntheis et t*h*esaolecen
sibus licet pro correbtione Iteretur una
tamen per omnem orbem terrae ecclesia
deffusa esse denoscitur Et Iohannis eñi In a
pocalebsy licet septē eccleseis scribat
tamen omnibus dicit uerū ad filemonem una ·
et at titū una et ad tymotheū duas pro affec
to et dilectione In honore tamen eclesiae ca
tholice In ordinatione eclesiastice
[11$^{r}$] d(e)*i*scepline s̄cificate sunt Fertur etiam ad
Laudecenses alia ad alexandrinos Pauli no
mine fincte ad he*re*sem marcionis et alia plu
ra quae In c(h)atholicam eclesiam recepi non
potest Fel enim cum melle misceri non con
cruit epistola sane Iude et superscrictio
Iohannis duas In catholica habentur Et sapi
entia ab amicis salomonis in honorē ipsius
scripta apocalapse etiam Iohanis et Pe
tri tantum recip(e)*i*mus quam quidam ex nos
tris legi In eclesia nolunt Pastorem uero
nuperrim e(t) temporibus nostris In urbe
roma herma conscripsit sedente cathe
tra urbis romae aeclesiae Pio ep̄s frat*re*(r)
eius et ideo legi eum quidē Oportet se pu
plicare uero In eclesia populo Neque inter
profe(*)tas conpletum numero Neque Inter
apostolos In finē temporum potest.
Arsinoi autem seu ualentini. uel mitiad(ei)*i*s
nihil In totum recipemus. Qui etiam nouū
psalmorum librum marcioni conscripse
runt una cum basilide assianum catafry
cum con*s*titutorem

A passage from Ambrose (*De Abraham*, 1.3.15) which follows the Muratorian Fragment in the codex (fo. 11$^r$, l. 24–fo. 11$^v$, l. 27) confirms the carelessness of the scribe because the entire fragment, some thirty-five lines, is accidentally repeated immediately after itself (fo. 11$^v$, l. 27–fo. 12$^r$, l. 25). Thus the codex contains two copies of the same text, one after another, presumably from the same original. Moreover in the codex fos. 11$^v$ and 12$^r$, which open opposite each other, both commence with the same line, so that twenty-five lines of the repeated passage are directly in front of each other. Yet the scribe appeared not to be conscious of the repetition. The substantial differences between the two versions of the repeated passage provide an index of the kind and frequency of scribal errors to be found in the Fragment.[5]

According to Westcott, there are in the duplicated portion 'thirty unquestionable clerical blunders including one important omission, two other omissions which destroy the sense completely, one substitution equally destructive of the sense, and four changes which appear to be intentional and false alterations'.[6] To these serious errors must be added the persistent misuse and omission of certain letters. It appears from the repetition of several obvious mistakes in the duplicated portion from Ambrose, namely 'ad cratia', 'docit', 'homilior', 'dilectis' (for *delictis*), that the scribe was particularly careless.

If such serious errors exist in a copy of only thirty-five lines, then it is very unlikely that similar errors in transcription would not occur in a passage like the Fragment which is almost two and a half times as long. The folio which precedes the Fragment also reveals the same kind of ignorance of construction, the same false criticism, and the same confusion of letters and terminations. Therefore the carelessness of this particular scribe is probably responsible for a significant portion of the barbarous transcription of the Fragment.

[5] Westcott, *Canon of the New Testament*, 522–3; note that he appears to have overlooked in his listing *dei* (fo. 11$^r$, l. 24) which was omitted in the repeated passage (fo. 11$^v$, l. 23).

[6] Ibid. 523.

## EXCERPTS FROM THE FRAGMENT

Excerpts from the Muratorian Fragment discovered in a Prologue to Paul's Epistles confirm that the poor Latin of the Fragment is not that of the original. The Prologue is contained in three eleventh-century and one twelfth-century Latin manuscript of the *Corpus Paulinum* at the Benedictine monastery on Monte Cassino, and was first published in *Miscellanea Cassinese*, ii (1897);[7] it includes parts of twenty-four lines of the Fragment, namely ll. 42–50 (*tali*); ll. 54 (*uerum*)–57 (*denoscitur*); ll. 63 (*fertur*)–68 (*concruit*); and ll. 81–5. The text is as follows (sentences in bold type are excerpts from the Fragment):[8]

**Primo omnium Corinthis scisma heresis interdicens. deinde Galathis circumcisionem, Romanis autem, ordinem scripturarum sed et praecipuum earum esse Christum intimans, prolixius scripsit. de quibus singulis necesse est nobis disputare, cum ipse beatus apostolus Paulus sequens precessoris sui Johannis ordinem, nonnisi nominatim, septem aecclesiis scripsit ordine tali** (nam) cum Romanis ita agit apostolus Paulus quasi cum incipientibus, qui post gentilitatem et initia fidei sortiantur et perveniant ad spem vitae aeter nae, multa de phisicis rationibus insinuat, multa de scripturis divinis; ad Corinthios prima consecutos iam fidem non recte conversantes obiurgat; ad Corinthios secunda contristatos quidem sed emendatos ostendit; Galatas in fide ipsa peccantes et ad Iudaismum declinantes exponit; Ephesios quia incipiunt et custodiunt laudat, quod ea quae acceperunt servaverunt; Philippenses quod in quo crediderunt servantes ad fructum pervenerunt; Colosenses collaudat quia velud ignotis scribit et accepto nuntio ab Epafra custodisse evangelium

[7] 'Fragmentum Muratorianum. Iuxta Codices Casinenses' (hereafter, 'Fragmentum Muratorianum'), 1–5, *Miscellanea Cassinese, ossia nuovi contributi alla storia, alle scienze e arti religiose, raccolti e illustrati per cura dei PP, Benedettini di Montecassino*, Anno I, Parte I, Fasc. I: Memorie e Notizie (Nova); Parte II, Fasc. I: Documenti (Vetera) (Tipografia di Montecassino, 1897); which presented the reading of Cod. Cas. 349, saec. xi (C), with critical notes.

[8] This edition is from A. Harnack, 'Excerpts aus dem Muratorischen Fragment (saec. xi et xii)' (hereafter, 'Excerpte'), *Theologische Literaturzeitung*, 23 (1898), 131–4, who presented the most common readings from the Benedictine texts.

gratulatur; Thesalonicenses prima in opere et fide crevisse gloriatur; in secunda praeterea quod et persecutionem passi in fide perseveraverint, quos et sanctos appellat, ut illos qui in Iudaeam Christum confessi persecutiones fortiter tolerarunt; (ad) Hebraeos, ad quorum similitudinem passi sunt Thesalonicenses, ut in mandatis perseveratnes persecutiones promptissime patiantur. **fertur etiam ad Laudicenses, aliam ad Alexandrinos, Pauli nomine ficte, ad heresim Marcionis, et alia plura quae in aecclesia catholica recipi non oportet. fel enim cum melle miscui non congruit, Arsinofa autem seu Valentini, vel Mitiadis, nihil in totum recipimus, qui etiam novum psalmorum librum Marcionis conscripserunt, una cum Basilide (sive) Asyano Catafrigum consitutorem, verum Corinthis, et Thesalonicensibus licet procorreptione uteretur, una tamen per omnem orbem terrae aecclesia catholica diffusa esse dinoscitur.** Triplex igitur Hebraeorum esse dinoscitur lingua. Heber unde Hebrei dicti sunt. Hanc linguam Moyses a domino legem accepit et tradidit, nam et Chaldeorum est alia, quam imperiti Iudaei vel Syri hebraeam fingunt, et ideo in multis male interpretes apud illos dissonat multa, apud nos autem auctor est beatus apostolus Paulus dicens, se Hebraeum ex Hebraeis, hoc est, de tribu Beniamin.

The Benedictine manuscripts, nos. 235 ($C^2$), 349 (C), 535 ($C^3$), 552 ($C^1$), contain only minor deviations among themselves. $C^2$ has some notable additions and omissions and changes in order, but none of these occur among the passages which correspond with the Muratorian Fragment.[9] The Latin of the excerpts in the later Benedictine manuscripts is significantly better than that in Muratori's Fragment and this suggests a source for the Benedictine manuscripts not directly dependent upon the Muratorian Fragment. Moreover, the Benedictine texts present several important new readings.

## THE LANGUAGE OF THE FRAGMENT

Several scholars, such as J. Donaldson, F. H. Hesse, A. Harnack, and A. A. T. Ehrhardt, have suggested that the Frag-

[9] 'Fragmentum Muratorianum', 1–5; Harnack, 'Excerpte', 132.

ment was originally composed in Latin.[10] Recent investigations by C. Mohrmann have demonstrated that the transition in language from Greek to Latin had begun in the Christian community of Rome as early as the middle of the second century.[11] An original composition in Latin is thus compatible with any time after that. But the most recent and detailed study by J. Campos argues, on the basis of a careful grammatical and philological analysis, that the Latin of the Fragment in fact originates from the later fourth century.[12] He carefully examined the spelling, vocabulary, and syntax of the Fragment's Latin and confirmed that many of the orthographic errors result from the common spelling and pronunciation of later Latin.[13] According to Campos:

1. The terminations *es* and *is* have been easily confused since the third century,[14] cf. 'Iohannis' for *Iohannes* (ll. 9, 15, 57), 'colosensis' for *colossenses* (ll. 52–3), 'tensaolenecinsis' for *thessalonicenses* (l. 53).

2. In tonic syllables *i* seems to have been written for the closed *e* in almost the entire empire since the third century,[15] cf. 'discriberet' for *describeret* (l. 16), 'comprindit' for *comprehendit* (l. 36), 'philippinses' for *philippenses* (l. 51).

3. The use of *u* for the long *o* also first appears in the third century and is more frequent in even later centuries,[16] cf. 'numeni' for *nomine* (l. 5), 'visurem' for *visorem* (l. 32); 'completum' for *completo* (l. 79).

4. The use of *o* for short *u* is frequent in the fourth century,[17] cf. 'decipolis' for *discipulis* (l. 9), 'foit' for *fuit* (l. 25), 'foturum' for *futurum*

[10] J. Donaldson, *A Critical History of Christian Literature and Doctrine*, 3 vols. (London, 1866), iii. 204, 210–11; F. H. Hesse, *Das Muratorische Fragment* (Giessen, 1873), 25–39; Harnack, 'Über den Verfasser und den literarischen Charakter des Muratorischen Fragments' (hereafter, 'Über den Verfasser'), *ZNW* 24 (1925), 1–16; A. A. T. Ehrhardt, 'The Gospels in the Muratorian Fragment', *Ostkirchliche Studien*, 2 (1953), 121–38.

[11] C. Mohrmann, 'Les origines de la latinité chrétienné à Rome', *VC* 3 (1949), 67–106, 163–83; cf. ead., 'Le Latin langue de la chrétiente occidentale', *Aevum*, 24 (1950), 133–61; ead., 'Quelques observations sur l'originalité de la littérature chrétienne', *Rivista di storia della Chiesa in Italia*, 4 (1950), 153–63; ead., 'L'étude de la latinité chrétienne: État de la question, méthodes, résultats', *Conférences de l'Institut de linguistique de l'Université de Paris*, 10 (1950–1), 125–41.

[12] J. Campos, 'Época del Fragmento Muratoriano', *Helmantica: Revista de Humanidades Clásicas*, 11 (1960), 485–96.

[13] Ibid. 491–3.

[14] Cf. H. Schuchardt, *Der Vokalismus des Vulgärlateins*, 3 vols. (Leipzig, 1866–8), i. 244–9, 258, 279–80; ii. 48–9.

[15] Cf. A. Audollent, *Defixionum Tabellae* (Paris, 1904), 535; A. Carnoy, *Le Latin d'Espagne d'après les inscriptions* (Louvain, 1902), 15–16.

[16] Cf. W. M. Lindsay, *The Latin Language* (Oxford, 1894), 33–4; Schuchardt, ii. 91–149.

[17] Cf. Lindsay, 29–30; Schuchardt, ii. 149–91.

(l. 26), 'sincolis' for *singulis* (l. 46), 'soi' for *sui* (l. 48), 'seconda' for *secunda* (l. 51).

5. In Italy the exchange of *e* for *i* is extensive during the fourth to sixth centuries,[18] cf. 'numeni' for *nomine* (l. 5), 'decipolis' for *discipulis* (l. 9), 'condescipulis' for *condiscipulis* (l. 10), 'decipulis' for *discipulis* (l. 22), 'profetetur' for *profitetur* (l. 34), 'corintheis' for *Corinthiis* (ll. 42, 54), 'prolexius' for *prolixius* (l. 46), 'desputari' for *disputari* (l. 47), 'nomenatim' for *nominatim* (l. 49), 'deffussa' for *diffusa* (l. 57), 'denoscitur' for *dinoscitur* (ll. 57–8), 'descepline' for *disciplinae* (l. 63), 'Laudecenses' for *Laodicenses* (l. 64), 'recepi' for *recipi* (l. 66), 'recipemus' for *recipimus* (l. 82).

6. The change of *it* to *et* and the inverse in verbal termination seems to have been common only since the second half of the fourth century,[19] cf. 'conscribset' for *conscripsit* (l. 6), 'incipet' for *incepit* (l. 8), 'licit' for *licet* (l. 16).

7. The use of *o* for the termination *um* is also very frequent in the *Peregrinatio Etheriae* (e.g. 4–5) and in Gregory the Great and Gregory of Tours,[20] cf. 'tertio' for *tertium* (l. 2), 'secundo' for *secundum* (l. 2), 'eo' for *eum* (l. 4).

Thus the Fragment reveals numerous examples of the spelling and pronunciation of Latin in the third and fourth centuries. Campos argued that the Latin of the Fragment originates from not earlier than the last decade of the fourth century, since some forms are not paralleled until very late in the second half of that century. Many of the orthographic mistakes of the Fragment attributed to later Latin suggest that an exemplar(s) of the Fragment was written by dictation, a common enough practice in many monastic scriptoria.

Campos, however, reinforced a late dating for the Latin of the Fragment by vocabulary, since the Fragment contains terms which first appear only from the end of the fourth century. For instance, *intimans* (l. 45) is a word that was employed by the author of the *Historia Augusta* (*c.* 400), but does not occur in classical or post-classical Latin.[21] *Visor* (l. 32) appears initially in Augustine (*c.* 386).[22] *Per ordinem* (ll. 33–4) is first found in the Old Testament Vulgate of Jerome (*c.* 392–407). The appearance of the word *palpaverunt* when quoting 1 John 1: 1 in the Fragment

[18] Cf. Carnoy, 15–17; Lindsay, 29–30; Schuchardt, ii. 1–91.

[19] Cf. Schuchardt, i. 258–60, 280–4.

[20] Cf. M. Bonnet, *Le Latin de Grégoire de Tours* (Paris, 1890), 131; Schuchardt, i. 164–5.

[21] Campos, 492–3.

[22] e.g. Augustine, *Contra Acad.* 2. 7, 19.

(ll. 30–4) also suggests a dependence upon Jerome's Latin. The Vulgate and other versions from the Fathers use *contrectaverunt*, *temptaverunt*, or *tractaverunt*, whereas Jerome adopted *palpaverunt* in his exegetical works.[23] The use of these Latin terms (and others)[24] would endorse a Latin original for the Fragment no earlier than the end of the fourth century. Campos argued that the Latin text discloses enough acquaintance with the Vulgate to suggest that it was probably not produced earlier than the first part of the fifth century.

A Greek original for the Fragment was suggested by Muratori when he first published the list in 1740.[25] This view received wide support, for example from Simon de Magistris, C. Bunsen, A. Hilgenfeld, T. Zahn, B. F. Westcott, G. Salmon, J. B. Lightfoot, and S. Ritter.[26] Several scholars, for example Bunsen, Hilgenfeld, and Zahn,[27] have attempted to reproduce the Greek original, a task which is made especially difficult because of the corrupt nature of the Latin text. Lightfoot suggested that the original document was written in Greek verse, like the corresponding lists of Amphilochius and Gregory of Nazianzus, and he produced a suggested Greek original for the Fragment in verse.[28]

The hypothesis of a Greek original has aided in understanding some of the difficult and confusing passages in the Fragment as simply poor translations into Latin. For example, S. P. Tregelles took note of the puzzling passage 'Et sapientia ab amicis salomonis in honorẽ ipsius scripta' (ll. 69–70), which

[23] e.g. Jerome, *In Hiezech.* 12, *In Abd.* 1.

[24] For more examples, see Campos, 492–6; G. Kühn, *Das Muratorische Fragment* (Zurich, 1892), 3–16, also argued for a 4th- or 5th-c. Latin translation from Greek for the Fragment.

[25] Muratori, iii. 851.

[26] S. de Magistris, *Daniel secundum LXX ex Tetraplis Origenis* (Rome, 1772), 467–9, quoted in M. J. Routh, *Reliquiae Sacrae*, 2nd edn., 5 vols. (Oxford, 1846–8), i. 431; C. Bunsen, *Analecta Ante-Nicaena*, 3 vols. (London, 1854), i. 142; A. Hilgenfeld, *Der Kanon und die Kritik des Neuen Testaments in ihrer geschichtlichen Ausbildung und Gestaltung, nebst Herstellung und Beleuchtung des Muratorischen Bruchstücks* (hereafter *Der Kanon*) (Halle, 1863), 40–1; T. Zahn, *Geschichte des neutestamentlichen Kanons* (hereafter *Geschichte*), 2 vols. (Leipzig, 1886–92), ii. 138–9; Westcott, *Canon of the New Testament*, 210–11; G. Salmon, 'Muratorian Fragment', *DCB* iii (London, 1882), 1000–3; J. B. Lightfoot, *AF* I. ii. 407; Ritter, 233.

[27] Bunsen, 142–54; Hilgenfeld, *Historisch-kritische Einleitung in das Neue Testament* (Leipzig, 1875), 97–8; Zahn, *Geschichte*, ii. 141–3.

[28] *AF* I, ii. 407.

is usually translated something like: 'and Wisdom written by friends of Solomon in his honour'.[29] This attribution of The Wisdom of Solomon to his 'friends' is nowhere else known. However, Tregelles observed that Jerome's preface to the Books of Solomon states: 'Aput Hebraeos nusquam est, quin et ipse stylus Graecam eloquentiam redolet, et nonnulli scriptorum veterum hunc esse Judaei Philonis affirmant.' Tregelles could find no writer before Jerome to make this assertion and believed that Jerome based it upon reading a Greek original of the Fragment. The proposed Greek original might have read: *καὶ ἡ Σοφία Σαλομῶνος ὑπὸ Φίλωνος εἰς τὴν τιμὴν αὐτοῦ γραφεῖσα*. It is thus assumed that the Latin translator confused *Φίλωνος* and *φίλων*, so as to translate *ab amicis* instead of *a Philone*. This is especially likely if, as Tregelles suggests, the termination *-ος* was written in much smaller letters as was often the case in very early manuscripts. Jerome may have added the qualifier of *Judaeus* to *Philonis* by an unconscious amplification from familiarity with the name of that Philo (cf. *De vir. ill.* 11). If he had seen a Greek original of the Fragment, then Jerome (*c.* 342–420) would be a *terminus ad quem* for the date of the Fragment.

P. Katz offered an additional example of a possible mistranslation in the Fragment.[30] He noted the enigmatic sentence 'epistola sane Iude et superscrictio Iohannis duas In catholica habentur' (ll. 68–9), which is usually translated something like: 'Certainly the epistle of Jude and two of the aforementioned John are held in the Catholic Church.' The reference would seem to imply an acceptance of Jude and 1 and 2 John. Yet 2 and 3 John are so closely related that one would expect either only 1 John to be named, or all three Johannine epistles, but not 1 and 2. Thus the mention of only two Johannine epistles is believed by many scholars to be particularly confusing. Westcott and Tregelles suggested the context of the Fragment must mean that the two epistles of John mentioned here are 2 or 3, where 1 John would have been implied already in a quotation about the Gospel of John earlier in the Fragment (ll. 26–31).[31]

[29] Tregelles, 50–3.

[30] P. Katz, 'The Johannine Epistles in the Muratorian Canon', *JTS*, NS 8 (1957), 273–4.

[31] Westcott, *Canon of the New Testament*, 216 n. 2; Tregelles, 49–50.

There is, however, some circumstantial evidence of 1 and 2 John circulating independently of 3 John.[32] Irenaeus, for instance, quoted freely from 1 John, and also from 2 John (e.g. *Adv. Haer.* 1.9.3; 3.16.5, 8), but there is no trace of 3 John in his writings. Cyprian and Tertullian also quoted frequently from 1 John, and at the same time in Africa, Aurelius Chullabi quoted from 2 John.[33] Again there is no trace of 3 John. The Latin epitome of Cassiodorus contains notes on the first two epistles of John only. In the Latin *Adumbrationes*, supposed extracts from Clement of Alexandria's Greek *Hypotyposes*, there are only notes on 1 John and a short summary of 'the Second Epistle of John'. It is certain that Clement knew at least one more Johannine epistle besides 1 John, since in one of his quotations he cited 1 John as 'the greater epistle' (*Strom.* 2.15.66). The Greek word μείζονι is comparative and not superlative, which in strictly correct classical Greek would imply that he knew only two. Papias made more than one quotation from 'the former (προτέρας) epistle of John' (Eusebius, *HE* 3.39.17). Likewise this expression of 'former epistle' would in correct classical Greek imply the existence of only two epistles. Yet in Hellenistic and Roman periods the comparative and superlative were frequently confused, and Eusebius himself has a similar expression in a context where he speaks explicitly of three Johannine letters (*HE* 3.24.17, 3.25.2). Moreover, Eusebius (*HE* 6.14.1) and Photius both stated that Clement commented on all the catholic epistles in his *Hypotyposes.* The brevity of 3 John may explain the silence about it. With the possible exception of one phrase in Papias (*HE* 3.39.17), there is no explicit mention of 3 John until the third century, and no clear citation from it until the fourth century. Moreover, whenever 3 John is disputed, 2 John is included with it in the dispute, but never 1 John.[34] Thus, the apparent grouping of only 1 and 2 John in the Fragment is confusing.

[32] A. E. Brooke, *A Critical and Exegetical Commentary on the Johannine Epistles* (Edinburgh, 1912), pp. lviii–lxii; T. W. Manson, 'Entry into Membership of the Early Church, Additional Note: The Johannine Epistles and the Canon of the New Testament', *JTS* 48 (1947), 32–3.

[33] *Sententiae Episcoporum*, no. 81, ed. W. Hartel, 459, quoted in Brooke, p. lix.

[34] Origen and Eusebius, *HE* 6.25.10 and 3.25.3, cf. 3.24.18; Amphilochius, *Iambi ad Seleucum*, 314–15; Jerome, *Der Vir. Ill.* 9, 18.

The interpretation of *catholica* in the passage is also unusual. Elsewhere in the Fragment the Church is always called *ecclesia catholica* (ll. 56, 61, 66, 73, 78), and a mere *catholica* would be uniquely interpreted here as 'Catholic Church'.[35] According to Katz, however, *catholica* frequently stood for *epistola catholica*, and 1 John was sometimes considered to be the catholic epistle *par excellence.* Origen, for instance, frequently spoke of a 'catholic epistle' in regards to not only 1 John, but also Jude, Barnabas, and 1 Peter. Dionysius of Alexandria also applied the word 'catholic' to 1 John, apparently to distinguish it from 2 and 3 John (Eusebius, *HE* 7.25.7, 10). Apollonius (*c.* 197) attributed to the heretic Themison the composition of a 'catholic epistle' in imitation of that of 'the Apostle', probably meaning John (Eusebius, *HE* 5.18.5). This title of 1 John was used long afterwards, for instance by Socrates and Theodoretus in the fifth century, especially in the form *Ἰωάννου ἡ καθολική*.[36]

In the light of these considerations, Katz concluded that the Fragmentist meant two epistles of John in addition to the catholic epistle 1 John. Noting that in the remainder of the sentence, 'Et sapientia ab amicis Salomoni in honorem ipsius scripta', *ab amicis* is most likely a mistranslation of *ὑπὸ Φίλωνος*, Katz suggested that the confusion with the Johannine epistles may also lie in the translation. He suggested a Greek original of *δύο σὺν καθολικῇ*, which was simply transliterated into *dua(e) sin catholica* in the Latin of the Fragment.[37] Katz added that the prevailing meaning of *σύν* at that time was 'in addition to' and not 'with', which would have been expressed by *μετά*. Katz's suggested Greek would be translated something like: 'Certainly the epistle of Jude and two [epistles] of the aforementioned John are held in addition to the catholic [epistle].'

The fact that several of the confusing passages in the Fragment may be explained by a mistranslation from Greek gives further strong support to the case for a Greek original for the Fragment. However, if the traditional dating of the Fragment is

[35] (*a*)*ecclesia catholica* in the Benedictine text (ll. 39–40) is probably the better reading for *ecclesia* alone (l. 56) in the Fragment.

[36] A. Jülicher, *An Introduction to the New Testament*, trans. J. Ward (London, 1904), 201.

[37] Katz, 274.

questioned, and a Greek original for the Fragment is presumed, then the Fragment would most likely have an Eastern provenance, since Latin replaced Greek as the language of the Western church by the third century.

## THE CODEX MURATORIANUS

The so-called Codex Muratorianus, which contains the Muratorian Fragment, is dated to the seventh or eighth century. This date is suggested by the age of the handwriting and ink of the Codex,[38] and by a two-line inscription on the first page. This inscription assigns the Codex to Columbanus (*c.* 543–615), presumably some time after 612 when he founded a monastery at Bobbio, and attributes the contents to John Chrysostom (*c.* 347–407):

> liber sc̃ti columbani de bobio[39]
> Iohis grisostomi

The Codex contains seventy-six leaves of rather coarse vellum, measuring 27 by 17 cm. It consists of nine gatherings of eight, and four other leaves. Fos. 6 and 74 are detached, and fos. 75 and 76 are conjugate. The fact that the last page (fo. 76ᵛ) is blank suggests that this was the original ending of the Codex. This is confirmed by the contents of fo. 76ʳ, consisting only of a notice of the sum paid to the copyist, in an ancient cursive handwriting which is not that of the scribe himself.

On the top of fo. 11ʳ the scribe wrote the letter I, and at the foot of fo. 17ᵛ he affixed the letter K. Thereafter he signed every eighth leaf on its conclusion with the next consecutive letter, except that he appears to have forgotten to insert the letter O at the foot of fo. 49ᵛ.[40] The final signature of R is found on fo. 73ᵛ. The introduction of these letters would appear to be a means of pagination for the Codex: the scribe intended to sign the first leaf of each gathering. If so, he did not begin until the eleventh

[38] Muratori, iii. 581; Westcott, *Canon of the New Testament*, 514–15.

[39] Buchanan, 538, appears to have missed the letter *m* in *columbani* in transcribing the inscription, although it is clearly present.

[40] The letter Q, which should appear at the bottom of fo. 65ᵛ is not apparent. If Buchanan, 538, read it there in 1907, then it must be assumed to have faded and become obscure.

leaf; his beginning with the letter I suggests that the Codex Muratorianus either was copied from a mutilated exemplar or else lost some of its pages. If the scribe of the Codex or its exemplar had began on the first page with the letter A, as many as fifty-six leaves may be missing. Since the eight-leaf cycle is not introduced until the eleventh leaf, there may have been at least two breaks in the first part of the Codex.

The inscription on the first page is in a different hand from the rest of the Codex. It is also inserted into the top margin over a titular superscription. This suggests that one break could have been at the very beginning of the Codex or its exemplar. According to E. S. Buchanan, the writing of the inscription is at least as old as the eighth century, perhaps even the seventh.[41] Therefore, if the inscription was added after the present Codex lost some initial folios, then those pages must have been lost within a century or so after the Codex was transcribed.

The number of lines on the first eighteen pages of the Codex is 24 or 25. Beginning with the page on which the Fragment commences (fo. $10^{r}$) the number of lines of the next sixteen pages (fos. $10^{r}$–$17^{v}$) is 31 or 32. The Fragment begins at the top of fo. $10^{r}$ in the midst of a sentence. The previous page in the Codex ends abruptly in the middle of a quotation from Eucherius. There is no significant vacant space either at the bottom of fo. $9^{v}$ or the top of fo. $10^{r}$. Thus some pages may be missing here in the Codex, as well as at the beginning.[42]

The Codex Muratorianus consists of a miscellaneous collection of Latin tracts followed by five early Christian creeds. The contents of the Codex are identified by titular superscription and/or the enlargement of the incipit. The folios containing the Muratorian Fragment ($10^{r}$–$11^{r}$), however, have no titular superscription and no enlargement of letters or spacing in the incipit.

DE TERRENIS (Eucherius, from *Formulae Spiritualis Intelligentiae*) $1^{r}$–$4^{v}$

[41] Buchanan, 537.

[42] A change in line-numbers does not necessarily suggest missing folios; e.g. the number of lines per page changes again, from 31 or 32 (fos. $10^{r}$–$17^{v}$) to an average of 26 or 27 (fos. $18^{r}$–$25^{v}$) and again to an average of 31 or 32 (from fo. $26^{r}$), without any apparent break in the text.

| | | |
|---|---|---|
| DE ANIMANTIBUS (Eucherius, from *Formulae Spiritualis Intelligentiae*) | | $4^{v}$–$8^{v}$ |
| DE NOMINIS (Eucherius, from *Formulae Spiritualis Intelligentiae*) | | $8^{r}$–$9^{v}$ |
| 'quibus tamen Interfuit' (*Muratorian Fragment*) | | $10^{r}$–$11^{r}$ |
| DE ABRAAM (Ambrose, from *De Abraham*) | | $11^{r}$–$12^{r}$ |
| DE EXPOSITIONE DIUERSARUM RERUM (Eucherius, *Instructiones ad Salonium*) | | $12^{r}$–$19^{r}$ |
| DE GENTIBUS | $13^{v}$–$14^{v}$ | |
| DE LOCIS | $14^{v}$–$15^{r}$ | |
| DE FLUMINIBUS ET AQUIS | $15^{r-v}$ | |
| DE MENSIBUS | $15^{v}$ | |
| DE SOLEPNITATIBUS | $15^{v}$–$16^{r}$ | |
| DE IDOLIS | $16^{r-v}$ | |
| DE UESTIBUS | $16^{v}$–$17^{r}$ | |
| DE DUPLICUS UESTIMENTIS | $17^{r}$ | |
| DE AUIBUS UEL UOLATILIBUS | $17^{r-v}$ | |
| DE BESTEIS UEL SERPENTIBUS | $17^{v}$ | |
| DE PONDERIBUS | $17^{v}$–$18^{r}$ | |
| DE MENSURIS | $18^{r-v}$ | |
| DE GRECIS NUMINIBUS | $18^{v}$–$19^{r}$ | |
| DE MATHEO EUANGE | | $19^{r}$–$28^{r}$ |
| DE DIE ET HORA | | $28^{r}$–$29^{v}$ |
| DE TRIBUS MENSURIS | | $29^{v}$–$30^{r}$ |
| DE PETRO APOSTOLO | | $30^{v}$–$31^{v}$ |
| DE REPARATIONE LAPSI (Chrysostom, *Paraeneses ad Theodorum*) | | $31^{v}$–$71^{v}$ |
| DE ABRAAM ('Ante hostium sedebat abraam') | | $71^{v}$–$73^{v}$ |
| FIDES SANCTI AMBROSI EPISCOPI | | $73^{v}$, $75^{r}$ |
| FIDES SANCTI LUCIFERI EPISCOPI | | $75^{r}$ |
| FIDES QUAE ES NICENO CONCILIO PROCESSIT | | $75^{r-v}$ |
| FIDES BEATI ATHANASI | | $75^{v}$ |
| EXPOSITIO FIDEI CHATOLICE[43] | | $74^{r-v}$ |

Over half of the pages of the Codex (82 out of 152) contain material from Chrysostom, which may account for the attribution to him in the inscription. Material from Eucherius of Lyons

[43] Fo. 74 is a detached leaf containing only *Expositio Fidei Chatolice*. As it currently stands in the Codex it is an intrusion, interrupting the sequence between fos. $73^{v}$ and $75^{r}$. If fo. 74 was a part of the Codex and stood with the other Creeds, then it must have originally appeared between fos. 75 and 76.

(d. *c.* 449) accounts for the next largest contribution (32 pages). The prominence given to Eucherius might suggest that the collection was made in southern Gaul, rather than in Italy. The vulgarisms in the Codex, according to Buchanan, support the hypothesis of a Gallic rather than an Italian origin.[44] If, as the inscription on the first leaf implies, this manuscript or its exemplar actually belonged to Columbanus, then he might well have commissioned the collection for himself or his monasteries some time while he was in Burgundy from 585 to 610.

All the datable contents in the Codex belong to the fourth or fifth century. The entries entitled 'De Terrenis', 'De Animantibus', and 'De Nominis' are chs. 3–5 of Eucherius' *Formulae Spiritualis Intelligentiae*, dated some time during his episcopacy (*c.* 432–50). The work titled 'De Abraam' is a fragmentary portion of Ambrose's homiletic treatise *De Abraham* (1.3.15–17), dating probably *c.* 382–8. The various tracts listed under the heading 'De Expositione Diuersarum Rerum' belong to the second book of Eucherius' *Instructiones ad Salonium* (2.3–14), also dated during his episcopacy. 'De Reparatione Lapsi' is a Latin translation of the longer of Chrysostom's *Paraeneses ad Theodorum lapsum*. This treatise dates from the four-year period when Chrysostom was an anchorite, probably some time between 373 and 381.

Both G. Mercati and C. H. Turner suggested that the two short pieces 'De Tribus Mensuris' and 'De Petro Apostolo', may be drawn from the same author as 'De Matheo Euange',[45] an exposition of the eschatological passage of Matt. 14: 20–44. Mercati attributed it to an anonymous chiliast, Turner to Victorinus of Pettau, whom he considered either as the original author or as the translator of a Greek source, perhaps Hippolytus. A. Souter, on the other hand, suggested Ambrosiaster as the author, a position which was later supported by C. Martini on the grounds of both its language and its theological content.[46]

[44] Buchanan, 539.

[45] G. Mercati, '1. Anonymyi Chiliastae in Matthaeum Fragmenta', *Varia Sacra* (Studi e Testi, 11; Rome, 1903), 1–49; C. H. Turner, 'An Exegetical Fragment of the Third Century', *JTS* 5 (1903–4), 218–41.

[46] A Souter, 'Reasons for Regarding Hilarius (Ambrosiaster) as the Author of the Mercati–Turner Anecdoton', *JTS* 5 (1903–4), 608–21; C. Martini, *Ambrosiaster: De Auctore, Operibus, Theologia* (Rome, 1944), 16–64.

Zahn argued for Ambrosiaster as the author of 'De Petro Apostolo' on the basis of a parallel with *Quaestio* 104.[47] Here too Martini supported the attribution by noting the affinities of 'De Petro Apostolo' with other passages from Ambrosiaster.[48] On the basis of linguistic and doctrinal elements, Martini also attributed 'De Tribus Mensuris' to Ambrosiaster, Buchanan suggested Ambrosiaster as a possible author for 'De Die et Hora'.[49] If Ambrosiaster wrote any of these works, then they would be dated generally from 363 to 384.

The 'Fides Beati Athanasi' in the Codex is an early recension of the Athanasian Creed, whose author and date are disputed. The creed probably derived from Gaul, perhaps in the region of Lérins. A Gallican origin is supported in that the Creed first appears in a sermon of Caesarius of Arles and has remarkable correspondence with the recently discovered *Excerpta* of Vincent of Lérins. A date for the Creed between 381 and 428 was generally accepted. However, J. N. D. Kelly argued that the Christological heresy attacked was Nestorianism, not Apollinarianism, and thus that the creed was composed after 428.[50]

The two creeds in the Codex attributed respectively to Ambrose (d. 397) and Lucifer (d. 370–1), 'Fides Sancti Ambrosi Episcopi' and 'Fides Sancti Luciferi Episcopi', are probably spurious, but would date no earlier than the late fourth century if genuine. The 'Fides Sancti Luciferi Episcopi' appears elsewhere as the work of Faustinus.[51] The entry 'Fides quae ex Niceno Concilio processit' is an early (Latin) recension of the Nicene Creed, which must be dated after the First Council of Nicaea in 325. The presence of an anathema and an explanation of *homoousios* in the version of the Codex would suggest a date before the later Niceno-Constantinopolitan Creed of 381.

This leaves in the Codex only the short work 'De Abraam' and the fragmentary detached leaf 'Expositio Fidei Chatolice' as unidentified. Otherwise all the works date from the fourth to

[47] Zahn, 'Ein alter Kommentar zu Matthäus', *NKZ* 16 (1905), 419–27.

[48] Martini, 65–7.

[49] Ibid. 68–73; Buchanan, 537.

[50] J. N. D. Kelly, *The Athanasian Creed* (London, 1964), 94–8.

[51] A. Hahn (ed.), *Bibliothek der Symbole und Glaubensregeln der alten Kirche* (Breslau, 1877), 277–8.

fifth centuries, save possibly for the Muratorian Fragment. The majority of the works are clearly late fourth-century. It is of course quite possible, if the Fragment dates from the late second-century, that an earlier work was included with the several later ones. However, if other arguments suggest a later date for the Fragment, then its inclusion in this Codex among such later works could only be considered as corroborative, at least for the Latin version.

## THE PROVENANCE OF THE FRAGMENT

The Muratorian Fragment is traditionally assigned to the Western church, emanating either from Rome or a church associated with Rome. The designation of Rome not only as *urbs Roma* (l. 76) but as *urbs* alone (l. 38) suggests to many such an origin for the Fragment. Likewise the absence of James and Hebrews in the list, and the presence of Revelation, would also commend a Western provenance.

Harnack argued that the Fragment was an official promulgation of Rome defining the contents of the New Testament for the rest of the Church.[52] Harnack read such phrases as 'we' and the 'Catholic church' as interchangeable in the Fragment, obviously implying Rome. Hence the terms 'a nobis' (l. 47), 'recipimus' and 'non recipimus' (ll. 72, 82), 'catholicam ecclesiam recipi non potest' (ll. 66–7), 'in catholica habentur' (l. 69), and 'quidam ex nostris' (ll. 72–3) were thought to designate Rome as the church to which the Fragmentist belonged. Harnack questioned whether any Western church (at the transition from the second to the third century) other than the Roman would have spoken thus.

H. Koch disputed the linguistic arguments of Harnack as overstated, and showed that the term *catholica ecclesia* did not necessarily have the restricted referent of Rome.[53] Numerous examples of *catholica ecclesia* are found in the third century, especially in Cyprian, used in reference to churches other than Rome.[54] Koch also showed that the terms *in urbe Roma* and

[52] Harnack, 'Über den Verfasser', 5–7.

[53] H. Koch, 'Zu A. v. Harnacks Beweis für den amtlichen römischen Ursprung des Muratorischen Fragments', *ZNW* 25 (1926), 154–60.

[54] e.g. Cornelius' letter to Fabian (Eusebius, *HE* 6.43.11); Cyprian, *Epistles*, 49.2, 66.5, 68.2, 730.9, 745.10.

*cathedra urbis Romae ecclesiae* were not the usual phrases of documents written in Rome. Rather, writings from Rome usually employed the phrase 'hic in urbe Roma' in reference to the city of Rome.[55] If the Fragment had originated from Rome, the expected phrase would have been something like 'pastorem *hic* in urbe Roma Hermas conscripsit . . .'. Sundberg noted that the meaning of the singular term *urbs* as Rome (l. 38) does not imply the place of the writing of the Fragment, but rather the place, namely, Rome (cf. Acts 28: 30–1), from which Paul's supposed journey to Spain would have originated (cf. Romans 15: 24, 28).[56] Thus, it is not necessary to think that the Fragment originated from Rome.

The supposition that the Fragment is Western because of the absence from the list of James and Hebrews, and the presence of Revelation, is also not well founded. Initially Revelation was as generally accepted in the East as it was in the West. Papias (*c.* 60–130) is said to have commented upon it,[57] and Melito of Sardis (d. *c.* 190) was the author of a lost work on Revelation (Eusebius, *HE* 4.26.2; Jerome, *De Vir. Ill.* 24). Theophilus of Antioch (*c.* 186) alluded to it (*Ad Autolyc.* 2.28) and is said to have used testimonies from it in a lost work against Hermogenes (Eusebius, *HE* 5.24.1). Apollonius of Hierapolis (*c.* 186) is also said to have used testimonies from Revelation (Eusebius, *HE* 5.18.13). Clement of Alexandria (*c.* 150–*c.* 215) quoted approvingly from it (*Paed.* 1.6; 2.11; *Strom.* 6.13, 25; cf. Eusebius, *HE* 6.14.1), and Origen cited it frequently as well (*De Princ.* 1.2.10; 4.1.25; *Contra Celsum* 6.6, 23; 8.17; *Comm. on John* 1.1, 2, 14, 23, 42; 2.4; 5.3, 4; 6.35; cf. Eusebius, *HE* 6.25.9).

Dionysius of Alexandria (d. *c.* 264) reveals the first doubts about the authority of Revelation. According to Dionysius some people rejected Revelation as the work of Cerinthus (Eusebius, *HE* 7.25.1–2). This would appear to be a reference to the Alogi. Dionysius, however, accepted the work and replied, 'But I could not venture to reject the book, as many brethren hold it in high esteem', and 'it is the work of some

[55] Koch, 159–60.

[56] Sundberg, 'Canon Muratori', 6–7.

[57] Cf. Andreas Caesariensis, *Apoc.* 34, *Serm.* 12; Oecumenius and Arethas, *Comm. in Apoc.* 12.7; all quoted in A. H. Charteris, *Canonicity* (Edinburgh, 1880), 338–9.

holy and inspired man', and 'I do not deny that . . . writer saw a revelation and received knowledge and prophecy' (Eusebius, *HE* 7.25.4, 7, 26). Yet on the basis of literary criticism Dionysius did concur that the author of Revelation was not the same John as the one who wrote the Gospel and Epistle (Eusebius, *HE* 7.25.1–27).

Similar reservations about Revelation may be reflected in the writings of Eusebius of Caesarea (*c.* 303–24). In one place Eusebius appeared to identify the author of Revelation as John the apostle and evangelist (*HE* 3.18.1), while in another place he acknowledged that if it was not the apostle, it was probably the presbyter John who saw the Apocalypse (*HE* 3.39.5–6). In his own list Eusebius enumerated Revelation among the *homologoumena*, but with the qualifier, 'if it really seem proper' (*HE* 3.25.2). A few lines later he declared that some rejected it, while others included it with accepted works (*HE* 3.25.4). In the previous chapter, Eusebius had noted that the opinions of most were still divided (*HE* 3.24.18). Eusebius' comments may reflect a hesitancy introduced by the remarks of Dionysius of Alexandria.[58]

None the less Pamphilus in Caesarea (*c.* 309) still quoted from Revelation (*Apol. pro Origene*), as did Methodius of Olympus (d. *c.* 311) (*On the Resurrection* 3.2.9; *Banquet* 1.5; 6.5; 8.4; 9.3). Revelation was also included in the Byzantine text of the New Testament, probably created by Lucian of Antioch (*c.* 312). It was also included in the probably Alexandrian Catalogue in the Codex Claromontanus, without scribal mark, and in Athanasius' thirty-ninth Festal Letter (367).

A thoroughgoing rejection of Revelation did not come about in the East until the second half of the fourth century. Cyril of Jerusalem is the first known writer to exclude Revelation without comment (*Catech.* 4.36). It is also omitted in the Apostolic Canons and the list (*Carm.* 12.31) of Gregory of Nazianzus (383–90); Amphilochius of Iconium (396 +) indicated that most people declared it to be spurious (*Iambi ad Seleucum* 316). Revelation is also absent from a Syrian catalogue of *c.* 400 and from the Peshitta version in Syriac, originating around the end of the fourth century. However, Epiphanius of

[58] Cf. R. Grant, *Eusebius as Church Historian* (hereafter *Eusebius*) (Oxford, 1980), 126–41.

Salamis still included Revelation in his list (*Haer*. 76.5) and so did Jerome (394), writing from Bethlehem (*Ad Paul. Ep.* 53). Revelation is also found in the Codex Alexandrinus (*c.*425).

Thus while some reservations about Revelation in the East are apparent earlier (Dionysius, Eusebius) the work was generally accepted into the second half of the fourth century (the catalogue in the Codex Claromontanus, Athanasius, Epiphanius, Jerome). Only well on in that century was the book more generally rejected in the East (Cyril, 'Apostolic Canons', Gregory of Nazianzus, Amphilochius, the Syrian catalogue, Peshitta). Thus the presence of Revelation in the Fragment would suggest a Western provenance only if the Fragment were thought to be dated after the late fourth century, by which time Revelation was absent from most Eastern lists.

The absence of James and Hebrews from the Fragment is striking, but the absence of 1 Peter is even more surprising, especially since the Revelation of Peter is listed (ll. 71–2). These absences have led many scholars to assume that references in the Fragment are missing. As has been noted previously, the Fragment is a barbarous transcription from a mutilated text. The scribe who accidentally repeated the passage from Ambrose following the Fragment omitted two and a half lines in copying it the second time. A similar omission within the Fragment may explain some of the remarkable absences.

Westcott, for instance, insisted that 1 Peter, James, and Hebrews 'could scarcely have been altogether passed over in an enumeration of books in which the epistle of St. Jude, and even Apocryphal writings of heretics, found a place'.[59] Likewise Tregelles argued that in regard to Hebrews and 1 Peter, 'we cannot suppose them to have been rejected by the author of the Fragment, or to have been writings with which he was unacquainted'.[60] It seems reasonable to suggest that the Fragment may have contained other references now lost, and that James and Hebrews (and 1 Peter) may have been among them.

C. Bunsen, for instance, supposed a defect in the Fragment after 'In catholica habentur' and before 'Et sapientia' (ll. 69–70), where mention was added of 1 Peter, James, and Hebrews, contrasting the composition of the latter with the Wisdom of

[59] Westcott, *Canon of the New Testament*, 216.

[60] Tregelles, 98.

Solomon which follows.[61] Zahn suggested a break in ll. 71–3; 'apocalapse Iohanis et Petri ⟨unam⟩ tantum recip(e)imus ⟨epistulam; fertur et altera⟩ quam quidam ex nostris legi In eclesia nolunt', in order to include 1 Peter.[62] Perhaps just as 1 John 1: 1–4 is quoted in the Fragment (ll. 26–34) as proof of the eyewitness character of the fourth evangelist, 1 Peter may have been mentioned earlier in the Fragment in the lost account of Mark's Gospel.

The possibility of omissions is supported by the supposition of other defects in the Fragment. Lightfoot, for example, suggested that there was a hiatus after 'Pauli nomine' (ll. 64–5) and before 'fincte', where he suspected other works of Marcion were referred to as forged, and not the Epistles to the Laodiceans and Alexandrians.[63] Westcott noted that the whole passage from 'et ideo' (l. 16) until 'futurum est' (l. 26) has no connection with what precedes that could be expressed by 'ideo', and similarly what follows is not connected with it by 'ergo'.[64] Likewise it appears that some words have been lost at the end of the sentence in l. 39 after 'ad spaniam proficescentis'. Westcott noted further that the present form of the Fragment seems to suggest that it was not originally continuous. Instead, he suggested that it had been made up of three or four different passages from some unknown author, and collected perhaps on the same principle as the quotations in Eusebius from Irenaeus, Clement, and Origen (*HE* 5.8; 6.24; 6.25.3–14).[65] Such a supposition may aid in explaining apparent omissions in the Fragment. Whatever the truth of such suggestions, judgements based on omissions in the Fragment are not conclusive.

In summary, the traditional assumption of a Western origin of the Fragment is questionable. Its association with Rome is disputed. The presence of Revelation is not remarkable, unless the Fragment was thought to be dated after the late fourth century. The absence of James and Hebrews (and 1 Peter) is inconclusive because of the probability of defects in the Frag-

[61] Bunsen, 152.

[62] Quoted in M. J. Lagrange, 'L'auteur du Canon de Muratori', *RBib* 35 (1926), 83–8, at 86.

[63] Lightfoot, *Saint Paul's Epistles to the Colossians and to Philemon* (New York, 1890), 290.

[64] Westcott, *Canon of the New Testament*, 527–8 n. 7.

[65] Ibid. 216–17.

ment. Thus the provenance of the Fragment remains uncertain.

## DATING THE FRAGMENT

The central passage upon which the traditional dating of the Fragment rests is:

Pastorem uero
nuperrim e(t) temporibus nostris In urbe
roma herma conscripsit sedente cathe
tra urbis romae aeclesiae Pio ep̃s frat*r*e(r)
eius

The plain sense of the statement is that Hermas wrote the Shepherd in Rome during the time while his brother, Pius, was bishop there. Pius (I) is known to have been bishop of Rome from *c.* 140 until his death *c.* 154. The phrase 'temporibus nostris' appears to express contemporaneity for the writing of the Shepherd with this established time-period of 140–54. The superlative 'nuperrim e(t)'—that is *nuperrime*—is then thought to confirm the temporal relationship between the composition of the Fragment and the writing of the Shepherd and the episcopacy of Pius.

The Fragment therefore appears to have been written some time shortly after the episcopacy of Pius (*nuperrime temporibus nostris*). Although Muratori dated the Fragment about 196,[66] Westcott believed that it could not be 'much later than 170 A.D.'[67] He argued that 'the statement in the text of the Fragment is perfectly clear, definite, and consistent with its contents, and there can be no reason either to question its accuracy or to interpret it loosely'.[68] G. Salmon suggested that *c.* 180 was 'the latest admissible date' contending 'that no one would speak of an event as having occurred "very lately and in his own time", if it was then more than twenty years ago.'[69] J. P. Kirsch, however, suggested the period of the Fragment's writing was 180×200.[70] Zahn also argued for a later date because the Fragment rejected Montanist writings.[71] C. Erbes, in the most

[66] Muratori, 851.

[67] Westcott, *Canon of the New Testament*, 209.

[68] Ibid. 209 n. 1.

[69] Salmon, 1000.

[70] J. P. Kirsch, 'Muratorian Canon', *The Catholic Encyclopedia*, x (London, 1911), 642.

[71] Zahn, 'Muratorian Canon', *The New Schaff-Herzog Religious Encyclopedia*, viii (New York, 1910), 53–6, at 54.

detailed discussion of the Fragment's dating, suggested an even later date. He concluded his study:

> Doch ist das gleichgültig für den gelieferten Nachweis der Abfassung des Muratorischen Fragments um das Jahr 220 u.Z., sowie für die dabei gewonnene Erkenntnis, daß der angeblich dem Paulus untergeschobene Brief an die Laodizener, alias an die Alexandriner, unsern gelegentlich dem Paulus selbst oder dem Barnabas zugeschriebenen Hebräerbrief meint, daß das an die Sekte des Marcion gerichtete 'mehrere Andere' auf den falschen Briefwechsel zwischen Paulus und den Korinthern geht, daß der kundige Autor schließlich mit den andern Schriften auch die Psalmen eines Marcion wie der konkurrierenden Gnostiker und Montanisten ablehnt.[72]

Erbes pointed out that if the Fragmentist did indeed compose his list as late as 220, and was about 70–5 years old at the time, then he could still have been born shortly before or during the episcopacy of Pius in Rome.[73] Thus despite the plain sense of the Fragment's statement, scholars have not been willing to date it 'quite recently' after Pius' episcopacy, but as much as sixty-five years later.

Besides Pius, the only other readily datable references in the Fragment are several names: Marcion (ll. 65, 83), Arsinous (l. 81), Valentinus (l. 81), Miltiades (?) (l. 81), Basilides (l. 84), and the Cataphrygians (ll. 84–5). These references are almost exclusively found in the last lines of the Fragment (ll. 81–5) which are particularly garbled and end abruptly:

> Arsinoi autem seu ualentini. uel mitiad(ei)*is*
> nihil In totum recipemus. Qui etiam nouũ
> psalmorum librum marcioni conscripse
> runt una cum basilide assianum catafry
> cum con*s*titutorem

There is obviously some confusion in these last lines since Basilides 'of Asia Minor' is mistakenly named as the founder of the Cataphrygians, and is thought to have composed a new psalm-book for Marcion, together with Arsinous, Valentinus, and Miltiades (?). Moreover, this confusion does not result from the poor transcription of the Fragment, since essentially the same reading reoccurs in the Benedictine texts (ll. 33–7).

[72] C. Erbes, 'Die Zeit des Muratorischen Fragments', *ZKG* 35 (1914), 331–62, at 362.
[73] Ibid. 361.

The confusion must be traced to an ancient common exemplar. The absence of any continuation of this passage from the Fragment in the Benedictine texts (l. 37) may also suggest that either this was the original ending of the Fragment, or else the Benedictine texts were derived along with the Fragment from a common mutilated exemplar.

The identification of some of the individuals named in these last lines is uncertain. Miltiades is the presumed referent of 'mitiad(ei)*i*s' (l. 81) in the Fragment (cf. Benedictine Prologue, l. 34, *Mitiadis* CC[1]; *Mi(ti)adis* C[2]; *Mitididis* C[3]); Marcion is usually assumed to be that of 'Marcioni' (l. 83). The reading of the Benedictine texts (*Marcionis*, l. 35) would seem to suggest a translation of 'a psalm-book of Marcion' (genitive rather than dative).

The referent of Arsinous (l. 81) is unknown. Credner conjectured that 'arsinoi' was a corruption of *Bardesanis.*[74] Bardesanes of Edessa (154–222) did take part in writing a large collection of Syriac hymns, and from the fourth century Bardesanes is attacked along with Marcion and/or Valentinus by Eastern fathers, e.g. the author of *De recta in Deum fide* (300+); Ephraem Syrus in his *madrash*es (*c.* 338–73); Theodoret of Cyrrhus in *Eranistes* (447). However, the presumption of an early dating and Western provenance from the Fragment led Hort to conclude that 'according to the best authorities, the great Syrian lived after the probable date of the fragment, and in any case he was not likely to be known to its author'.[75] If so, then the reference is unknown.

Ferguson remarked that these references are all second-century.[76] Yet there is nothing definitive about a later writer mentioning earlier ones. Moreover, the individuals named are specifically literary, having a book or books especially associated with them. It may be this factor, rather than their dates, which accounts for their mention in a listing of the New Testament works. Indeed, a sufficient period of time might be required to allow for the spread and infiltration of these heretical works into orthodox communities and for their subsequent delineation and exclusion from the acceptable

[74] Credner, *Zur Geschichte des Kanons*, 91.

[75] F. J. A. Hort, 'Arsinous', *DCB* i (London, 1877), 174.

[76] Ferguson, 677–83.

collection. In any event, the date of the Fragment cannot be confidently deduced from these references alone. Moreover, if the Fragment's original ending is mutilated, then further references may have followed those which have survived.

The reference to the Shepherd of Hermas, therefore, remains the crux of traditional dating of the Fragment at the end of the second century. The plain sense of that reference (ll. 73–7) suggests that the Fragment was written shortly after the episcopacy of Hermas' brother Pius (*c.* 140–*c.* 154) during which time Hermas wrote the Shepherd. However, the issues involved in the traditional dating of the Shepherd are more complex than they appear at first sight and will be dealt with at length in Ch. 2.

## THE AUTHORSHIP OF THE FRAGMENT

The question of authorship of the Fragment is unresolved. The attribution of authorship is usually made on the basis of an assumed date and provenance, and a supposed Greek original. Muratori, when he published the Fragment in 1740, proposed the Roman presbyter Gaius (Caius) as the author.[77] Simon de Magistris attributed the Fragment to Papias.[78] Bunsen suggested Hegesippus (*c.* 154–*c.* 180).[79] J. Chapman argued for Clement of Alexandria.[80] Harnack, who previously argued for Rhodon (*c.* 180–92) as the author of the Fragment, later proposed either Pope Victor I (189–98) or Zephyrinus (198–217), or one of their clerks on their behalf.[81] Lightfoot suggested

[77] Muratori, iii. 851; Gaius can be discounted because it is now known that he opposed, as works of Cerinthus, the Fourth Gospel and Revelation, which the Fragment accepts as by the Apostle John, cf. J. Gwynn, 'Hippolytus and his "Heads against Caius"', *Hermathena* 6 (1886–8), 397–418; for a history of the problem of Gaius, cf. T. H. Robinson, 'The Authorship of the Muratorian Canon', *The Expositor*, 7th ser., 1 (1906), 481–95.

[78] De Magistris, 467–9. Previously the date of Pius' episcopacy was less certain; it was sometimes supposed to be as early as AD 127, cf. Tregelles, 64; J. Barmby, 'Pius I', *DCB* iv (London, 1887), 416–17. However, the later dating of Pius' reign from *c.* 140 to *c.* 154 could now preclude consideration of Papias, cf. J. N. D. Kelly, *The Oxford Dictionary of Popes* (Oxford, 1986), 10.

[79] Bunsen, 142. This suggestion was disputed by Donaldson, 207–10.

[80] J. Chapman, 'Clément d'Alexandrie sur les Évangiles, et encore le Fragment de Muratori', *RBén* 21 (1904), 369–74.

[81] Harnack, 'Über den Verfasser', 15.

Hippolytus (*c.* 180–*c.* 236) as the author, which has remained the most widely favoured proposal.[82] Bartlet, having suggested that the author belonged to the later School of John, 'in the generation after Papias and Polycarp—men like Melito of Sardis, Apollinaris of Hierapolis, and, somewhat later, Polycrates of Ephesus',[83] identified him specifically with Melito.[84] Earlier, G. Kühn had suggested Polycrates of Ephesus.[85]

But Hippolytus is the suggestion most discussed. Some scholars have continued to argue for Hippolytean authorship,[86] while still others have disputed it.[87] Harnack, for instance, opposed Lightfoot's reading of the inscription on Hippolytus' chair, and noted the absence of any mention in Hippolytus of the Revelation of Peter, the Pauline epistles to the Alexandrians, and the Laodiceans, the Wisdom of Solomon, Valentinus Arsinous, or the new psalm-book of the Marcionites, all referred to in the Fragment.[88] But as Hans von Campenhausen noted, 'the principal objection remains the one that it is simply impossible to ascribe to a man like Hippolytus the muddle-headed remarks to be found in the Muratorian Canon'.[89]

The numerous proposals for and arguments about authorship reveal the difficulty involved in attributing the Fragment and the lack of scholarly consensus. Westcott concluded that 'there is no sufficient evidence to determine the authorship of the Fragment . . . such guesses are barely ingenious'.[90]

[82] Lightfoot, *AF* I. ii. 378–13.

[83] V. Bartlet, 'Melito the Author of the Muratorian Canon', *The Expositor*, 7th ser., 2 (1906), 214–24, at 215.

[84] Ibid. 214–24.

[85] Kühn 33 n. 1.

[86] Zahn, 'Miscellanea: II. Hippolytus, der Verfasser des muratorischen Kanons', *NKZ* 33 (1922), 417–36; N. Bonwetsch, 'Hippolytisches', *Nachrichten von der Königlichen Gesellschaft der Wissenschaften zu Göttingen* (Berlin, 1924), i. 27–32 ('Nachtrap') 63–4; Lagrange, 'L'auteur'; id., 'Le canon d'Hippolyte et le fragment de Muratori', *RBib* 42 (1933), 161–86.

[87] Chapman, 369–74; Harnack, 'Über den Verfasser'; N. A. Dahl, 'Welche Ordnung der Paulusbriefe wird vom Muratorischen Kanon vorausgesetzt?', *ZNW* 52 (1961), 39–53, at 45; I. Frank, *Der Sinn der Kanonbildung. Eine historische-theologische Untersuchung der Zeit vom I. Clemensbrief* (Freiburger Theologische Studien, 90; Freiburg i. B., 1971).

[88] Harnack, 'Über den Verfasser', 8–9.

[89] H. von Campenhausen, *The Formation of the Christian Bible*, trans. J. A. Baker (Philadelphia, 1972), 245 n. 198.

[90] Westcott, *Canon of the New Testament*, 209–10.

## CONCLUSIONS

The Muratorian Fragment was first published in 1740 as an example of a barbarous scribal transcription. The beginning and probably the end of the Fragment are missing. A substantial portion of its poor Latin may be credited to the carelessness of the scribe of the Codex Muratorianus, which is especially apparent in a repeated passage of Ambrose following the Fragment. Excerpts of the Muratorian Fragment discovered in three eleventh- and one twelfth-century Latin manuscripts of the *Corpus Paulinum* at the Benedictine monastery on Monte Cassino confirm that the poor Latin of the Fragment is not that of the archetype.

The Latin of the Fragment has been dated by grammatical and philological analysis to the late fourth century. The vocabulary of the Fragment supports a date no earlier than the last decade of the fourth century for the Latin. If Latin is not the language of the Fragment's autograph, then the Fragment is probably a translation from Greek. The hypothesis of a Greek original has aided in understanding some of the difficult and confusing passages in the Fragment as simply poor translations into Latin. However, if the traditional dating of the Fragment is questioned and a Greek original for the Fragment is assumed, then the Fragment would most likely have an Eastern provenance.

The codex in which the Fragment is found is a seventh- or eighth-century manuscript of the Bobbio monastery. Missing leaves in the Codex may account for the mutilated beginning of the Fragment, but not the abrupt ending. The attributable contents of the Codex Muratorianus are all dated in the fourth and fifth centuries. Almost two-thirds of the pages of identifiable material in the Codex are from Eastern sources.

The traditional Western origin of the Fragment is questionable. H. Koch has shown that the Fragment most probably did not originate from the city of Rome. The presence of Revelation in the Fragment is not remarkable, unless it was thought to be late fourth century. The absence of James and Hebrews (and 1 Peter) is inconclusive because of the probability of defects in the Fragment. If omissions are allowed, then no argument may be drawn from the absence of James or Hebrews. Thus the provenance of the Fragment remains uncertain.

A plain reading of the Fragment suggests that it was composed shortly after the period which it attributes to Hermas' writing the Shepherd, namely, the episcopacy in Rome of Hermas' brother Pius. However, few scholars have been willing to date the Fragment so early, and have instead argued for composition anywhere between 170 and 220. Dating the Fragment by other references is inconclusive, and there has been no scholarly consensus about its authorship. Therefore a careful analysis of the traditional dating of the Fragment is needed.

# 2

# THE SHEPHERD OF HERMAS

THE crux of the traditional dating of the Fragment is the phrase 'nuperrim e(t) temporibus nostris' (l. 74). What the original Greek for the phrase may have been is uncertain. Ferguson was careful in his opposition to Sundberg to note that since the text is generally recognized as a translation, 'arguments from the language employed in the Muratorian Fragment have limited value'.[1] Likewise there may be 'limited value' in dating the Fragment upon this simple three-word Latin phrase. The Latin translation, shown by the Benedictine text to have gone through several editions, is suspect in various places, as suggested by Tregelles and Katz (see Ch. 1), and was transcribed by a hand that has clearly shown itself, in the words of Westcott, 'either unable or unwilling to understand the work which he was copying, and yet given to arbitrary alteration of the text before him from regard simply to the supposed form of words'.[2]

Sundberg has reinterpreted the Fragment's key dating phrase.[3] To begin with, Sundberg translated *nuperrime* not as a relative superlative (e.g. 'very recently') with reference to the Fragmentist, but as an absolute superlative (e.g. 'most recently') with reference to the preceding books in the list. The meaning then of *nuperrime* would be that the Shepherd of Hermas is not comparable with the preceding works in the list in terms of antiquity of authorship. Sundberg did not insist that this is the only correct interpretation but that this is a viable alternative. Even Ferguson acknowledged this to be a possible translation.[4] This alternative would somewhat free the dating

[1] Ferguson, 678; Donaldson, 209, suggested that the reference to Hermas in the Fragment was an interpolation by a supposed Roman or African translator made expressly for the purpose of dismissing the Shepherd.

[2] Westcott, *Canon of the New Testament*, 523.

[3] Sundberg, 'Canon Muratori', 11.

[4] Ferguson, 677–8.

of the Fragment from temporal association with the writing of the Shepherd.

Sundberg also wished to broaden the traditional interpretation of 'temporibus nostris' which reads these words as implying immediate contemporaneity. Sundberg noted the practice in the early Church of distinguishing the Apostles and their teaching from all that came after them. There is evidence that by the time of Hegesippus this distinction had taken on a particularly sacred temporal aspect, for he considered the Church a pure and uncorrupted virgin throughout the time of the Apostles and their hearers (cf. Eusebius, *HE* 3.32.6–8; 4.22.4). Eusebius (*HE* 3.31.6) similarly spoke of 'the Apostles themselves and the apostolic age' as a distinct group and time.

Sundberg noted with particular interest a reference in Irenaeus (*Adv. Haer.* 5.30.3) which reads in part: '. . . for that [the revelation to John] was seen not a very long time ago, but almost in our own generation (τῆς ἡμετέρας γενεᾶς) towards the end of the reign of Domitian' (cf. Eusebius, *HE* 5.8.6). The phrase, 'not a very long time ago, but almost in our own generation', was an odd statement for Irenaeus to make considering that the time-span involved was almost a hundred years. Sundberg read the 'almost' as suggesting that Irenaeus was trying to make a point about the lateness of Revelation, that it was written about the end of the apostolic period, i.e. 'almost in our own generation'. This quotation would thus involve a clear distinction between the apostolic age and 'our time'. As such it provides the precedent with which Sundberg wished to read 'temporibus nostris' in the Fragment as meaning 'our time' as distinguished from apostolic time.[5]

Ferguson interpreted the quotation from Irenaeus somewhat differently. He read the 'in our own generation' as referring only to Irenaeus' own lifetime (*c.* 130–*c.* 200), and the 'almost' as meaning only that Revelation was written shortly before Irenaeus' time.[6] But the quotation suggests that Revelation was written over thirty years before Irenaeus' birth, which might be stretching the limits of 'almost'. Still Ferguson went on to suggest two other examples where ἡ ἡμετέρα γενεά meant

[5] Both Donaldson, 212; and Zahn, 'Muratorian Canon', 54; recognized that the Fragmentist may have been using the phrase, or some part of it, to refer to the apostolic age.

[6] Ferguson, 678.

only within one's lifetime, and not specifically post-apostolic time (1 Clem. 5; Eusebius, *HE* 5.16.22; cf. 3.32.8). Ferguson provided no rationale for Irenaeus' use of the phrase, 'not a very long time ago', in reference to a revelation almost a hundred years earlier. The phrase would again make more sense if it referred to the post-apostolic age and not to Irenaeus' own lifetime. Moreover, Ferguson acknowledged that the early Church certainly distinguished apostolic from post-apostolic times. He declared 'our times' was not the usual way of speaking about the post-apostolic era, but offered no alternative.

Sundberg's interpretation is then at least plausible, and possibly has a precedent. The Fragmentist may well have meant only to distinguish between apostolic and post-apostolic times with his use of 'temporibus nostris'. The real point of the argument in the Fragment's statements about the Shepherd is not that it is heretical, but that it was written too late to be considered apostolic. The temporal references of 'nuperrime' and 'temporibus nostris' in this case should perhaps then be read as relating only to the Shepherd of Hermas and the apostolic age, and not to the date of the Fragment itself. The argument in the Fragment for a late dating of the Shepherd need not correlate it with the lifetime of the Fragmentist, but only with that of Pius of Rome. The language of the Fragment can be read as making its case against it without reference to the dating of the Fragmentist. Sundberg proposed the interpretation, 'but Hermas wrote the Shepherd most recently (that is, later than the apostolic books previously mentioned), in our time (that is, not in apostolic time), in the city of Rome, while his brother Pius was the bishop occupying the episcopal chair of the church of the city of Rome'.[7] The traditional dating of the Muratorian Fragment at the end of the second century by virtue of the phrase 'nuperrime temporibus nostris' is thus dubious.

The phrase occurs within a series of statements in the Fragment (ll. 73–80) about the Shepherd of Hermas:

Pastorem uero
nuperrim e(t) temporibus nostris In urbe
roma herma conscripsit sedente cathe
tra urbis romae aeclesiae Pio ep̃s frat*r*e(r)

[7] Sundberg, 'Canon Muratori', 11.

> eius et ideo legi eum quidẽ Oportet se pu plicare uero In eclesia populo Neque inter profe(*)tas conpletum numero Neque Inter apostolos In finẽ temporum potest.

These statements in the Fragment appear to be making four declarations: (i) that Pius (I) was the brother of Hermas; (ii) that the Shepherd of Hermas was written while Pius was bishop of Rome; (iii) that the Muratorian Fragment was written shortly thereafter; and (iv) that at that time the Shepherd was received as a secondary work, which deserved to be studied privately but could not be read publicly in the churches.

In order to determine the accuracy of the third declaration, upon which the traditional dating of the Fragment is centred, namely that the Fragment was written shortly after Pius' episcopacy, it will be useful to investigate the accuracy of the other three statements. A careful study of the Shepherd of Hermas is needed so as to evaluate the temporal relationship between (*a*) Hermas' writing of the Shepherd, (*b*) Pius' episcopacy, and (*c*) the Muratorian Fragment.

## DATING THE SHEPHERD

The Muratorian Fragment (ll. 73–7) clearly declares that Hermas wrote the Shepherd while his 'brother' Pius was bishop of Rome. Yet all the other evidence for determining its date suggests a period much earlier than the middle of the second century. The Jewish-Christian elements in it suggest that Hermas was of Jewish descent, while the first line of the book (1. 1) implies that he was also a slave.[8] The most probable time for a Jewish slave to have been brought to Rome was after the capture of Jerusalem in AD 70.

In Vision III (13. 1) there is a hint that some of the apostles were still alive. In one sentence the 'apostles' are listed with 'the bishops, teachers, and deacons'. This sentence is followed by one which reads: 'Some [of them] have fallen asleep while others

[8] The numbering of citations employed here was introduced by M. Whittaker, *Der Hirt des Hermas*, rev. edn. (GCS 48, Berlin, 1967), and is found in most modern editions of the Shepherd.

are still living' (13.1). This may suggest that some of the apostles were still living. Later in Similitude IX, however, the apostles appear to have all died (92.4; 93.5). Thus the Shepherd may have been written during the transition to the post-apostolic age, about the end of the first century.

Hippolytus, in his quarrel with Callistus (*Haer.* 9.8), quoted the book of Elchasai to the effect 'that there was preached unto men a new remission of sins in the third year of Trajan's reign' (AD 99/100). This could possibly be the Shepherd. In the first part (Vis. I–IV), the problem of repentance is applied directly to Hermas' household. The second part (Vis. V–Sim. X) is more clearly dominated by the Shepherd as the angel of repentance. The doctrine of a second repentance is the general theme of the Mandates, especially in IV and XII, and culminates in Similitude VIII. If Hippolytus was referring to the Shepherd, then the work could be clearly dated at the turn of the first century.

In Vision II Hermas is instructed by the heavenly figure of the elderly lady to write down his visions for the 'elders'.

> So you shall write two little books and you shall send one to Clement and one to Grapte. Then Clement will send one to the other cities, for that has been entrusted to him. And Grapte will instruct the widows and the orphans. But in this city you yourself shall read it aloud with the elders who stand at the head of the church. (8.3.)

Grapte is otherwise unknown and may have belonged to an order of widows, deaconesses, or virgins.[9] The Clement here is most probably Clement of Rome (*c.* 92–101). 1 Clement was written *c.* 96 by Clement in the name of the Roman church to the church at Corinth.[10] This precedent may account for Hermas' description of Clement as one who had authority to send letters and would imply a date for the Shepherd after 96.

Hermas' description of 'the elders who stand at the head of the church' (8.3) suggests that there was not yet a monarchical bishop in Rome. Elsewhere he speaks of 'officials of the church' (*προηγεμόνες*), 'bishops' (*ἐπίσκοποι*), and 'elders' (*πρεσβύτεροι*), always in the plural.[11] This is particularly revealing if

[9] Cf. 1 Tim. 3.11, 5.3–16; Jas. 1.27, Rom. 16.1, Pliny, *Epis.* 10.97; Ignatius, *Smyr.* 13.1; Polycarp, *Phil.* 4.3, 5.14.

[10] Cf. Dionysius of Corinth, in Eusebius, *HE* 4.23.11; Irenaeus, *Adv. Haer.* 3.3.3.

[11] Cf. 6.6, 8.2, 9.8, 13.1, 17.7, 43.1, 104.2.

Hermas' brother Pius is supposed to be just such a monarchical bishop (ll. 75–7).

A monarchical episcopate at Rome probably did not yet exist in the time of Clement.[12] In 1 Clement only two orders are enumerated, bishops and deacons (cf. 42). Moreover the term *ἐπίσκοποι* is still synonymous with *πρεσβύτεροι* as it is in the New Testament[13] and appears to be in the Shepherd. Yet in the first or second decade of the next century, as exemplified by the epistles of Ignatius, the two terms begin to designate distinctive offices, and a widespread monarchical episcopacy is evidenced, at least in Asia Minor.[14] The absence of a monarchical episcopacy in the Shepherd might suggest a date before the epistles of Ignatius (*c.* 110).

The only specific literary reference in the Shepherd is to the apocryphal Eldad and Modad (7.4). The two men are known from Numbers (11.26–9), but their prophecies are unrecorded there. The book of Eldad and Modad is also referred to in the Palestinian Targums (*Jerus.* 1; 2) of the first century AD. The close resemblance of the references in the Shepherd and the two Targums suggests the same source. Elsewhere the work is unknown, although in 1 Clem. 23.3–4 (cf. 2 Clem. 11.2–3) a long quotation, not found in the Old Testament, is thought by Lightfoot and Holtzman to be from the book of Eldad and Modad.[15]

There is an absence of mention in the Shepherd of any of the early documents to or from Rome, e.g. Romans (*c.* 58), Mark (*c.* 65), 1 Peter (*c.* 65). Nor does there appear any mention or influence of the later prominent teachers at Rome, e.g. Valentinus (*c.* 136), Cerdo (*c.* 140), Marcion (*c.* 140), Justin (*c.* 148). While the significance of these absences is questionable, they perhaps fit best with a date at the very beginning of the second century, sufficiently removed from the earlier writings and the later teachers.

'A great tribulation' appears at hand in Visions I–IV (6.7,

[12] Lightfoot, *Saint Paul's Epistle to the Philippinans* (London, 1888), 95–9; cf. Jerome, *Ep.* 69.3, 146.

[13] Cf. Acts 20.17, 28; Titus 1.5–7; 1 Pet. 5.1–2.

[14] Cf. Ignatius, *Polyc.* 5.6, *Ephes.* 2; Polycarp, *Phil.* 1, 5, 6; Hegesippus, in Eusebius, *HE* 4.22; Irenaeus, *Adv. Haer.* 3.3.3.

[15] Lightfoot, *AF* 1. ii (London, 1890), 80–1 n. 2; cf. J. T. Marshall, 'Eldad and Modad, Book of', *A Dictionary of the Bible*, i (Edinburgh, 1898), 676.

7.4, 22.1, 23.5, 24.6). Which persecution is meant is uncertain. The Neronian persecution (*c.* 64) would probably not have been anticipated,[16] and there is a reference to a past persecution in 9.9, which would preclude the Neronian persecution as the 'tribulation to come'. That this past persecution was Nero's is perhaps confirmed by the description of what was suffered, namely, 'whips, prisons, great persecutions, crosses, wild beasts, for the sake of the Name' (10.1). The 'tribulation to come' could have occurred any time thereafter, as the persecution of Christians appears intermittent and sporadic from Nero to Diocletian.[17]

Attempts have been made to identify the 'tribulation to come' more specifically with the persecutions of either Domitian (*c.* 95) or Trajan (*c.* 112). Trajan's correspondence with Pliny reveals Christian trials in Bithynia (Pliny, *Ep.* 96–7). There is no evidence, however, that the persecution spread to Rome or anywhere else. In writing to the emperor, Pliny notes: 'Having never been present at any trials of Christians, I am unacquainted with the method and limits to be observed either in examining or punishing them' (Pliny, *Ep.* 96). Pliny acknowledges that there have been trials of Christians before the time of his writing (*c.* 112), perhaps in Rome before he left (*c.* 104). There are hints of such trials in the Similitudes, for example: 'those who suffered for the sake of the law . . . those who were persecuted for the sake of the law and did not suffer' (69.6–7), and 'those who were questioned when arrested by the authorities and did not deny, but suffered readily . . . but as many as were cowardly and became doubtful and considered in their hearts whether they should deny or confess, and suffered' (105.4; cf. 50.3). If Pliny was referring to trials before he left Rome (*c.* 104) then the tribulation in the Shepherd may have been in the early years of Trajan's reign (98–117), around the turn of the century.

The persecutor of the tribulation to come is described by Hermas as the 'beast', a synonym for Rome in much apo-

[16] Cf. H. M. Gwatkin, *Early Church History to AD 313*, i (London, 1909), 73–90; H. B. Workman, *Persecution in the Early Church* (London, 1906), 364–5; W. M. Ramsay, *The Church in the Roman Empire* (London, 1893), 226–51.

[17] W. H. C. Frend, *Martyrdom and Persecution in the Early Church* (Oxford, 1965), 210–35.

calyptic literature (cf. Revelation). Yet the beast does not appear to harm the faithful: 'And the beast came on with a rush as if it could destroy a city . . . stretched itself out on the ground and did nothing but thrust out its tongue' (22.9). This may be a reference to a threatened persecution under Trajan which may never have materialized in Rome itself.[18] None the less in Similitude VIII, 'apostates', 'betrayers', and 'blasphemers', have been produced (72.4, 62.3, cf. 96.1).

There is evidence of a persecution in Rome under Domitian (*c.* 95), but it may not have been directed specifically at Christians.[19] Nevertheless Domitian's demand to be called 'Dominus et Deus' could produce among Christians what the faithful might well call 'apostates, blasphemers, and betrayers'. If the persecution in the Shepherd was under Domitian, then the reference in 10.1 would refer naturally to the martyrs of Nero's persecution.

Hermas himself, who had been originally prosperous in trade (14.7, 28.5, 50.1), lost his business in the persecution (20.2), having been betrayed, it would seem, by his children (3.1, 6.2, 7.1). At the time of the Visions he seems to have been employed in cultivating a farm (9.2; 50.5, 7; 66.1). Zahn, who placed the persecution under Domitian, ingeniously conjectured that Hermas was one of those victims of the tyranny of Domitian to whom Nerva made restitution by giving land instead of the goods of which they had been despoiled.[20] The persecution mentioned in the Shepherd might best be assigned then to Domitian (95), or the early years of Trajan (*c.* 100).

The internal evidence of the Shepherd supports an early date for all its parts. The first section (Visions I–IV) appears to be written before a threatened persecution under Domitian or perhaps Trajan. The second section (Vision V–Similitudes VII, X) appears to have been written shortly thereafter to describe the nature of repentance for Christians in the persecution. Similitude IX seems to have been written to unify the work and threaten those who had been disloyal to the church and left it.

[18] Ramsay, 252–319; Gwatkin, 115–34.

[19] D. McFayden, 'The Occasion of the Domitianic Persecution', *AJT* 24 (1920), 46–66; cf. R. L. P. Milburn, 'The Persecution of Domitian', *CQR* 139–40 (1944–5), 154–64.

[20] Zahn, *Der Hirt des Hermas*, 133–4; cf. Eusebius, *HE* 3.20.10.

Two of the Greek fragments that preserve portions of the Shepherd are themselves dated from the second century (P. Mich. 130, P. Iand. 4). Metzger has recently noted that an international conference of classical scholars held at Dublin in 1984 generally agreed that the latter of these two documents should itself be dated to the earlier second century rather than later. As Metzger observed, 'The implication of the latter opinion, if sustained, for the date of the origin of the *Shepherd* is obvious.'[21]

Only the tendentious evidence of the Muratorian Fragment suggests a later date for the Shepherd. An early date makes other references of the work more easily intelligible; for example, the mention of Clement of Rome, the lack of a monarchical episcopacy, a persecution under Domitian or Trajan, and the absence of later Roman history. B. H. Streeter noted that 'scholars of the sharpest critical acumen have allowed themselves to be terrorised, so to speak, into the acceptance of a date which brings to confusion the history of the Church in Rome, on the evidence of an authority no better than the Muratorianum'.[22] Consequently numerous scholars have dismissed the dating of the Shepherd suggested by the Fragment; for example Donaldson, C. Bigg, W. Wilson, Streeter, W. Coleburne, Sundberg.[23] Others will acknowledge that certain parts of the book were most likely written at or before the turn of the first century, but they wish to allow that other parts may have been written as late as 140, the earliest possible date to concur with the Fragment's statements; for example, Harnack, S. Giet, L. W. Barnard, Snyder, J. Reiling.[24]

[21] B. M. Metzger, *The Canon of the New Testament* (Oxford, 1987), 63 n. 36; my thanks to Albert Sundberg for bringing this to my attention.

[22] B. H. Streeter, *The Primitive Church* (London, 1929), 205.

[23] Donaldson, 209; C. Bigg, *The Origins of Christianity* (Oxford, 1909), 72–3; W. Wilson, 'The Career of the Prophet Hermas', *HTR* 20 (1927), 21–62, at 59; Streeter, *The Primitive Church*, 204–8; W. Coleburne, 'A Linguistic Approach to the Problem of Structure and Composition of *The Shepherd of Hermas*' (hereafter 'Linguistic Approach'), *ANZTR* 3 (1969), 133–42, at 139–40; Sundberg, 'Canon Murator', 12 n. 33a.

[24] Harnack, *Geschichte der altchristlichen Literatur bis Eusebius* (hereafter, *Altchristliche Literatur*), 4 pts. in 2 vols. (Leipzig, 1958), ii. 1, 258–9; S. Giet, *Hermas et les Pasteurs* (Paris, 1963), 285–93; L. W. Barnard, 'The Shepherd of Hermas in Recent Study', *HeyJ* 9 (1968), 29–36, at 32; G. F. Snyder, 'The Shepherd of Hermas', *The Apostolic Fathers*, vi (London, 1968), 24; J. Reiling, *Hermas and Christian Prophecy* (Leiden, 1973), 24.

The Fragment plainly states that 'Hermas wrote the Shepherd most recently in our own times in the city of Rome, while the bishop Pius, his brother, was seated on the throne of the church of the city of Rome' (ll. 73–7). If the Shepherd was written, not, as the Fragment says, while Pius was bishop of Rome, but thirty or more years before, then the Fragment is making a grave misstatement on a point essential to its argument for the rejection of the work. It is more reasonable to assume that the whole statement in the Fragment is in error.

## MULTIPLE AUTHORSHIP

The recognition of the possibility of different editions of the Shepherd has raised the question to modern scholars of multiple authorship.[25] In 1963 S. Giet proposed that the existing text consists of three different works by three authors who wrote at different times.[26] According to Giet, the first and oldest of these comprised Visions I–IV and was probably written by Hermas himself early in the second century. The second work consisted of only Similitude IX and was probably written by the brother of Pius of Rome, *c.* 140–54. The third work was of distinctly Jewish-Christian tendency and was written several years after Similitude IX, namely, *c.* 155–60. This third work comprised the remainder of the text, namely, Vision V, the Mandates and Similitudes I–VIII. The unknown third author Giet called 'Pseudo-Pasteur' (named after an attribution in the *Liber Pontificalis*) who passed himself off as the original Hermas of the Visions.

The Shepherd, however, is a rambling prophetic work which cannot be easily systematized. The style of the entire work is a masterpiece of inconsistencies. Giet's attempt to portray Similitude IX as by an 'orthodox' theologian and then attempting to identify this theologian with the brother of Pius is very

[25] The possibility of different editions of the Shepherd have been acknowledged since the study of M. Dibelius, *Der Hirt des Hermas* (Tübingen, 1923). Textual evidence supports his conclusions since Vision V is given different titles in different manuscripts, and appears to be the beginning of the work in the Michigan papyrus and the Sahidic version; cf. K. Lake, 'The Shepherd of Hermas', *HTR* 18 (1925), 279–80.

[26] Giet, 280–309.

questionable. There was probably no rigid idea of 'orthodoxy' in the second century, and though the Similitude does portray a more developed Christology and ecclesiology, there is no internal evidence in Similitude IX to date the work so late as the middle of the second century. Similitude IX reinterprets the tower in Vision III, and if it is a separate work, it is obviously later than Visions I–IV. However, Similitude IX need not be seen as much later than the beginning of the second century. While the apostolic period is apparently over in Similitude IX, it seems to have been written in the generation that immediately followed 'the apostles and teachers of the proclamation of the Son of God' (92.4; cf. 93.5). A date around the episcopacy of Pius (*c.* 140–*c.* 154) would appear to be a bit late. Giet, it appears, was simply trying to correlate the reference in the Fragment with the obvious literary divisions of the Shepherd.

The editorial references in the Shepherd suggest that Similitude IX was later than Vision V–Similitudes I–VIII and Similitude X (25.5; 77.5; 78.1) rather than earlier, as Giet suggested.[27] Similitude IX appears to have been inserted among the Similitudes, causing them to be renumbered and rearranged. Therefore the work of the so-called Pseudo-Shepherd would likewise have to be dated in the generation following the apostles. Giet's date of *c.* 155–60 again appears too late.

Another scholar, W. Coleburne, also attempted to define multiple authors for the Shepherd. Coleburne envisaged at least six authors for the work, breaking the text into seven parts—Visions I–IV (called V), Vision V (called R), Mandates I–XII.3.3 (called M), Mandate XII.3.3–6.5 (called E), Similitudes I–VII (called S), Similitude VIII (called S8), and Similitude IX (called S9).[28] The divisions are based primarily

[27] Some editions of the Shepherd vary in their numbering of the Similitudes. In addition, the Athos Codex, the Palatina Latin version, and the Ethiopian translation all have textual variations at Mandate XII (46.3) which suggest to some scholars that the last part of Mandate XII (46.4–49.5) may originally have been the first Similitude, and been renumbered when Similitude IX, which has an apparently more developed Christology and ecclesiology, was inserted; cf. J. Armitage Robinson, *Barnabas, Hermas, and the Didache* (London, 1920), 27; Snyder, 6–7.

[28] Coleburne, 'Linguistic Approach'; cf. id., 'The Shepherd of Hermas: Case for Multiple Authorship and Some Implications', *StudPat* 10/1 (1970), 65–70.

upon linguistic evidence from what Coleburne calls his *apparatus discernendi.* Similitude X is not considered by Coleburne since no significant fragments of the Greek text are known.

Interestingly, none of Coleburne's six authors is dated near the middle of the second century. He placed V during the persecution of Domitian, *c.* 95. According to his theory of composition, M and S must be even earlier, perhaps *c.* 60, in response to the controversy about the remission of sins after baptism found in Hebrews 6: 4–6. No clear evidence of dating R and E is found, but they must be placed after M and S but before V. S8 is placed by Colburne in the last years of the first century and the reign of Nerva. For S9 the well-ordered reign of Trajan would seem a possibility, *c.* 100, but not much later, according to Coleburne, or else it would fall into the period of monarchical episcopacy. He dismissed the reference to Hermas in the Muratorian Fragment, but suggested that the apostolic Hermas of Romans 16. 14, noted by Origen, may have been the author of the original work M. The author of V then reintroduced the name of Hermas around AD 95 as a 'concession to a strong Roman tradition'.[29]

Neither Giet's nor Coleburne's suggestion of multiple authorship has received strong support from other scholars, although there is general agreement that different editions may have appeared. Giet's interpretation has been subjected to a severe and detailed criticism by R. Joly, who completely rejected it.[30] A. Hilhorst, who has seen Coleburne's unpublished *apparatus discernendi*, disputed the conclusions based upon it.[31] Differences in composition do not rule out the possibility of a single author, which is still the generally favoured thesis.[32] Moreover, a significant time-span is neither suggested nor needed for the completion of later additions. Attempts to expand substantially the time of composition of the Shepherd are not founded upon internal evidence, which consistently suggests a date around AD 100 for all the parts. The time of

[29] Id., 'Linguistic Approach', 141.

[30] R. Joly, 'Hermas et le Pasteur', *VC* 21 (1967), 201–18.

[31] According to Reiling, 24 n. 1.

[32] L. Pernveden, *The Concept of the Church in the Shepherd of Hermas*, trans. I. and N. Reeves (Lund, 1966), 291–300; Barnard, 29–36; Reiling, 22–4.

composition is expanded substantially only because of later traditions about who Hermas was, traditions which associate him with Rom. 16: 14 and Pius of Rome.

## TRADITIONS ABOUT AUTHORSHIP

The Shepherd of Hermas is written as autobiography and often in the first person. The author is quickly (1.4) and repeatedly identified as 'Hermas' although all the specific references occur only within Visions I–IV (1.4; 2.2, 3, 4; 4.3; 6.2; 7.1 (*bis*); 9.6, 9; 16.11; 22.4, 7). If a single author is assumed for the work, there are four traditions about its authorship.

1. First there is the unlikely notion that the Apostle Paul was the author. The transcriber of the Ethiopic version suggested this in a marginal note, probably based on nothing more substantial than the identification of Paul with the god Hermes in Acts 14: 12.[33]

2. G. Gaab and Zahn first proposed as author of the Shepherd an otherwise unknown contemporary of Clement of Rome (*c.* 96).[34] This proposal is based primarily upon the reference to Clement in 8.3. All the internal evidences for dating the work would also be consistent with such a suggestion; the lack of a monarchical episcopacy, the reference in Hippolytus, a possible persecution in Rome under Domitian or in the early years of Trajan, and the absence of later Roman history.

3. A third possibility is to identify the author with the Hermas to whom a salutation is sent by Paul at the end of his epistle to the Romans (Rom. 16: 14). That the Shepherd is to be located in Rome is almost certain. The opening line of the book declares it: 'The one who brought me up sold me to a certain Rhoda in Rome' (1.1). Other geographical references are clearly Roman: the road to Cumae (1.3, 5.1), the Via Campana (22.2). The Clement of 8.3 is most probably Clement of Rome. Moreover, tradition offers no origin for the Shepherd other than Rome. The Muratorian Fragment depicts Hermas as the brother of a bishop of Rome, and Origen and others equate

[33] G. H. Schodde, *Hêrmâ Nabî: The Ethiopic Version of Pastor Hermae Examined* (Leipzig, 1876), 5.

[34] G. Gaab, *Der Hirt des Hermas* (Basle, 1866), 67–70, cf. 71–124; Zahn, *Der Hirt des Hermas*, 285–312, cf. 44–61.

him with the Hermas of Rom. 16:14. However, it should be noted that all the Roman references occur in the first part of the Shepherd, that is Visions I–IV.[35]

Origen, in his *Commentary on Paul's Epistle to the Romans* (*c.* 244), in a section which is known only from the Latin translation of Rufinus (*c.* 397), is the earliest extant witness to attribute the authorship of the Shepherd to the apostolic Hermas:

'Salutate Asyncritum . . . fratres.' De istis simplex est salutatio nec aliquid eis insigne laudis adiungitur. Puto tamen, quod Hermas iste sit scriptor libelli illius, qui Pastor appellatur, quae scriptura valde mihi utilis videtur et ut puto divinitus inspirata. Quod vero nihil ei laudis adscripsit, illa opinor est causa, quia videtur, sicut scriptura illa declarat, post multa peccata ad paenitentiam fuisse conversus; et ideo nec opprobrium ei aliquod adscripsit, didicerat enim scripturam non improperare homini convertenti se a peccato. Neque laudis aliquod tribuit, quia adhuc positus erat sub angelo paenitentiae, a quo tempore opportuno Christus rursus deberet offerri. (*Commentary on Romans* 10.31.)

Eusebius (*HE* 3.3.6) and Jerome (*De Vir. Ill.* 10) both repeat the tradition.

It is unlikely that the Hermas mentioned in Romans is the same Hermas who wrote the Shepherd. To begin with the date of Romans (*c.* 54–7) appears too early for the Shepherd. Secondly the work itself shows no trace that the author wished to be taken for the Hermas associated with the Apostle Paul. If the author was seeking a pseudonym, the obscure reference in Romans seems an unlikely choice for a later writer. But most important is the question of the integrity of Rom. 16.

New Testament scholars have debated the authenticity of this chapter on a number of grounds, especially its long list of names (vv. 1–15).[36] It would be surprising to discover that Paul

[35] In Similitude IX (78.4) Arcadia appears to be the subject of the vision and the only other geographical reference in the Shepherd, cf. R. Harris, 'Hermas in Arcadia', *JBL* 21 (1887), 69–83; id., *Hermas in Arcadia and Other Essays* (Cambridge, 1896), 1–20; and J. Armitage Robinson, *A Collation of the Athos Codex of The Shepherd of Hermas* (Cambridge, 1888), app. B, 'Hermas in Arcadia', 30–4. However, the possible independence of this part of the Shepherd diminishes the importance of the reference in placing the work.

[36] Gamble, *The Textual History of the Letter to the Romans* (Studies and Documents 42; Grand Rapids, Mich., 1977); T. W. Manson, 'St. Paul's Letter to the Romans—and Others', *BJRL* 31 (1948), 224–40, at 237; E. J. Goodspeed, 'Phoebe's Letter of Introduction', *HTR* 44 (1951), 55–7; J. Knox, 'A Note on the Text of Romans', *NTSt* 2

had so many Christian friends and would commend the deaconess Phoebe (v. 1) to a church he had never visited. If Rome was the intended recipient of the chapter, then at least nine of the twenty-six people mentioned there must have emigrated from the East where Paul would have known them, namely, Prisca and Aquila (vv. 3–5), Epaenetus (5), Andronicus and Junias (7), Ampliatus (8), Stachys (9), Rufus and his mother (13). It would hardly have served Paul's purpose in Romans if he had greeted emphatically so many old friends instead of the leading personalities of the congregation. The warning against trouble-makers (17–18) also accords better with a church for which Paul had pastoral responsibility rather than the church at Rome, where he was a stranger, and which he addressed earlier with a measure of diffidence and with every effort to avoid the appearance of criticism (1: 10–12; 12.3–5; 15.14–15, 18–20). A significant consensus of modern scholarship is that chapter 16 was not originally written for the church at Rome, and may not have originally been a part of the Epistle.[37]

If ch. 16 was not intended for the church at Rome, then the Hermas mentioned by Paul in 16: 14 could not be the Hermas of the Shepherd. For the Hermas of Romans (16: 14) would then not have resided in Rome, as the Hermas of the Shepherd did. Moreover, the association of the apostolic Hermas in Romans with the Hermas of the Shepherd would not have been made except where and when ch. 16 had been attached to the remainder of the Epistle. Yet ch. 16 appears not to have been a part of the version of Romans that circulated in the West at the end of the second century.

The evidence of the early church in the West suggests a recension of Romans with neither ch. 15 nor ch. 16. Marcion, for instance, appears to have used a text of Romans that concluded at the end of ch. 14.[38] According to chapter-lists in

(1955–6), 191–3; J. Munck, *Paul and the Salvation of Mankind*, trans. F. Clarke (London, 1959), 198.

[37] e.g. R. H. Fuller, *A Critical Introduction to the New Testament* (Letchworth, 1971), 51–3; and Perrin–Duling, *The New Testament: An Introduction*, 114; Collins, *Introduction to the New Testament*, 142.

[38] Origen wrote that from 14.23 Marcion 'usque ad finem cuncta dissecuit' in Romans (*Comm. on Romans* 10. 43), and Tertullian is silent about chs. 15 and 16 in his review of Marcion's work (*Adv. Marc.* 5.13–14).

Cyprian, the Old Latin version placed the doxology (16:25–7) after chapter 14, suggesting a natural conclusion to the work. The same placement occurs in some Latin Vulgate manuscripts.

| *Extent* | *Date* | *Source* |
|---|---|---|
| 1–14 | *a.* 160 | Marcion |
| 1–14, 16:25–7 | *a.* 258 | Cyprian |
| | *c.* 400 | Vulgate MSS 1648, 1792, 2089; ch.-lists in A, F |

Thus Marcion's recension may have been prevalent in the West; alternatively, the absence of chs. 15 and 16 was not his doing but represented an early form in which the text reached him.[39] There is no quotation from either ch. 15 or ch. 16 in the writings of Irenaeus, Tertullian, or Cyprian, although their works are considerable and the chapters were known to Clement of Alexandria.

If Romans was known with only chs. 1–14 in the West at the end of the second and beginning of the third centuries, then this may be further evidence against dating the Muratorian Fragment at that time, because it reveals possible acquaintance with ch. 15. The Fragment explained the absence in Acts of any account of Paul's missionary journey to Spain by insisting that Luke was not present when the Apostle set out and only recorded the things he witnessed (ll. 35–9). In doing so, the Fragment employed the uncommon Latin form *spania* for Spain (l. 39), instead of the familiar *Hispania*. *Σπανία* was the word employed by Paul in Rom. 15:24, 28 when describing his plans for a visit to Spain, and was probably the word present if there was a Greek original of the Fragment. It may have been simply transliterated in the Latin translation.[40] If so, then the Fragmentist was probably familiar with Rom. 15 in Greek, and that was not likely in the West at the end of the second and beginning of the third century.

T. W. Manson suggested that it was in Alexandria that ch. 16 was added to Romans.[41] The earliest manuscript to

[39] Marcion, of course, was not incapable of expunging ch. 15, especially with the laudatory reference to the Old Testament (v. 4) and Old Testament quotations (vv. 3, 8–12, 21), but there is no reason to assume that he also expunged ch. 16.

[40] A similar transliteration, as noted earlier, has been suggested by P. Katz, see ch. 1 n. 32.

[41] Manson, 235–6.

include it is the Egyptian 𝔭46 (*c.* 200), the exemplar of which appears to have ended after ch. 15.[42] The earliest reference to ch. 16 also comes from Egypt in Clement of Alexandria (*Paed.* 1.6, cf. 3.12). Perhaps it was only in the East and shortly before the time of Origen that an identification of the Hermas mentioned in Romans with the Hermas of the Shepherd could have been made, because before then, and elsewhere, ch. 16, containing the name of Hermas, does not appear to have been part of the Epistle. The identification of the two Hermae may have originated with Origen himself or a contemporary.

Origen's association of the Hermas mentioned in Romans with the author of the Shepherd occurs in his *Commentary on Romans*, written towards the end of his life (*c.* 244). Although Origen referred to the Shepherd many times, nowhere else did he make this claim about its authorship. Nor does any writer before Origen (save possibly for the Fragmentist) appear to identify the author with the Hermas of Romans, or for that matter with anyone else. In the *Commentary*, Origen appears to justify Paul's salutation to Hermas by conjecturing 'puto tamen' that this may be the Hermas of the Shepherd and then praising the work himself ('et ut puto divinitus inspirata'). Origen similarly conjectured that the Clement mentioned in Paul's Epistle to the Philippians (4: 3) was Clement of Rome (*Comm. on John* 6.36). Both these conjectures are unlikely. It is probable that Eusebius derived his account of the apostolic Hermas from Origen, and Jerome derived his from Eusebius. Therefore Origen may be the ultimate source of the tradition which associates the Hermas of Romans with the author of the Shepherd, and which would then date no further back than the middle of the third century.

The Muratorian Fragment may bear an indirect and a reluctant testimony to knowledge of the Eastern tradition of the apostolic authorship of the Shepherd. The Fragment allowed private reading of the book, but wished to exclude it among canonical works specifically because Hermas, in the view of the

[42] H. A. Sanders, *A Third-Century Papyrus Codex of the Epistles of Paul* (University of Michigan, 1935), 16–17 and pl. iii; note that the scribe put a line and a couple of dots like a semicolon, otherwise unknown in the MS, after the 'Amen' of the doxology (16.25–7), which has been placed at the end of ch. 15, as if the epistle ended at that point in the exemplar.

Fragmentist, was not apostolic. The Fragment's whole contention was that the Shepherd was written 'most recently, in our own time', by Pope Pius' brother, and 'therefore it ought indeed to be read, but it cannot to the end of time be read publicly in the church to the people, either among the prophets, whose number is settled, or among the apostles' (ll. 77–80). There would be no need to deny so emphatically the apostolicity of Hermas in the Fragment, unless a tradition associating Hermas with an apostle was known. Such a tradition is unknown before Origen and may well have originated with him. If the Fragmentist betrays an awareness of that tradition then the Fragment would have to be dated after Origen. Additionally the tradition of the apostolic Hermas appears to be a particularly Eastern one, based upon what is an Eastern recension of Romans which included ch. 16, and passed on among Fathers writing in the East, namely Origen, Eusebius, Jerome (in Bethlehem). If the Fragment reveals an awareness of the tradition of the apostolic Hermas, then this would be more easily understood if the Fragment was an Eastern document.

4. A fourth tradition of authorship identifies the Hermas of the Shepherd as the brother of Pius, bishop of Rome. This association is found in three major sources.

### 1. *The Muratorian Fragment*

As we have seen, the Fragment ascribes the Shepherd to Pius' brother:

Pastorem uero
nuperrim e(t) temporibus nostris In urbe
roma herma conscripsit sedente cathe
tra urbis romae aeclesiae Pio ep̃s frat*re*(r)
eius

This tradition is also found in an early list of popes up to Liberius (352–66), commonly called the Liberian Catalogue.[43]

Sub huius [*Pii*] episcopatu frater eius Ermes librum scripsit in quo mandatum continetur, quod ei precepit angelus, cum venit ad illum in habitu pastoris.

[43] L. Duchesne, *Le Liber Pontificalis*, 2 vols. (Paris, 1886–92), i. 1–12.

The third appearance of the kinship of Hermas and Pius is in an early Latin poem against the Marcionites called *Carmen adversus Marcionitas*, attributed to Tertullian:[44]

> post hunc [*Hyginum*] deinde Pius, Hermas cui germine frater,
> angelicus pastor, cui tradita verba locutus . . . (3.294–5.)

It is unlikely that the Hermas of the Shepherd was the brother of Pius. The Hermas of the Shepherd appears to have been a foundling slave (1.1), who would be unlikely to know who his parents or siblings were. 'Hermas' is a Greek name, while 'Pius' is Latin. Hermas wrote in Rome before a monarchical episcopacy was established there, casting further doubt on his brother's being a monarchical bishop. Hermas never mentioned a brother in the Shepherd although he frequently referred to the leaders of the church and to the members of his family, that is his wife and children. Hermas appeared to be writing at a considerably earlier time than that of Pius' episcopacy and it is also unlikely that the Shepherd, if written under Pius, would have been regarded as inspired so quickly in the church, for instance by Irenaeus, Clement, Tertullian, while at the same time with no apparent recollection or tradition of its authorship. The purpose of linking Hermas with Pius in the Fragment appears to be to combat a supposed apostolicity for Hermas, a tradition which cannot be traced earlier than Origen.

The traditional dating of the Muratorian Fragment is in jeopardy if the Shepherd was not written in the middle of the second century, and if Hermas is not Pius' brother. For it is unlikely that a contemporary witness ('nuperrime temporibus nostris') would be so mistaken in information vital to its argument concerning the position of Hermas, which, moreover, other contemporary witnesses could or would dispute. However, if the Fragment was written later, then it is more easily understood how a mistake could be made, and not disputed. Later generations would be unlikely to remember exactly when the Shepherd was written or who the brothers of Pius were, and would possess a highly popular work claimed as authoritative by predecessors, but for reasons perhaps unknown. Supposing

[44] M. Müller, *Untersuchungen zum Carmen adversus Marcionitas* (Ochsenfurt, 1936), 7–38.

a later date for the tradition that Hermas was the brother of Pius would also explain the high regard in which the Shepherd was held by the early Church, since the work would probably not have been so highly received if it was thought to be dated from the middle of the second century. Later generations would also be more likely to conjecture that the apostolic Hermas was the author, if the tradition that Hermas was the brother of Pius was unknown and no other tradition was established.

The plain sense of the words 'nuperrime temporibus nostris' in the Fragment suggests a contemporary account of Hermas as the brother of Pope Pius and as writing the Shepherd in the middle of the second century. Yet there is more reason to suspect that these words were misleadingly translated or transcribed than to suggest that the Shepherd was indeed written while Pius was bishop in Rome or that Pius was Hermas' brother. The attempt to explain the statements in the Fragment as exaggerated anti-Montanist polemic still assumes that the Fragment was written in the late second century.[45] It is an attempt to keep the traditional date of the Fragment, while correcting or explaining the misinformation about the date of the Shepherd. But if the information about Hermas is in fact incorrect, then it is unlikely that the Fragment was written at the end of the second century. Such a misstatement about the Shepherd would be better understood as being made by later generations unfamiliar with the work itself or its author, but interested only in discrediting Hermas' claim to be apostolic, in response to a tradition which may not have originated until the time of Origen (*c.* 244). The dating of the other sources associating Hermas and Pius confirm the tradition as later.

## 2. *The Liberian Catalogue*

The Liberian Catalogue is one of several tracts in a collection of documents gathered together and edited for the use of Christians at Rome in the fourth century by a compiler whom Theodor Mommsen dubbed the 'Chronographer of 354'.[46]

[45] Cf. Harnack, *The Origin of the New Testament*, trans. J. R. Wilkinson (London, 1925), 83–5.

[46] Th. Mommsen, *Über den Chronographen vom Jahre 354* (Leipzig, 1850).

The Liberian Catalogue comprises a chronological account of the bishops of Rome from St Peter to Liberius (352–66). The length of each episcopate is given in years, months, and days. The names of the emperors are also given, and historical notes are sometimes added recording important events in the life of the Roman church. There is in the list a marked break at Pontian (230–5). The method of reckoning the imperial reign is more specific thereafter, suggesting perhaps that a later editor worked with an earlier piece that listed only the years, and not the months and days.[47] There are no historical notices in the earlier portion, with two exceptions: the date of St Peter's crucifixion, and the reference to Hermas.

There are numerous historical notes from Pontian to Lucius (253–4). A break in the Catalogue may be suggested after Lucius, since there is an absence of historical notices for the remaining part of the Catalogue with one exception, namely Julius (337–52). Thus the first continuator of the earliest part of the list ending at Pontian seems to have written under Stephen (254–7), the successor of Lucius, and to have described the events of the twenty years intervening possibly from personal knowledge, if not official sources.

A third break towards the end of the Catalogue is also possible. Lightfoot noted that four other works in the collection of the Chronographer of 354 were compiled about 334, specifically, the *Commemoration-Days of Bishops and Martyrs*, the *Chronicle of the World*, the *Chronicle of the City*, and the *Regions of the City*. Lightfoot contended that an earlier list of the popes incorporated into the Liberian Catalogue ended about the same time, evidenced by the lack of historical notes from Lucius until Julius.[48] The immediate predecessor of Julius was Marcus (336), who was bishop for less than a year and about whom there may have been nothing to note. The second continuator of the original list may have compiled his catalogue at the end of the episcopate of Sylvester (314–35), *c.* 334.

The Chronographer of 354 was probably the final editor of the Liberian Catalogue. He could have added the last three names (Marcus, Julius, Liberius) and the historical note about Julius. The note about Julius is the most elaborate notice in the

[47] Lightfoot, *AF* I. i. 264–6.

[48] Ibid. 263–4.

whole document, even containing an enumeration of the churches built by him. This note is most probably the work of a contemporary. The Chronographer may not have included notes for Marcus (336) and Liberius (352–66), because the reign of the former was too brief and the latter was just beginning. At which point then, was the tradition about Hermas being the brother of Pius introduced into the Liberian Catalogue: 231–5, 254–7, 334, 354?

Lightfoot argued that Hippolytus was the editor of the original list (231–5) from which the Liberian Catalogue is derived and that he introduced the historical note about Hermas being the brother of Pius.[49] Inconsistencies and errors within the Liberian Catalogue, however, suggest that the original list, from Peter to Pontian, contained only the names of the bishops and their durations of office in years, all the other information, in particular the names of emperors and historical notes, being added by the later editors.[50] This would also fit the description in the table of contents of the *Liber Generationis*, namely 'Nomina episcoporum Romae et quis quot annis praefuit'. There is a note respecting the fate of 'Hippolytus the presbyter' in the historical information about Pontian in the Liberian Catalogue which may suggest that the second editor knew that his primary source was from Hippolytus. Hippolytus' opponent, Pope Callistus (217–22), is thought to have relied heavily upon the Shepherd for defence of his position on repentance, and Hippolytus, it is argued, would gladly have discredited the work if he knew any reason to. Some scholars, as was noted earlier, have argued that Hippolytus was the author of the Fragment itself and therefore was familiar with the Hermas–Pius tradition.[51]

While Hippolytus may have been the author of the original list of the Liberian Catalogue, there are serious objections to the claim that the note about Hermas' being the brother of Pius was introduced into the list at that time. There are only two historical notes in the earliest part of the list, the date of Peter's crucifixion and the Hermas–Pius tradition. Lightfoot denied that Hippolytus introduced the first note, especially

[49] Lightfoot, ibid. 261–2, argues that the *Liber Generationis* is a translation of the named, but previously unknown *Chronica* of Hippolytus.

[50] Mommsen, 585–98.

[51] See ch. 1 nn. 82, 86.

since Hippolytus appears to have dated the Crucifixion in AD 28 whereas the compiler of the Liberian Catalogue dates it AD 29. None the less Lightfoot allowed the solitary note relating to Hermas to have been part of the original list.[52] If Hippolytus was the author and included more than just names and dates, a historical note about Callistus or Zephyrinus might have been more likely. Hippolytus refused to accept the teaching of Pope Zephyrinus and rejected his successor Callistus as a heretic, which seems inconsistent with their recognition in the Liberian Catalogue as genuine popes, without comment. The rejection of the Shepherd by Hippolytus is based upon its supposed use by Callistus, deduced from a vague reference in Tertullian (*De Pud.* 10). Callistus is no longer accepted as Tertullian's opponent, who is now thought to have been Bishop Agrippinus of Carthage.[53] Moreover, this tradition about Hermas' brother does not seem to be known to any other Church father of that time, such as Irenaeus, Clement, or Origen.

The only evidence for the prior existence of the tradition about Hermas and Pius is the assumption that the Muratorian Fragment was a late second-century document. But the main reason for presuming that date is its reference to Hermas and his brother. If the Fragment is thought to be later, then there is little reason to credit Hippolytus or a contemporary with inserting a single historical note into the original list of the Liberian Catalogue. It was most probably added by a later editor. It is unlikely to have been inserted by the supposed editor of 334, since he is noted for his lack of historical information. The two editors who are believed to have added historical notes are those of 254–7 and 354. In either of these two cases, the author of the historical note could have been responding to Origen's association of the Hermas of the Shepherd with the Hermas of Rom. 16: 14.

The tradition about Hermas in the Liberian Catalogue might have been added at the same time as the historical notice on Peter's crucifixion, the only other note in the earliest part of the list. The note on Peter reads: 'Passus autem cum

[52] Lightfoot, *AF*, I. i. 300.

[53] C. Figgini, 'Agrippino o Callisto?', *Scuola cattolica* 6/3 (1924), 204–11; W. Koehler, 'Zum Toleranzedikt des römischen Bischofs Calixt', *ZKG* 61 (1942), 124–35.

Paulo die iii Kl. Iulias, cons. ss. imperante Nerone'.[54] The striking aspect of this note is that Peter and Paul are said to have been killed together under Nero. Jerome (*c.* 394) is the earliest witness to confirm the tradition that Peter and Paul were executed together (*De Vir. Ill.* 5). In the Acts of Peter (*c.* 180), Paul is clearly not even in Rome when Peter was killed.[55] The idea that they suffered together was probably an inference from the union of their names by Clement (1 Clem. 5), Ignatius (*Rom.* 4), Gaius (Eusebius, *HE* 2.25), and Tertullian (*Praescript.* 36; *Scorp.* 15). Dionysius may have encouraged the tradition with the statement that they 'suffered martyrdom at the same time' (κατὰ τὸν αὐτὸν καιρόν) (Eusebius, *HE* 2.25.8). Prudentius (*c.* 400), perhaps aware of the conflicting traditions in the Acts of Peter and the Liberian Catalogue, represented the Apostles as suffering on the same day one year apart (*Peristeph.* 12.5). Since the tradition that Peter and Paul were martyred together is otherwise unknown before the end of the fourth century, it was probably added to the Liberian Catalogue by the editor of 354 rather than the editor of 254–7. If the historical note about the Shepherd was added by the same editor who added the note about Peter, then the tradition that Hermas was the brother of Pius would not have been introduced into the Liberian Catalogue until the fourth century and the final edition.

### 3. *Carmen adversus Marcionitas*

The tradition that Hermas was the brother of Pius is also present in the third book of the *Carmen adversus Marcionitas*, a poem in opposition to Marcionism, containing 1,302 hexameters written in poor Latin in five books. The poem was first published in 1564 among the works of Tertullian.[56] Although there is some dependence upon Tertullian's *Adversus Marcionitas* (*c.* 212), there is little foundation for an attribution to him. Thus the author is generally known as Pseudo-Tertullian.

Within the poem there is a list of the bishops of Rome, by which the advent of Cerdo and Marcion to Rome is dated. A

[54] R. A. Lipsius, *Chronologie der römischen Bischöfe* (Kiel, 1869), 41–3; Duchesne, i, p. ix.

[55] Acts of Peter 40 (11).

[56] G. Fabricius, *Poetarum Veterum Ecclesiasticorum Opera Christiana* (Basle, 1564).

statement that Pius and Hermas were brothers is found within the mention of Pius' episcopacy:

> hac cathedra Petrus, qua sederat ipse, locatum
> maxima Roma Linum primum considere iussit.
> Post quem Cletus et ipse gregem suscepit ovilis.
> Huius Anacletus successor sorte locatus.
> Quem sequitur Clemens; is apostolicis bene notus.
> Euaristus ab hoc rexit sine crimine gregem.
> Sextus Alexander Sixto commendat ovile;
> post expleta sui qui lustri tempora tradit
> Telesphoro; excellens hic erat, martyrque fidelis.
> Post illum doctus legis, certusque magister,
> cum vestri sceleris socius, praecursor et auctor
> aduenit Romam Cerdo . . .
> iamque loco nono cathedram suscepit Hyginus.
> Post hunc deinde Pius, Hermas cui germine frater,
> angelicus pastor, cui tradita verba locutus,
> aque pio suscepit Anicetus ordine sortem.
> Sub quo Marcion hic ueniens . . . (3.276–85, 293–7.)

The order of bishops given in the poem is unique among early lists, but reveals the separation of Cletus and Anacletus (Anencletus) into two persons, as does the Liberian Catalogue:

| Irenaeus[57] | Eusebius[58] | Liberian Catalogue[59] | Optatus/ Augustine[60] | Pseudo-Tertullian[61] |
|---|---|---|---|---|
| Peter | Peter | Peter | Peter | Peter |
| Linus | Linus | Linus | Linus | Linus |
| *Anacletus* | *Anencletus* | Clement | Clement | *Cletus* |
| Clement | Clement | *Cletus* | *Anacletus* | *Anacletus* |
| Evaristus | Evaristus | *Anacletus* | Evaristus | Clement |
| Alexander | Alexander | Evaristus | Alexander | Evaristus |
| Sixtus | Sixtus | Alexander | Sixtus | Alexander |
| Telesphorus | Telesphorus | Sixtus | Telesphorus | Sixtus |
| Hyginus | Hyginus | Telesphorus | Hyginus | Telesphorus |
| Pius | Pius | Hyginus | Anicetus | Hyginus |
| Anicetus | Anicetus | Anicetus | Pius | Pius |
| Soter | Soter | Pius | Soter | Anicetus |
| Eleutherius | Eleutherius | Soter | Eleutherius | |

[57] Irenaeus, *Adv. Haer.* 3.3.3.

[58] Eusebius, *HE* 3.2, 4, 13, 15, 21, 34; 4.1, 4, 5, 10, 11, 19, 30; 5.22, 28; 6.21, 23, 29, 39; 7.2, 5, 27, 30, 32; *Chronicon* according to all three recensions (Armenian, Hieronymian, and Syrian), cf. Lightfoot, *AF* I. i. 208, 221.

[59] Duchesne, 2–5.

[60] Cf. Optatus, *De schism. Don.* 2.2.3; Augustine, *Ep.* 53.2.

[61] *Carmen adv. Marc.* 3.276–97.

The separation of Cletus and Anacletus (Anencletus) into two different persons was probably a scribal error originating in one of the revisions of the Liberian Catalogue, from which it passed into the Felician Catalogue and later editions of the *Liber Pontificalis.*[62] It is more likely that Pseudo-Tertullian should be dependent for his papal list on an edition of the Liberian Catalogue than that an editor of the Catalogue should rely upon the *Carmen adversus Marcionitas.* Thus the *Carmen adversus Marcionitas* was probably dependent upon one of the editions of the Liberian Catalogue, directly or indirectly. Both works indeed are possibly Roman in origin. However, in Pseudo-Tertullian Cletus and Anacletus are placed before Clement, while in the Liberian Catalogue they occur after him (the *Liber Pontificalis* inserted Clement between them). Likewise Anicetus is after Pius in Pseudo-Tertullian, as in most lists, but before him in the Liberian Catalogue. Thus a case of direct dependence cannot be established between the Liberian Catalogue and the *Carmen adversus Marcionitas.* The variations between the lists suggest that the dependence was mediated by some other source or influence.

If Pseudo-Tertullian was dependent upon one of the editions of the Liberian Catalogue for its duplication of Cletus and Anacletus (Anencletus), then it is probable that he received the tradition of Hermas' being the brother of Pius from the same source. If the Hermas–Pius tradition was introduced into the Liberian Catalogue at the same time as the historical note about Peter's crucifixion, then it was probably introduced into the final edition of 354. Thus the *Carmen adversus Marcionitas* was perhaps dependent upon the final edition of the Liberian Catalogue.

The date of the *Carmen adversus Marcionitas* is disputed. Suggested dates for the work have varied from the mid-third to the early sixth century.[63] W. Brandes and Harnack noted that

[62] Tertullian does not appear to have made this duplication himself, cf. *Praescript.* 32.

[63] W. Brandes, 'Zwei Victoringedichte des Vatic. Regin. 582 und das Carmen adversus Marcionitas', *Wiener Studien*, 12 (1890), 310–16, at 312–13; F. Oehler, *Tertulliani omnia* (Leipzig, 1853), ii. 782; E. Huckstadt, *Über das pseudotertullianische Gedicht Adversus Marcionem* (Leipzig, 1875), 51–7; A. Hilgenfeld's review, *ZWT* 19 (1876), 154–9; Duchesne, xi. n. 2; A. Waitz, *Das pseudotertullianische Gedicht Adversus Marcionem* (Darmstadt, 1900), 14–29 (for a summary of their argument, cf. Harnack, *Altchristliche Literatur*, ii. 2, 445); Harnack, ibid. 445–9.

Pseudo-Tertullian wrote: 'Filius, immenso *genitum de lumine lumen*' (4. 29) and 'De patre principium, *genitum de lumine lumen*' (5. 199).[64] They could find no example of this important formula, 'genitum de lumine lumen', before the Council of Nicaea in 325. Thus a date for the *Carmen adversus Marcionitas* before that time is perhaps unlikely. More recently K. Holl argued for an even later dating.[65] Besides 'genitum de lumine lumen', Holl noted the phrase 'cum patre semper erat, unitus gloria et aevo' (5. 201). This phrase, according to Holl, hints at Arian objections to the theological use of *coaevus* and *aequaevus*, which did not appear in Western theology before 360. Holl went on to argue on other accounts for a date for the *Carmen adversus Marcionitas* in the last quarter of the fifth century, or the first quarter of the sixth.

The variety of suggested dates witnesses to the difficulty of reaching a firm conclusion, but most recent scholars have opted for a date in the fourth century, after 325.[66] Overall, there seem good grounds for claiming that the *Carmen adversus Marcionitas* is probably later than the Liberian Catalogue, and probably dependent upon it for its tradition of Hermas' being the brother of Pius.

In summary, both the Liberian Catalogue and the *Carmen adversus Marcionitas* as witnesses for the Hermas–Pius tradition are much later than the traditionally dated Muratorian Fragment. Both witnesses are probably to be dated some time after Origen's *Commentary on Romans* (*c.* 244) and the tradition could have arisen in response to the apostolic Hermas tradition suggested by Origen. Perhaps Pius did have a brother named Hermas, a common enough name at that time. A later generation could easily confuse the two. But it is unlikely that the Hermas of the Shepherd was the brother of Pius; and it is also unlikely that a supposedly contemporary source like the Fragment, as traditionally dated, would make such an error. If the Fragment were to be dated in the fourth century, then the mistake would be more understandable, and the witness it

[64] Brandes, 310–11; cf. Harnack, *Altchristliche Literatur*, ii. 2. 442 n. 4.

[65] K. Holl, 'Über Zeit und Heimat des pseudotertullianischen Gedichts adv. Marcionem', *Gesammelte Aufsätze*, iii (Tubingen, 1928), 13–53.

[66] Harnack, *Altchristliche Literatur*, ii. 2. 445–9; Holl, loc. cit.

would present to the Hermas–Pius tradition would be contemporaneous with the other surviving testimonies.

## RECEPTION IN THE CHURCH

Attestation of the Shepherd among the churches is early and widespread. The oldest extant testimony is Irenaeus of Lyons (*c.* 130–*c.* 200), who simply quoted a passage from the work with the words, 'Well said the Scripture' (ἡ γραφή: *Adv. Haer.* 4.20.2; cf. Eusebius, *HE* 5.8.7), in the midst of quotations from Genesis, Malachi, Ephesians, Matthew, Revelation, 1 Peter, and Colossians. The fact that Irenaeus did not name the source may suggest that he was quoting a well-known text. None of the other scriptural references was identified either. Additionally, the first reference to Genesis was also introduced as from the 'Scripture' (*Scriptura*: 4.20.1).

The mutilated beginning of the *Stromateis* of Clement of Alexandria opens in the middle of a sentence from the Shepherd, and about ten times elsewhere he quoted from the book,[67] always with a complete acceptance of the reality and divine character of the revelations made to Hermas. Clement also quoted from the Shepherd in the *Eclogae propheticae* (45). The context of these references was often clearly among scriptural passages, e.g. John, Ephesians (*Strom.* 1.17); Romans, Deuteronomy, Isaiah (2.9); Ezekiel, Matthew, Romans (6.6); Psalms, Luke, Matthew, Mark (*Eclog. proph.*). Clement appeared to regard the Shepherd as inspired, for in one place he wrote: 'Divinely [θείως] therefore the power which spoke to Hermas by revelation said . . .' (1.29); elsewhere he wrote: 'And it is well said by the shepherd . . .' (6.6).

The Shepherd seems to have been translated into Latin by Tertullian's time (*c.* 160–*c.* 225), since he described it by the Latin title *Pastor* and not by a Greek title, as he usually did when he was referring to Greek writings. In *De oratione* (16), he disputed the practice of sitting down immediately after prayer,

[67] *Strom.* 1.1.1. (Shepherd 25.5), 1.85.4 (43.3), 1.181.1 (12.3), 2.3.5 (11.4), 2.43.5–44.4 (93.5–7), 2.55.3–4 (16.3–5, 7; cf. 30.2; 31); 4.74.4 (23.5); 6.46.5 (93.6); 6.131.2 (5.3–4).

for which he knew no other reason except that Hermas is said to have sat upon a bed after praying (25.1). The Shepherd seems to have been a very influential work in the Church at that time, and Tertullian did not dispute its authority, only the unreasonableness of converting a narrative statement into a rule of discipline. Thus Tertullian appears to have accepted the book at that point.

The evidence of Irenaeus in Lyon, Clement in Alexandria, and Tertullian in North Africa suggests that the Shepherd was widely accepted among the churches at the end of the second century and the beginning of the third, although none of these writers appears to have known the origin of the book or anything about its author. Such a combination of widespread acceptance with unknown origins would not be remarkable if the work was written *c.* 100 by a relatively unknown author and if the Muratorian Fragment was of a later date. However, it is remarkable if Shepherd was composed during Pius' episcopacy and if the tradition that Hermas was his brother was known at the end of the second century, as would be the case in some areas of the Church at least with the traditional dating of the Muratorian Fragment.

Twenty years after his comments in *De oratione*, and after his conversion to Montanism (*c.* 207), Tertullian came to reject the Shepherd, vehemently attacking it as 'the book that loves adulterers' and noting that 'every' synod, even of the non-Montanists, has habitually counted it 'spurious' ('sed cederem tibi, si scriptura Pastoris, quae sola moechos amat, diuino instrumento meruisset incidi, si non ab omni concilio ecclesiarum, etiam uestrarum, inter apocrypha et falsa iudicaretur', *De Pud.* 10). This reference suggests that Tertullian's opponent had cited the Shepherd in his defence. As previously mentioned that opponent was formerly thought to have been Pope Callistus but is now generally believed to have been Bishop Agrippinus of Carthage.[68]

Tertullian's remarks in *De Pudicitia* (*c.* 220) are the first indisputable criticisms of the Shepherd. *De Pudicitia* is a polemic against the penitential discipline of the church, a position which contradicted Tertullian's own earlier views in *De Paenit-*

[68] See above, n. 53.

*entia* (*c.* 203). Indeed in *De Pudicitia*, Tertullian introduced a class of sins for which there is no forgiveness, the *irremissibilia.* Among these was idolatry, and thus there was no scope for repentance of idolatry, a position which conflicts with the principal theme of the Shepherd. It is not surprising that the Montanist Tertullian railed against the popular and influential work. His statement that it was rejected by every synod of the churches, even those of the non-Montanists, however, cannot be objectively verified, and might be thought of as an example of his famous rhetoric. Later in *De Pudicitia* (§ 20) Tertullian commented on Hebrews ('extat enim et Barnabae titulus ad Hebraeos'), noting that this work was at least 'more received' than the Shepherd, suggesting something less than the previously described universal rejection for the book ('et utique receptior apud ecclesias epistola Barnabae illo apocrypho Pastore moechorum').

Tertullian's reasons for rejecting the Shepherd are clearly sectarian and it should not be thought that there was widespread rejection of the work. A. Jülicher noted that: 'The "Shepherd" of Hermas was treated by practically all the Greek theologians of the third century who had occasion to use it as a canonical document.'[69] Even in the West it must have remained popular, for some twenty manuscripts still exist in an Old Latin version of the second or third century. There is strong evidence of a familiarity with the work in the *Passio SS. Perpetuae* et *Felicitatis* (202/3).[70] While the Shepherd was not directly cited at all by Cyprian (d. 258), this is not particularly surprising.[71] Cyprian had a comparatively rigorist position in regard to the repentance of the *sacrificati* and *thurificati* of the Decian persecution, and would not have taken kindly to the more lenient repentance allowed in the Shepherd. There is a clear allusion to Similitude II, however, in Commodian: 'Sicut ulmus amat vitem, sic ipsi pusillos' (*Instruct.* 1.30). The Shepherd was not unfavourably mentioned in the Liberian Catalogue or the *Carmen adversus Marcionitas* (*c.* 475–*c.* 525). John

[69] A. Jülicher, *An Introduction to the New Testament*, 521.

[70] J. Armitage Robinson, *The Passion of S. Perpetua* (TxSt 1/2; Cambridge, 1891), 26–36.

[71] There are possibly some allusions in Cyprian to the Shepherd despite the absence of direct references; cf. Zahn, *Der Hirt des Hermas*, 181 n. 2; Harnack, *Altchristliche Literatur*, i. 1. 52–3.

Cassion (*c.* 360–435) also cited it in his *Collationes Patrum* (13.12) *c.* 420.

Moreover, in the pseudo-Cyprianic *Adversus Aleatores* there are numerous allusions to the Shepherd,[72] and at one point it is specifically cited as 'divine scripture' (*dicit enim scriptura divina*, 2). The *Adversus Aleatores* is a sermon written in late Latin against *dicing*. The date of the work is disputed, and it is not found among the earliest manuscripts of Cyprian, such as the catalogue dated 359 discovered by Mommsen. The tract is not quoted as Cyprian's until the fourteenth century. At one time Harnack assigned it to Pope Victor,[73] but this position received little support.[74] Harnack himself later expressed doubt about his dating, writing:

> Ich habe früher die pseudocyprianische Schrift *Ad aleatores* dem Victor vindiziert (Texte u. Unters. V, Heft 1), bin aber jetzt gegen diese Hypothese skeptisch geworden. Ist sie nicht von Victor, so ist sie von einem novatianischen römischen Bischof aus d. JJ. 260–309.[75]

The first official notice of dicing in the Church is at the Council of Elvira (*c.* 300), canon 79. The late Latin of the work is similar to other documents found amongst the Cyprianic correspondence.[76] Koch therefore held that the *Adversus Aleatores* was written by a bishop of North Africa after Cyprian's time, perhaps *c.* 300.[77]

If the *Adversus Aleatores* is dated after Tertullian's *De Pudicitia*, as seems evident, then there is continued evidence in the Latin church of a high regard for the Shepherd as *scriptura divina*. The only extant rejection of the work is limited to the Montanists, although their influence combined with the Novatianist controversy may account for a decline in its use in the West.

[72] Harnack, *Der pseudocyprianische Tractat de Aleatoribus* (TU 5/1; Leipzig, 1889), 126–8.

[73] Ibid. 92–125; cf. H. Ryder, 'Harnack on the "De Aleatoribus"', *The Dublin Review*, 3rd ser., 22/43 (1889), 82–98.

[74] See bibliography in Harnack, *Altchristliche Literatur*, ii. 2. 370–2 and n. 3.

[75] Id., *Lehrbuch der Dogmengeschichte*, 5th edn., i (Tübingen, 1931), 483 n. 4.

[76] (i) The letter of the Roman clergy *sede vacante* to the Carthaginian clergy on the flight of Cyprian (*Ep.* 8); (ii) a letter of the Roman Celerinus to the Carthaginian Lucian (*Ep.* 21); (iii) Lucian's answer (*Ep.* 22); (iv) a letter of the Confessors to Cyprian (*Ep.* 23); (v) a letter of Caldonius to Cyprian and his clergy (*Ep.* 24).

[77] Koch, 'Zur Schrift Adversus aleatores', *Festgabe K. Müller* (Tübingen, 1922), 58–67.

It is in the East that more general, non-sectarian reservations about the Shepherd developed. Origen certainly had a high regard for the work. In *De Principiis* (*c.* 220–30), he quoted it along with the Psalms and 2 Maccabees as 'ex scripturarum auctoritate' (1.1.5). In his *Homilies on Luke* (*c.* 233–4), having quoted from an apocryphal work which he knew might be disputed, Origen added that anybody offended by this work could find the same doctrine in *The Shepherd* (*Hom. on Luke* 35), implying that it was a widely acknowledged source. In his *Commentary on Romans* (*c.* 244), Origen called the Shepherd 'divinely inspired' (*divinitus inspirata*). Six times he referred to it without commenting on its inspiration.[78] Yet Origen was also aware that the work had its despisers. Later in *De Principiis* he described the Shepherd as τῷ ὑπό τινων καταφρονουμένῳ βιβλίῳ (4.1.11), but it is obvious that he himself was not one of these despisers. Who the despisers were is not certain, and these comments may reflect nothing more than Montanist dissatisfactions.

The fact that Origen interjected a personal opinion in his *Commentary on Romans*, 'et puto divinitus inspirata', perhaps suggests a continued controversy about the book. In his *Commentary on Matthew* (*c.* 246), Origen described the Shepherd as φερομένης μὲν ἐν τῇ ἐκκλησίᾳ γραφῆς, οὐ παρὰ πᾶσι δὲ ὁμολογουμένης (14.21). Remarks which exist only in Rufinus' loose translation express similar hesitation about the work later in Origen's life. For instance, in the *Commentary on Matthew* (*c.* 246) the phrase 'si cui placeat illum legere librum' (2.53), is found. In Origen's *Homilies on Numbers* (246–54) we read: 'si cui tamen scriptura illa recipienda videtur' (8.1), and in *Homily I on Psalm 38* (*c.* 247) is found, 'si cui tamen libellus ille recipiendus videtur (1)'. What exactly occasioned this new-found hesitation in Origen is not known; but it would seem that despite the apparent hesitation, Origen still approved of the work. It seems unlikely that Origen became aware of opposition to the Shepherd when he visited Rome around 212,[79] since he does not appear to have revealed any personal hesitancy until some thirty years later, 244–54. However, while in Rome, he may

[78] *De Prin.* 1.3.3; 3.3.4; *Comm. on John* 1.17; *Hom. on Joshua* 10.1; *Hom. on Ezekiel* 13.3; fragment on Hosea in *Philoc.* 8.3.

[79] Chadwick, 276.

have learnt of the Montanist disparagement of the work reflected in his comment in *De principiis.* Since Origen revealed no knowledge of the tradition of its authorship recorded in the Fragment, it seems unlikely that the Fragment's objections could have been the source of Origen's apparent later hesitancy.[80] It is possible that Origen became hesitant about the Shepherd when he moved to Caesarea (*c.* 232), if the work was not accepted there.[81] Origen's later remarks do not so much suggest that the Shepherd had been rejected, as only that it was not received.

Eusebius of Caesarea (*c.* 260–*c.* 340) appears to mark the turning-point for the status of the Shepherd. While relating the tradition of the apostolic Hermas' authorship in his *Church History*, Eusebius noted that the work had been disputed by some, and thus on their account it could not be placed among the acknowledged books (ὁμολογούμενα, 3.3.6). Still, Eusebius made it clear that others considered the work quite indispensable, especially to those who needed instruction in the faith (3.3.6). Eusebius reported that it had been publicly read in churches, and that some of the most ancient writers used it (3.3.6; cf. 5.8.7). Immediately after these comments on the Shepherd, Eusebius wrote: 'This will serve to present the divine writings that are undisputed as well as those that are not universally acknowledged' (ταῦτα εἰς παράστασιν τῶν τε ἀναντιρρήτων καὶ τῶν μὴ παρὰ πᾶσιν ὁμολογουμένων θείων γραμμάτων εἰρήσθω, 3.3.7). The Shepherd obviously belonged to the latter class of works, those that were not universally acknowledged. A little later in the *Church History* (3.25.1–5), Eusebius, in listing books of the New Testament, placed it among the spurious (νόθοι) works,[82] along with the Acts of Paul, the Revelation of Peter, Barnabas, the Didache, and perhaps Revelation, and the Gospel according to the Hebrews. On the one hand, these works were distinguished from the accepted writings (ὁμολογούμενοι), namely the four gospels, Acts, the epistles of Paul, 1 John, and 1 Peter, and from the

[80] J. Ruwet, 'Les "Antilegomena" dans les œuvres d'Origène', *Biblica*, 23 (1942), 18–42, at 33–5.

[81] Cf. Chadwick, 276–7.

[82] 'Spurious' is considered the better translation of νόθος throughout this work, cf. Lampe, 918, s. v. νόθος B. 4.

disputed books (ἀντιλεγόμενοι), namely James, Jude, 2 Peter, and 2 and 3 John. On the other hand, these writings were also distinct from those which were cited by the heretics under the name of the Apostles, namely the Gospels of Peter, Thomas, Matthias, and of any other besides them, and the Acts of Andrew and John and the other Apostles, which 'are not to be placed even among the spurious writings [νόθοι], but are all of them to be cast aside as absurd and impious' (3.25.6–7). Unlike Origen, who while acknowledging a dispute about the Shepherd continued to accept the work, Eusebius, in acknowledging the dispute, clearly placed it in a secondary class.

A parallel situation appears to be reflected in the list of the Codex Claromontanus ($D^p$). In this list of New Testament works, the scribe drew a line before the last four entries, namely Barnabas, the Shepherd, the Acts of Paul, and the Revelation of Peter. This line suggests a dispute about these works. The contents of this secondary class in the list of the Codex Claromontanus is almost identical with that of Eusebius (3.25.4). Revelation, which Eusebius noted that some rejected (ἀθετοῦσιν) and others counted among the accepted books (ὁμολογούμενοι), is here placed among the latter. The Gospel according to the Hebrews, which Eusebius acknowledged that some had classed in the spurious group, although he himself seemed reluctant so to do, is absent altogether from the list. The remaining works which Eusebius had grouped all together are exactly those which are distinguished in this list, although the order is different: the Acts of Paul, the Shepherd, the Revelation of Peter, and Barnabas. The presence of these works in the list suggests an Eastern origin, perhaps associated with the school of Alexandria. The absence of the reservations about James, Jude, 2 Peter, and 2 and 3 John that Eusebius expressed (*HE* 3.25.3) would perhaps suggest a later date.

In the Codex Sinaiticus (א), the Shepherd again appears to be in a secondary class. Following the books of the New Testament and Barnabas, a space of over one and a half columns is left vacant, after which the Shepherd was added.[83] Such a gap may suggest a secondary class for the Shepherd.[84] There are

[83] Lake, *Codex Sinaiticus*, 141b–142.

[84] There is a similar gap after Acts in Codex Sinaiticus which may cast doubt upon the interpretation of the one before the Shepherd.

divisions indicated in the margin of the Gospels in the Codex Sinaiticus which are a device derived from Eusebius for forming a harmony of the Gospels.[85] Thus this codex, like the catalogue in the Codex Claromontanus, was probably later than Eusebius.

Athanasius (*c.* 296–373) in an earlier work, the *De Incarnatione Verbi Dei* (probably best dated *c.* 318), called the Shepherd 'most edifying' (ὠφελιμωτάτης) (3), and quoted it between Genesis and Hebrews. In his paschal letter of 339, however, Athanasius appeared more hesitant. When he quoted from Mandate I (26.1) among citations from Deuteronomy, Hebrews, Isaiah, John, the epistles to Timothy, Romans, and other books, he introduced it with an apology in the style of Origen, 'if any man is not offended at his testimony' (*Ep. Fest.* 11.4). Perhaps the Arian appeal to Mandates I (cf. *Ep. ad Afros* 5) led Athanasius still later to emphasize that the Shepherd was 'not in the canon'; for example at *De Decretis* 18 (350/1). In his famous paschal letter of 367 Athanasius clearly placed it among a secondary class of works that were not in the canon but were none the less useful for catechetical instruction (*Ep. Fest.* 39.7). Distinct from apocryphal writings (ἀπόκρυφοι), this secondary class also included the Didache, and several Jewish works, namely Wisdom, Sirach, Esther, Judith, and Tobit.

Jerome (*c.* 342–420) in his preface to the Books of Kings (*Prologus Galestus*) (391), also placed the Shepherd among Jewish writings, specifically Wisdom, Sirach, Judith, and Tobit, which 'non sunt in canone'. In his *Lives of Illustrious Men* (392), Jerome noted that while the Shepherd was almost unknown in the West, it was read publicly in some churches in Greece (*De Vir. Ill.* 10). He noted that it was in fact a useful book ('re vera utilis liber') and many of the ancient writers quoted from it as authoritative ('multique de eo scriptorum veterum usurpavere testimonia'). Yet if the Shepherd was the work referred to in book 1 of his *Commentary on Habakkuk* (392), then Jerome appears to have viewed it there as foolish, 'Ex quo liber ille apocryphus stultitiae condemnandus est, in quo scriptum est, quemdam angelum nomine Tyri praeesse reptili-

[85] B. M. Metzger, *The Text of the New Testament* (Oxford, 1964), 46.

bus' (1: 14) (cf. Shepherd 23:4). Still in book 2 of his *Commentary on Hosea* (406), he wrote with a hesitancy reminiscent of Origen and Athanasius: 'Unde et in libro Pastoris, *si cui tamen placet illius recipere lectionem*, Hermae primum videtur ecclesia a cano capite, deinde adulescentula et sponsa crinibus adornata' (7.9).

Rufinus (*c.* 345–410) also mentioned the Shepherd in a secondary class. In his *Commentary on the Apostles' Creed* (397/8) Rufinus presented a list of books of the Old and New Testaments. Thereafter he added some works that he called 'ecclesiastical': 'sciendum tamen est quod et alii libri sunt qui non canonici sed ecclesiastici a maioribus appellati sunt' (*Comm. in Symb. Apost.* 38). The characteristic of this class of books was that they could freely be read in the churches, but could not be appealed to as authoritative ('Quae omnia legi quidem in ecclesiis voluerunt, non tamen proferri ad auctoritatem ex his fidei confirmandam'). In this group, Rufinus included Wisdom, Sirach, Tobit, Judith, and the books of the Maccabees (1, 27), 'in Novo vero Testamento libellus qui dicitur Pastoris seu Hermas, qui appellatur Duae viae vel Judicium Petri'. Rufinus also recognized another class of works, the 'apocrypha', which were those which could not be read in the churches: 'Ceteras vero scripturas Apocryphas nominarunt, quas in ecclesiis legi noluerunt'.

Within the Muratorian Fragment, the Shepherd was also clearly placed in a secondary class. It was excluded from among the prophets and apostles, whose number was complete (ll. 78–80). Yet while its private reading was still encouraged, it ought not to be read publicly in church (ll. 77–8). It was reported to have been read in churches by Eusebius (*HE* 3.3.6), Jerome (*De Vir. Ill.* 10), and Rufinus (*Comm. in Symb. Apost.* 38). Despite Origen's hesitancy, it was only with Eusebius that the Shepherd was put in a secondary class of limited acceptance. Eusebius clearly noted that it 'has been disputed by some, and on their account cannot be placed among the acknowledged books' (3.3.6). Origen appears never to have gone so far. But throughout the fourth century in the East, the Shepherd is found in such a secondary class: in Eusebius, Athanasius, the list in the Codex Claromontanus, the Codex Sinaiticus, and Rufinus (whose tradition was at least influenced by the East). Thus the statements about it in the

Fragment would not be particularly remarkable if the latter was dated in the fourth century in the East.

Ferguson denied that Eusebius was the turning-point in regard to the status of the Shepherd. Instead he suggested that Eusebius' statements 'are in a historical context; he was reporting a situation which we know goes back at least to the time of Tertullian'.[86] Yet Tertullian's remarks are quite different from those of the Fragment and it is hard to correlate Tertullian's description of the Shepherd as 'the book that loves adulterers', with the encouragement in the Fragment that the Shepherd ought to be read privately. Tertullian, after his conversion to Montanism, rejected the work utterly, while the Fragment maintained a limited acceptance of it. While the Montanists may have introduced a dispute about the book, its acceptance was not limited in the Church at large, as far as is known, until Eusebius. Thereafter the Shepherd remained accepted, but in a secondary class, throughout the fourth century.

Ferguson suggested that: 'The approval which Irenaeus gave the work and Clement of Alexandria's regard for it as inspired could be the very use against which the *Canon Muratori* was protesting, or alternatively the very kind of private use which the author approved.'[87] Yet it cannot be both. Irenaeus and Clement of Alexandria appear unaware of any dispute or restriction of the work. If Ferguson cannot correlate Irenaeus' and Clement's use of the Shepherd with either the private reading the Fragment approves or the public reading it rejects, then Irenaeus and Clement cannot be used, as Ferguson wishes, as contemporary confirmation of the Fragment's views and evidence of its date.

Tertullian's rejection of the Shepherd was clearly a sectarian and isolated incident, not a general trend. In the West the work was still quoted or alluded to by Tertullian's opponent, Bishop Agrippinus of Carthage, by Commodian, John Cassian, and especially by the author of *Adversus Aleatores*, who expressly cited the work as 'divine scripture'. Moreover, it was not unfavourably mentioned in the Liberian Catalogue or by the author of the *Carmen adversus Marcionitas*; and some twenty Old Latin manuscripts of the work survive. In fact apart from

[86] Ferguson, 679. [87] Ibid. 678–9.

Tertullian's complete renunciation of the Shepherd in *De Pudicitia*, there is no extant unfavourable remark about it in the West until Jerome (if considered Western), who at one point appeared to call it 'foolish' but at another time 'useful'. It was only in the East, and after Origen's time, that questions about the work caused it to be excluded from among the universally acknowledged writings and placed into a secondary class of limited acceptance. The statements about the Shepherd in the Muratorian Fragment imply that it was received into just such a secondary class. Thus its attitude towards the Shepherd suggests a fourth-century date for the Fragment.

## CONCLUSION

While the traditional dating of the Muratorian Fragment has been based on its statements about the Shepherd of Hermas, those statements themselves appear to be erroneous or misleading on several accounts. First, the dating of the Shepherd in the Fragment during the episcopacy of Pius (*c.* 140–*c.* 154) is uncorroborated and most probably incorrect. All other evidence suggests a date around AD 100: the apparent reference to Clement of Rome, the lack of a monarchical episcopate, and the mention of a persecution most readily identified with the time of Domitian or the early years of Trajan. The fact that the work was so widely and approvingly disseminated, among Irenaeus, Tertullian (in his Catholic phase), and Clement of Alexandria, would also discourage a dating in the middle of the second century.

Secondly, the tradition of authorship for the Shepherd presented in the Fragment, namely by Pius' brother, is also unlikely to be correct, and is otherwise unknown until the fourth century, when this tradition appears in the Liberian Catalogue (354) and the *Carmen adversus Marcionitas* (354+). The insistence in the Fragment that Hermas was not apostolic would suggest a knowledge of the tradition of the apostolic Hermas' authorship, which probably originated with Origen (*c.* 244). This is a peculiarly Eastern tradition, evidenced by Origen, Eusebius, Jerome (in Bethlehem), and was probably dependent on an Eastern recension of Romans which included ch. 16. Even ch. 15 may have been unknown in the West at the time when the Fragment is traditionally dated, and yet the Fragmentist appears to have known it.

Thirdly, the reception of the Shepherd in the church as depicted by the Fragment militates against the traditional dating of the latter. It is paralleled most clearly by Eastern sources of the fourth century, namely Eusebius, Athanasius, the list in Codex Claromontanus, and the Codex Sinaiticus. The attitude of limited acceptance reflected in the Fragment contrasts both with the complete rejection of the work by the sectarian Tertullian and the strong acceptance of the work by Irenaeus, Clement of Alexandria, and Origen.

If these statements in the Fragment about the Shepherd are erroneous or misleading, then the apparent statement in the Fragment that it was composed shortly after the episcopacy of Pius is dubious itself. The traditional dating of the Fragment, dependent on the key phrase 'nuperrime temporibus nostris', which Sundberg has attempted to reinterpret, is also rash in view of the known poor transcription and the suspected careless translation of the manuscript. Thus the traditional dating of the Muratorian Fragment has no sure foundation, and the place of the Fragment within the history of the New Testament canon needs to be reconsidered.

# 3

# THE FORMATION OF THE CANON

WHEN a survey is undertaken of the history of the Christian canon as a whole, the Muratorian Fragment as traditionally dated emerges as an anomaly in the development of the New Testament. Albert Sundberg suggested that 'in order to write a coherent and accurate history of the development of the New Testament it becomes necessary to distinguish between the terms "scripture" and "canon" as *termini technici* in the history of canon'.[1] He contends that scholars often fail to make this distinction and instead treat the two terms as synonymous. He defines 'scripture' as religious literature that is appealed to for religious authority. 'Canon' is then a closed collection of 'scripture', to which nothing can be added and from which nothing can be subtracted. Whereas the concept of canon presupposes the existence of scriptures, the concept of scripture does not necessarily entail the notion of canon. It is entirely possible to possess scriptures without having a canon, and this was in fact the situation in the first few centuries of the Church.

## THE OLD TESTAMENT

Sundberg's distinction between scripture and canon is based on the fact that the literature received from Judaism was treated as authoritative in the early Christian church, together with the view now widely held that the Jewish literature received by Christianity was not a closed collection.[2] Until the nineteenth century, most scholars thought that the Jewish canon was completed in the days of Ezra and Nehemiah long before Jesus and the rise of Christianity.[3]

[1] Sundberg, 'Revised History', 453–4.
[2] See Introd. n. 1.
[3] Sundberg, *Old Testament*, 12–13.

The studies of A. Kuenen in the late nineteenth century made it especially difficult to defend the closing of the Jewish canon by Ezra and the Great Synagogue.[4] The witnesses to the tradition of 2 Maccabees (*c.* 90–50 BC) and 2 (4) Esdras (AD *c.* 100) are significantly removed from the period of Ezra (*c.* 397 BC) and Nehemiah (*c.* 444 BC), so as to represent only a later tradition about the origins of the Jewish scriptures.

While the Law and the Prophets may have been long established among the Jewish scriptures, the remaining books of the Jewish canon do not appear to have been defined in the pre-Christian era. Ben Sira, for example, in the prologue to his translation of Ecclesiasticus (*c.* 130 BC) mentions the sacred writings three times, each time leaving the last element of the collection undefined. Likewise in 2 Macc. 15:9 Judas is noted as 'encouraging [his men] from the Law and the Prophets . . .'. A reference to Nehemiah's 'memoirs' and library (2. 13–15) suggests that a collection of 'writings' in addition to the Law and the Prophets may have also been known to the author. Philo of Alexandria (AD *c.* 49) mentions 'the Laws, and the words foretold by the prophets, and hymns and the other writings, by which knowledge and piety are multiplied and perfected' (*De vita contempl.* 25). The New Testament frequently refers to the Law and the Prophets without mention of the 'writings' (e.g. Matt. 5:17, 7:12, 11:13, 22:40; Luke 16:29, 31, 24:27; John 1:45; Acts 13:15, 28:23). In Luke, Jesus is said to have begun with the Law and the Prophets, but what he went on to is unspecified: 'And beginning with Moses and all the Prophets he [Jesus] interpreted to them in all the Scriptures the things concerning himself' (24:27). A few verses later the Psalms are included: 'in the Law of Moses and the Prophets and the Psalms . . .' (24:44). Thus the Law and the Prophets appear to have been defined elements within the Jewish scriptures before the Christian era. But the 'writings', the remaining element, still appear undefined to New Testament writers.

The numerous quotations from and allusions to the books of the Jewish canon which appear in the New Testament cannot be distinguished from the numerous quotations from and

[4] A. Kuenen, 'Über die Männer der großen Synagoge', *Gesammelte Abhandlungen zur biblischen Wissenschaft von Dr. Abraham Kuenen* (Freiburg, i. B., 1894), 125–60.

allusions to Jewish scriptures outside the canon.[5] Similarly, references by the early writers of the Christian churches, both in the East and West, do not neatly distinguish between the works of the Jewish canon and other Jewish scriptures. The books now called 'deuterocanonical' by Roman Catholics and 'apocryphal' by Protestants were in the early Church employed in ways indistinguishable from the books included in the Jewish canon. Thus the Jewish canon appears not to have been closed in the days of the New Testament writers.[6]

The discoveries at Qumran confirm this point. In a way similar to Christian writings, the works found at Qumran included quotations from and allusions to the books of the Jewish canon which are indistinguishable from quotations from and allusions to other Jewish scriptures outside the canon.[7] Thus in both a Jewish sectarian group that came to an end in Palestine about AD 68, and in a primitive Christianity that arose within Judaism in Palestine after 30 AD, there is a similar treatment of Jewish religious writings. It does not seem likely that the one group influenced the other.[8] Moreover, there is no known restriction against the use of this wider body of Scriptures in Judaism before the end of the first century AD.

When the Jewish canon was closed is not certain. It is not until the end of the first century AD, after the Christians had separated from the synagogues, that there is any clear evidence of the establishment of the Jewish canon. Josephus (*c.* 100) is the first extant witness for a closed Jewish canon. In *Contra Apionem* (1. 37–41) he considers the Jewish canon closed, the text inspired and inviolable, the period of time within which these books originated fixed, and the number of the books established (at 22). Josephus' polemic, however, may suggest that an established Jewish canon was a recent innovation. The exact contents of Josephus' collection remain uncertain, and

[5] e.g. Sir. 5. 11 (Jas. 1:9); 2 Macc. 6–7 (Heb. 11:35–6); Wisd. 2:13, 18 (Matt. 27:43); 5.17 (Eph. 6:11, 13); 7:26 (Heb. 1:3); 9:15 (2 Cor. 5:4); 13:1–9, 14:22–31 (Rom. 1:20–32); cf. Bleek, 'Ueber die Stellung der Aprokyphen des alten Testamentes im christlichen Kanon', *Theologische Studien und Kritiken*, 26 (1853), 268–354.

[6] B. Childs, *Introduction to the Old Testament as Scripture* (London, 1979), 53.

[7] B. J. Roberts, 'The Dead Sea Scrolls and the Old Testament Scriptures', *BJRL* 36 (1953–4), 75–96; J. A. Sanders, 'Cave 11 Surprises and the Question of Canon', *McCormick Quarterly*, 12 (1968), 84–98.

[8] Sundberg, *Old Testament*, 101–2.

the last element of the canon appears untitled as 'the remaining four [books] contain hymns to God and the maxims of life for men'. 2 (4) Esdras 14:19–48 (*c.* 100) also suggests a closed Jewish canon. Here ninety-four Jewish works are alluded to. Twenty-four books are to be made public while the remaining seventy are 'to be delivered in secret to the wise'. The twenty-four books would appear to be the Jewish canon. Indeed it was probably to limit the contents of the Jewish canon against so many other writings and influences that it was finally closed. Thus at the turn of the first century AD (*c.* 100), Josephus and 2 (4) Esdras are the earliest surviving witnesses to a closed Jewish canon, though they disagree about the exact number of works included, for Josephus has twenty-two while 2 (4) Esdras has twenty-four.

Disputes about which works were included in the Jewish canon continued into the second and third centuries AD. Ecclesiastes and the Song of Solomon were discussed at Jamnia (AD *c.* 90). Esther and Ezekiel were still disputed in the third century.[9] Ecclesiasticus, although not part of the Jewish canon, was quoted three times in the Talmud apparently as Scripture.[10] According to the Gemara, some rabbis still did not admit Proverbs, Esther, Ezekiel, and Ruth.[11] Thus, while the concept of a closed Jewish canon apparently became accepted in Rabbinic circles from the end of the first century AD, the exact contents of that canon continued to be disputed for some time.

Confusion about the exact contents of the Jewish canon is evidenced by Christian writers as well. Melito (*c.* 170) provided a list of the books of the Jewish canon in answer to frequent questions from his brother [bishop?] Onesimus, who 'desired to have an accurate statement of the ancient books as regards their number and order' (Eusebius, *HE* 4.26.13–14). Apparently unable to fulfil this request in Sardis, Melito 'went East

[9] S. Leiman, *The Canonization of the Hebrew Scripture* (Hamden, Conn., 1976), 120–1; R. Meyer, 'The Canon and the Apocrypha in Judaism', *TDNT* iii (1965), 978–87, at 984.

[10] Hagigah 13a; Yebamoth 63b; Babakama 92b; cf. Erubin 54a (*The Babylonian Talmud*, trans. I. Epstein, 34 unnumbered vols. (London, 1935–52), 73, 426, 536, cf. 375).

[11] A. Jeffrey, 'The Canon of the Old Testament', *The Interpreter's Bible*, i (New York, 1952), 32–35, at 39; G. F. Moore, *Judaism*, i (Cambridge, 1927), 242–7.

and came to the place where these things were preached and done'. In his list of twenty-one books, Melito oddly omits mention of Esther and Lamentations and places Ezekiel after Daniel.

Later, Origen also provided a list of the Jewish canon. 'But it should be known that there are twenty-two canonical books, as the Hebrews have handed them down; the same as the number of the letters of their alphabet ... These are the twenty-two books according to the Hebrews ...' (Eusebius, *HE* 6.25.2). Origen included a transliteration in Greek of the Hebrew titles to parallel the names of the books as known in the Septuagint. He appears to have omitted the book of the Twelve Prophets, since his intended list of twenty-two books includes only twenty-one Hebrew titles; unless indeed one reads e.g. ⟨*οἱ Δώδεκα προφῆται, Τρησαώρ·*⟩ *Ἰώβ*. He also noted the book of the Maccabees at the end of his list.

Both lists that Melito and Origen presented are clearly Jewish catalogues and not Christian ones. Origen drew a clear distinction between 'their scriptures' (those of the Jews) and 'our scriptures' (those of the Church), both with respect to the reading of the text (cf. *Ad Africanum* 5, 9, 13) and with respect to the number of books. He noted, for instance, that the Jews did not use Tobit and Judith, to which the churches did appeal (*Ad Africanum* 13.3). Origen appears to have suggested confinement by Christians to the Jewish canon only for polemic purposes with Jewish opponents (*Ad Africanum* 5.13). A similar need may lie behind Melito's list, for he is known to have made a collection of 'testimonies' from the Jewish canon (Eusebius, *HE* 4.26 12, 14).

The extant evidence suggests that the Jews defined their canon (*c.* 100) some time after the Christians had separated from the synagogues and that the Christians inherited a larger body of Jewish scriptures than the later Jewish canon. The Eastern church felt the impact of the newly established Jewish canon more clearly than the Western. Melito, implicitly, and Origen, explicitly, attempted to correlate Christian usage with the Jewish twenty-two-book list, at least for polemical purposes. Like their successors, they related, in varying combinations, separate Septuagint works to the Hebrew titles of the Jewish canon (see Table 3.1). In Epiphanius there are three

TABLE 3.1. *Eastern Christian lists of the Old Testament*

| Melito | Origen | Athan. | Cyril | Epiph.[1] | Epiph.[2] | Epiph.[3] | Gregory | Amphil. |
|---|---|---|---|---|---|---|---|---|
| Gen. | Gen. | Gen. | Gen. | Gen. | Gen. | Gen. | Gen. | Gen. |
| Exod. | Exod. | Exod. | Exod. | Exod. | Exod. | Exod. | Exod. | Exod. |
| Num. | Lev. | Lev. | Lev. | Lev. | Lev. | Lev. | Lev. | Lev. |
| Lev. | Num. | Num. | Num. | Num. | Num. | Num. | Num. | Num. |
| Deut. | Deut. | Deut. | Deut. | Deut. | Deut. | Deut. | Deut. | Deut. |
| Josh. | Josh. | Josh. | Josh. | Josh. | Job | Josh. | Josh. | Josh. |
| Judg. | { Judg. | Judg. | { Judg. | Judg. | Pss. | Job | { Judg. | Judg. |
| Ruth | { Ruth | Ruth | { Ruth | Ruth | Prov. | Judg. | { Ruth | Ruth |
| 1–4 Kgs. | 1–2 Kgs. | 1–2 Kgs. | 1–2 Kgs. | Job | Eccles. | Ruth. | 1–4 Kgs. | 1–4 Kgs. |
| 1–2 Chr. | 3–4 Kgs. | 3–4 Kgs. | 3–4 Kgs. | Pss. | Song | Pss. | 1–2 Chr. | 1–2 Chr. |
| Pss. | 1–2 Chr. | 1–2 Chr. | 1–2 Chr. | Prov. | Josh. | 1 Chr. | 1–2 Esd. | 1–2 Esd. |
| Prov. | 1–2 Esd. | 1–2 Esd. | 1–2 Esd. | Eccles. | { Judg. | 2 Chr. | Job | Job |
| Eccles. | Pss. | Pss. | Esther | Song | { Ruth | 1 Kgs. | Pss. | Pss. |
| Song | Prov. | Prov. | Job | 1 Kgs. | 1–2 Chr. | 2 Kgs. | Eccles. | Prov. |
| Job | Eccles. | Eccles. | Pss. | 2 Kgs. | 1–2 Kgs. | 3 Kgs. | Song | Eccles. |
| Isa. | Song | Song | Prov. | 3 Kgs. | 3–4 Kgs. | 4 Kgs. | Prov. | Song |

| | | | | | | | | |
|---|---|---|---|---|---|---|---|---|
| Jer. | Isa. | Job | Eccles. | 4 Kgs. | Twelve | Prov. | Twelve | Twelve |
| Twelve | { Jer. | Twelve | Song | 1 Chr. | Isa. | Eccles. | Isa. | Isa. |
| Dan. | { Lam. | Isa. | Twelve | 2 Chr. | Jer. | Song | Jer. | Jer. |
| Ezek. | { **Ep.** | { Jer. | Isa. | Twelve | Ezek. | Twelve | Ezek. | Ezek. |
| Esd. | (Twelve) | { **Baruch** | { Jer. | Isa. | Dan. | Isa. | Dan. | Dan. |
| (Esther) | Dan. | { Lam. | { **Baruch** | { Jer. | 1–2 Esd. | Jer. | | Esther |
| | Ezek. | { **Ep.** | { Lam. | { Lam. | Esther | Ezek. | | |
| | Job | Ezek. | { **Ep.** | { **Ep.** | | Dan. | | |
| | Esther | Dan. | Ezek. | { **Baruch** | | 1 Esd. | | |
| | | | Dan. | Ezek. | | 2 Esd. | | |
| | | | | Dan. | | Esther | | |
| | | | | 1 Esd. | | | | |
| | | | | 2 Esd. | | | | |

Entries preceded by a brace are listed under a single heading.
Entries in **bold** type are not in the Jewish Canon.
Entries in parentheses are missing.

*Sources*: Melito, in Eusebius, *HE* 4.26.14; Origen in Eusebius, *HE* 6.25.2; Athanasius, *Ep. Fest.* 39.4; Cyril of Jerusalem, *Catech.* 4.35; Epiphanius[1], *Adv. Haer.* 1.1.8; Epiphanius[2], *De Mens. et Pond.* 4; Epiphanius[3], *De Mens. et Pond.* 23; Gregory of Nazianzus, *Carm.* 1.12.5; Amphilochius, *Iambi ad Seleucum* 2.51–88.

different attempts to correlate Christian usage of Jewish scriptures with the Jewish canon. These variations suggest that while the tradition of a twenty-two-book Jewish canon was received from Palestine, no clear tradition of the contents or of how the Jews arranged or counted their scriptures was known to the churches. There is in the Christian and Jewish lists a general disagreement about contents, order, and grouping. No extant Christian list of the Old Testament agrees with the Masoretic Jewish canon until the Synod of Dort in the seventeenth century. These differences indicate the fluidity that once existed, and further confirm that the early church did not inherit an established Jewish canon.

The Eastern Fathers of the fourth century appear to have accepted the proposition that the Old Testament of the Church should be limited to the Jewish canon. This conviction, however, was at first not completely integrated into their usage, for the Eastern Fathers continued to use works from the larger body of Jewish scriptures throughout the fourth century.[12] There is no marked difference, for instance, between Athanasius' use of the books of the Jewish canon and those of the larger body of Jewish scriptures.[13] Quotations from the non-canonical Jewish scriptures are introduced with formulae regularly used with the books of the Jewish canon.[14] A similar practice is to be found in the writings of Cyril of Jerusalem and Gregory of Nazianzus.[15]

The early Eastern codices of the Old Testament from the

[12] E. Schürer, *A History of the Jewish People*, rev. G. Vermes, F. Millar, and M. Goodman, iii. 2 (Edinburgh, 1987), gives patristic citations, including those from the 4th c., for each book of the so-called Apocrypha and Pseudepigrapha.

[13] Wisd 1:45 (*Letters* 4.4); 1:11 (*Def. before Const.* 5); 2:21 (*Hist. of Arians* 71); 2:23 (*Incarn. of the Word* 5); 6.18 (ibid. 4); 3:57 (*Def. of his Flight* 19); 7:25 (*Def. of Nicene Definition* 11; *On the Opinion of Dionysius* 15); 7:27 (*Letters* 1.1; 10.4); 9:2 (*Discourse* 2.19, 45); 13:5 (*Against the Heathen* 35); Sir. 1:25 (*Life of Anthony* 28); 4:28 (*Def. against Arians* 90); 7:25 (*Def. before Const.* 2); 18:17 (*Letters* 14. 5); Tobit 4.18 (*Def. before Const.* 17); 2 (4) Esdras 4:36 (*Discourse* 2.20); 4:40 (*On the Opinion of Dionysius* 25); 4:41 (*Def. before Const.* 11).

[14] Tobit 12.7 (*Def. against Arians* 11); Sir 7:13 (*Hist. of Arians* 52); 30:4 (*Def. against Arians* 66); Wisd. 1:11 (*Def. against Arians* 3); 7:25 (*On the Opinion of Dionysius* 9; *Discourse* 2:79); 13.5 (*Discourse* 2:32).

[15] Cyril; Wisd. 6:16 (*Catech.* 16:19); 13.5 (*Catech.* 9:2, 16); Sir. 3:21–2 (*Catech.* 6.4; 11.19); 4:31 (*Catech.* 13. 8); Baruch 3:35–7 (*Catech.* 11.15); 2 Macc. 7:1 (*Orat.* 43.74); Wisd. 7:26 (*Orat.* 37.18); Sir. 3:12 (*Orat.* 37.18). Gregory: *Orat.* 29.16–17, 37.18, 43.74–5, 45.15.

fourth and early fifth centuries (see Table 3.2) similarly include works from the larger body of Jewish scriptures.[16] There is no separation within these codices between the works of the Jewish canon and other writings. Thus while the Eastern Fathers may have accepted the proposition that the Old Testament of the Church should be limited to books of the Jewish canon, they did not at first completely integrate this conviction into their usage.

The Western Fathers of the fourth century do not appear to have felt compelled to limit their use of Jewish scriptures to the Jewish canon. The earliest evidence of The Jewish canon among Christians in the West is in Hilary of Poitiers (d. 368), who was probably following Origen's list. Elsewhere, though, he employed Tobit, Judith, Wisdom, Baruch, and Susanna in a way corresponding to his use of Jewish canonical works.[17] Augustine, in a radical contrast to the Eastern practice of the fourth century, postulated an equal and identical divine inspiration for both the Jewish canon and the Christian Old Testament of the Septuagint (*City of God* 18.42–3). The later church councils of the West at Hippo (393) and Carthage (397, 412) confirmed Augustine's witness to a larger body of Jewish writings than the Jewish canon. Thus the presence of the Jewish canon was ultimately not decisive in the Western church's Old Testament canon. (See Table 3.3)

Jerome in Bethlehem, in contrast to Augustine and Western fathers in general, rejected whatever was not originally written in Hebrew. Specifically he rejected the Wisdom of Solomon, Sirach, Judith, Tobit, and 1 and 2 Maccabees (*Prol. Gal.*). Rufinus (*c.* 380) compromised by placing the books Jerome rejected in a special class known as the 'ecclesiastical writings', which, he held, could be read in church, but could not be used to establish doctrine (*Comm. in Symb. Apost.* 38).

In summary, it is clear that not only did the Church not inherit a canon of Scripture from Judaism, but that the Church

[16] See J. Cozza-Luzi, *Nouum Testamentum e Codice Vaticano 1209 Nativi Textus Graeci primo omnium phototypice Repraesentatum* (Rome, 1889); H. and K. Lake, *Codex Sinaiticus*, i (Oxford, 1911); E. M. Thompson, *Facsimile of the Codex Alexandrinus*, 4 vols. (London, 1879–83).

[17] Judith (*In Psalm.* 125:5); Tobit (*In Psalm.* 118:2.8); Sir. (*In Psalm.* 66:9, 140:4); Baruch (*In Psalm.* 68:19, *de Trinitate* 4.42).

TABLE 3.2 *Early Christian codices of the Old Testament*

| Vaticanus | Sinaiticus | Alexandrinus |
|---|---|---|
| . . . Genesis | . . . Genesis . . . | Genesis |
| Exodus | | Exodus |
| Leviticus | | Leviticus |
| Numbers | . . . Numbers . . . | Numbers |
| Deuteronomy | | Deuteronomy |
| Joshua | | Joshua |
| Judges | | Judges |
| Ruth | | Ruth |
| 1–4 Kings | | 1–4 Kings |
| 1–2 Chronicles | . . . 1 Chronicles . . . | 1–2 Chronicles |
| 1–2 Esdras | . . . 2 Esdras | Hosea |
| Psalms . . . | Esther | Amos |
| Proverbs | **Tobit** | Micah |
| Ecclesiastes | **Judith** . . . | Joel |
| Song of Solomon | **1–4 Maccabees** | Obadiah |
| Job | Isaiah | Jonah |
| **Wisdom** | Jeremiah | Nahum |
| **Sirach** | Lamentations . . . | Habakkuk |
| Esther | Joel | Zephaniah |
| **Judith** | Obadiah | Haggai |
| **Tobit** | Jonah | Zechariah |
| Hosea | Nahum | Malachi |
| Amos | Habakkuk | Isaiah |
| Micah | Zephaniah | Jeremiah |
| Joel | Haggai | **Baruch** |
| Obadiah | Zechariah | Lamentations |
| Jonah | Malachi | **Epistle of Jeremy** |
| Nahum | Psalms | Ezekiel |
| Habakkuk | Proverbs | Daniel |
| Zephaniah | Ecclesiastes | Esther |
| Haggai | Song of Solomon | **Tobit** |
| Zechariah | **Wisdom** | **Judith** |
| Malachi | **Sirach** | 1–2 Esdras |
| Isaiah | Job | **1–4 Maccabees** |
| Jeremiah | | Psalms[a] |
| **Baruch** | | **Ps. 151**[b] |
| Lamentations | | Job |
| **Epistle of Jeremy** | | Proverbs |
| Ezekiel | | Ecclesiastes |
| Daniel | | Song of Solomon |
| | | **Wisdom** |
| | | **Sirach** |

Entries in **bold** type are not in the Jewish canon.
Suspension-points indicate losses in the manuscript.

[a] Before the Psalms are placed an epistle of Athanasius to Marcellinus on the Psalter, and a summary of the contents of the *Psalms* by Eusebius.

[b] After the Psalms, there are placed a number of canticles extracted from other parts of the Bible.

was forced to determine an Old Testament canon for itself.[18] Sundberg's distinction between 'scripture' and 'canon' is useful in distinguishing between the time when the Church's Old Testament scriptures were undefined, and the fourth century, when the churches were struggling with fixing an Old Testament canon. The establishment of the Jewish canon does not seem to have prompted the Christians at first to define their own Old Testament. The early lists of the Jewish canon of Melito and Origen appear to have been devised only for polemic purposes. Only in the fourth century did the Eastern Fathers attempt to limit their Old Testament scriptures to the Jewish canon. The Western Fathers, on the other hand, were content to establish an Old Testament canon without limitation by the Jewish canon. In the West, Jewish non-canonical scriptures like Judith, Tobit, Sirach, and the books of the Maccabees found their way into the Christian Old Testament canon. Whether in the West or the East, the crucial period in the formation of the Christian Old Testament canon was the fourth century.

The Muratorian Fragment as traditionally dated at the end of the second century contrasts greatly with the establishing of the Old Testament in the fourth century. The Fragment clearly represents a New Testament canon. To accept its traditional date would suggest that the Church was engaged in defining a New Testament canon more than 150 years before it began fixing an Old Testament canon. While this is not impossible, it is unlikely, and it must have been such a consideration that encouraged Sundberg to reconsider the date of the Fragment.

## COMMENTS, COLLECTIONS, CATALOGUES

The references that scholars use to trace the development of the New Testament are of differing forms. If the differences are not acknowledged, then misleading theories can be established in the history of the Canon. For example, Charles Buck sought to establish that the early Pauline corpus began with Corinthians

[18] A. Jepsen, 'Kanon und Text des Alten Testaments', *Theologische Literaturzeitung*, 74 (1949), 65–74.

TABLE 3.3. *Western Christian lists of the Old Testament*

| Hilary | Jerome[1] | Jerome[2] | Rufinus | Augustine | Carthage |
|---|---|---|---|---|---|
| 5 Moses | Genesis | Genesis | Genesis | Genesis | Genesis |
| | Exodus | Exodus | Exodus | Exodus | Exodus |
| | Lev. | Lev. | Lev. | Lev. | Lev. |
| | Numbers | Numbers | Numbers | Numbers | Numbers |
| | Deut. | Deut. | Deut. | Deut. | Deut. |
| Joshua | Job | Joshua | Joshua | Joshua | Joshua |
| Judges | Joshua | Judges | Judges | Judges | Judges |
| Ruth | Judges | Ruth | Ruth | Ruth | Ruth |
| 1–2 Kgs. | Ruth | 1–2 Kgs. | 1–2 Kgs. | 1–4 Kgs. | 1–4 Kgs. |
| 3–4 Kgs. | Sam. | 3–4 Kgs. | 3–4 Kgs. | 1–2 Chr. | 1–2 Chr. |
| 1–2 Chr. | 3–4 Kgs. | Isaiah | 1–2 Chr. | Job | Job |
| 1–2 Esd. | Twelve | Jer. | 1–2 Esd. | **Tobit** | Psalms |
| Psalms | Isaiah | Ezekiel | Esther | Esther | 1–5 Sol. |
| Proverbs | Jer. | Twelve | Isaiah | **Judith** | Twelve |
| Eccles. | Ezekiel | Job | Jer. | **1–2 Macc.** | Isaiah |
| Song | Daniel | Psalms | Ezekiel | 1–2 Esd. | Jer. |

| | | | | | |
|---|---|---|---|---|---|
| Twelve | Psalms | Proverbs | Daniel | Pss. | Ezekiel |
| Isaiah | **Song** | Eccles. | Twelve | Prov. | Daniel |
| { Jer. | Sol. | Song | Job | Song | **Tobit** |
| { Lam. | Esther | Daniel | Psalms | Eccles. | **Judith** |
| { **Ep. Jer.** | 1–2 Chr. | 1–2 Chr. | Proverbs | **Wisdom** | Esther |
| Daniel | Ezra–Neh. | 1–2 Esd. | Eccles. | **Sirach** | 1–2 Esd. |
| Ezekiel | | Esther | Song | Twelve | **1–2 Macc.** |
| Job | | | | Isaiah | |
| Esther | | | | Jer. | |
| (**Tobit**) | | | | Daniel | |
| (**Judith**) | | | | Ezek. | |

Entries preceded by a brace are listed under a single heading.
Entries in **bold** type are not in the Jewish canon.
Entries in parentheses are recorded with 'some add'.

*Sources*: Hilary, *Prolog. in Lib. Ps.* 15; Jerome[1], *Ep.* 53.8; Jerome[2], *Praef. in Lib. Sam. et Mal.*; Rufinus, *Comm. in Symb. Apost.* 35; Augustine, *De Doct. Christ.* 2.13; Council of Carthage (397), canon 26; 1–5 Sol. probably comprises Prov., Eccles., Song, **Sirach**, **Wisd.**

*Note*: Jerome's lists, and perhaps Rufinus' list as well, might be better understood as reflecting Eastern concerns.

and ended with Romans.[19] To support his thesis, Buck provided a table comparing entries found in the Muratorian Fragment, Tertullian, and Origen.

| *Fragment* | *Tertullian* | *Origen* |
|---|---|---|
| Corinthians | Corinthians | Corinthians |
| Ephesians | Galatians | Ephesians |
| Philippians | Philippians | Colossians |
| Colossians | Thessalonians | Thessalonians |
| Galatians | Ephesians | Philippians |
| Thessalonians | Romans | Romans |
| Romans | | |
| Philemon | | |

Buck, however, failed to acknowledge the differences in the form of his sources. He had to construct the lists for Tertullian (*Adv. Marc.* 4.5) and Origen (*Contra Celsum* 3.19–20) from narrative material. In order to create his list for Origen, Buck introduced Corinthians at the head by virtue of an unnamed Pauline quotation at the end of the previous chapter in Origen. Buck's assignment of a specific order for the letters in Tertullian is dubious since in the same chapter Tertullian named the four Gospels in the unusual sequence of John, Matthew, Mark, Luke, and elsewhere listed the Pauline letters in a different manner (*Praescript.* 36). Both Origen's and Tertullian's lists are incomplete, as Buck noted: 'Although it is impossible to say where Colossian and Philemon occurred in Tertullian's corpus, or Galatians and Philemon in Origen's, it is certain that these letters occurred in their respective lists' (pp. 352–3). The Fragmentist, unlike Tertullian and Origen, quite clearly intended to catalogue the complete Pauline corpus in a specific order without significant narration or omission. Buck, however, included only a partial list from the Fragment in his table, omitting any mention of the epistles to Timothy and Titus.

Buck's comparison is flawed in failing to appreciate the differences in format between his sources, and to allow for the possible implications of these differences. It will be helpful to build upon Sundberg's differentiation of 'scripture' and 'canon' by introducing some technical distinctions between the forms which references used in studying the development of

[19] C. Buck, 'The Early Order of the Pauline Corpus', *JBL* 68 (1949), 351–7.

the New Testament take. It is recognized of course that context is the ultimate cause of form. However, general forms are still distinguishable. For the sake of convenience, three categories are here proposed: 'comments', 'collections', and 'catalogues'.

## 1. *Comments*

Comments are the most ambiguous of the three categories proposed, and simply refers to any mention of works as authoritative or as Scripture. The reference may often be to only two or three works, and may frequently be in the context of some other discussion. There is usually no intention of completeness in this category, and this is its most distinctive feature.

Buck's reference to Paul's letters from Tertullian (*Adv. Marc.* 4.5) is a good example of a comment. The mention of Paul's epistles occurs in the context of a discussion about Luke's gospel. The reference betrays no intention of completeness, which explains why other Pauline letters accepted by Tertullian are not mentioned, specifically Colossians and Philemon, and why this list differs in order and content from his remarks on Paul's letters in *De Praescriptione Haereticorum* (36).

## 2. *Collections*

Collections are more definite than comments: they have clear and distinct boundaries, which include certain specifiable works. Yet the boundaries are by definition not rigid. Collections are easily altered, and thus they do not imply as firm boundaries as their form suggests. Collections are specific, but not final, for they are often amended and enlarged. They are by definition not closed.

The group of Pauline letters represented by the so-called Marcionite prologues is a good example of what I mean by a collection. In their original form the prologues probably represented a collection of the Pauline letters to the seven churches, in Galatia, Corinth, Rome, Thessalonica, Laodicea, Colossae, and Philippi. This collection probably did not include Hebrews or the Pastoral Epistles. The prologue to Ephesians may have originally had the form of a prologue to Laodiceans and Philemon may have been originally incorporated with

Colossians. At a later stage, or stages, the original prologues were translated into Latin and new prologues were composed for Philemon and for the second letters to the Corinthians and to the Thessalonians. Subsequently, prologues for Hebrews and the Pastoral Epistles (1 and 2 Timothy, Titus) were added, and an Ephesians prologue replaced the one to Laodiceans. Thus while the original prologues constituted a distinct collection with definite boundaries, the collection itself was easily altered and enlarged.

### 3. *Catalogues*

The category of catalogues is the most distinct since by its very nature it is precise and definite. The boundaries which it declares are explicitly fixed and more permanent than the boundaries of collections. This is evident in catalogues when works beyond the boundaries are sometimes noted and dismissed. In its pure form, a catalogue is simply an accepted list, to which nothing can be added or subtracted.

The Muratorian Fragment is a good example of a catalogue. The Fragmentist quite clearly intended to list the Pauline corpus in a specific order, without omission. He stated that Paul wrote first to the Corinthians, then to the Galatians, and then to the Romans (ll. 42–5). It would seem that he intended to list Paul's letters in the order in which he considered them written. He did not carry this through, however, but started over again, saying that following the example of his predecessor John (ll. 46–50), Paul wrote in a similar pattern to seven churches in the following order: Corinthians, Ephesians, Philippians, Colossians, Galatians, Thessalonians, and Romans (ll. 50–4). He then added that: 'he [Paul] wrote to the Corinthians and to the Thessalonians once more for their reproof' (ll. 53–5). After a couple of lines, again noting John's writing to seven churches (ll. 57–9), the Fragmentist awkwardly continued: 'But to Philemon one, and to Titus one, and to Timothy two, [written] out of goodwill and love, are yet held sacred to the glory of the Catholic church for the ordering of ecclesiastical discipline' (ll. 59–63). The Fragmentist intended to present not only a specific order for Paul's epistles, but also a complete list, noting for example those letters which were rejected as forgeries, such as those to the Alexandrians and the Laodiceans.

The Fragment is more than a catalogue of Paul's epistles, it is a catalogue of New Testament works. Other writings are declared accepted by the Fragment, just as some are equally rejected. While the concept of a fixed boundary is evident in the Fragment, the determination on which side of the boundary some works fall is still uncertain. For example, in the Fragment it is acknowledged that some do not want the Revelation of Peter read in the churches (ll. 71–3) and that the Shepherd ought to be read privately, but not publicly (ll. 73–80). None the less the Fragment implies an explicitly fixed boundary that is more permament than that of collections.

These distinctions in form are particularly useful in differentiating the implications of the context and nature of sources when comparing different canonical listings. They also hint at the development of the Canon. The movement from comments to collections to catalogues is instructive in the formation of the Christian Bible. The boundaries of the elements of the canon are fixed gradually just as the boundaries of these categories are gradually defined. Comments generally precede collections in the formation of the Christian canon, just as collections generally precede catalogues.

Sundberg, in urging a revised history of the New Testament canon, suggested three phases: (i) the rise of Christian literature to the status of Scripture; (ii) the conscious collection of Christian writings into closed subcollections; and (iii) the formation of the New Testament list.[20] These three stages can be correlated with the categories here introduced, except that collections remain 'open'. Sundberg's 'scripture' and 'canon' reflect concepts in the formation of the Canon. 'Comments', 'collections', and 'catalogues' represent the shapes these concepts took in the development of the Canon. The formats of 'comments' and 'collections' usually imply the concept of 'scripture', just as the presence of 'catalogues' usually implies

[20] See Introd. n. 2. Note that the Fourfold Gospel is the only 'subcollection' (Sundberg's term), or better still 'subcanonical collection', which is closed independently of the cataloguing of the 4th c. The 'closing' of the other subcanonical collections—the Old Testament, the Pauline letters, and the catholic epistles—does not appear distinct from the final phase of establishing a New Testament list.

the concept 'canon'. Thus it is entirely possible to make comments about Scriptures and/or to possess a collection of Scriptures without also having a catalogue or intending a canon. This was in fact the situation in the first few centuries of Christian Church.

## MARCION'S COLLECTION

In the nineteenth century some scholars, like Zahn, argued that the Church already had a New Testament canon before the time of Marcion.[21] Zahn demonstrated through the comments of the Church Fathers that the majority of New Testament writings were read and valued throughout much of the Christian Church at an early date. This kind of evidence does not necessarily imply a canon as here defined, but suggests only that New Testament writings were beginning to be seen as authoritative religious literature, that is, as Scripture.

J. Knox in his famous monograph suggested that Marcion (d. *c.* 160) was the creator of the New Testament. He argued that 'it is apparent that the non-Marcionite churches, at the time when Marcion set up his "Gospel and Apostle" and wrote his *Antitheses*, had no Scripture except what we call the Old Testament'.[22] He concluded that after Marcion 'Christian writings had for the first time become Christian Scripture'.[23] Knox wished to assert more than that Marcion was the first promoter of Christian 'Scripture'. But despite noting that 'a canon is by necessity a "closed" canon',[24] he failed to distinguish carefully between scripture and canon in his argument, and, like Harnack before him, concluded that 'Marcion is primarily responsible for the idea of the New Testament [canon].'[25] Even E. C. Blackman, who disputed much of the influence on the Canon which Harnack and Knox attributed to Marcion, still acknowledged that 'The first closed New Testament canon of which we have knowledge was made by Marcion.'[26]

[21] Zahn, *Geschichte*, ii. 434.

[22] Knox, *Marcion and the New Testament* (hereafter *Marcion*) (Chicago, 1942), 24.

[23] Ibid. 26.

[24] Ibid. 25.

[25] Ibid. 31; cf. Harnack, *Marcion: Das Evangelium vom fremden Gott* (hereafter *Marcion*) (TU 45; Leipzig, 1921).

[26] E. C. Blackman, *Marcion and His Influence* (London, 1948), 23.

Did Marcion introduce a canon of Scripture, or did he simply promote among the churches a collection of Christian scriptures as opposed to the already extant collection of Jewish scriptures? Were Marcion's scriptures closed? The nature of Marcion's work as an editor and collector of Christian scriptures suggests that neither the content nor text of his scriptures was fixed. Marcion's basic intent appears to have been to recover a lost tradition by editing the sources known to him. There is no direct evidence that Marcion knew or excluded other gospels.[27] So far as is known, Marcion never polemized against the other gospel traditions. Although Tertullian accused Marcion of rejecting certain Pauline epistles, there is no evidence that Marcion knew them. Thus Marcion appears to have accepted and edited the scriptures known to him.

Although Marcion may have made certain changes and adjustments in the gospel of Luke and the Pauline epistles which he received, this was not a radical procedure. Matthew and Luke not only expanded their Marcan source but also revised and corrected it; in the same way the Fourth Evangelist reshaped his material with theological intent. Tatian, too, in compiling the Diatessaron appears to have made major excisions from his sources. Other Pauline editors are also known to have conflated and rearranged the texts known to them. Marcion's activities seem no different than those of other collectors of Christian scriptures at that time.

Marcion apparently never handed down his Collection as traditional or 'revealed', for his editorial work was carried on by his disciples.[28] It is probable that later Marcionites admitted into their scriptures verses from the gospels of Matthew, Mark, and John. Ephraem Syrus said that the Marcionites had not rejected Matthew 23:8 (*Song* 24.1). John 13:34 and 15.19 are quoted by the Marcionite Marcus in Adamantius' *Dialogue* (2.16, 20). Similarly, Adamantius (2.15) accuses the Marcionites of corrupting Matthew 5:17. Origen in his *Commentary on Matthew* (15.3) quoted a Marcionite interpretation of Matt. 19:12. The followers of Marcion may also have added to the texts of their received epistles. It is probable that the doxology

[27] Knox, *Marcion*, 163–5.

[28] Adamantius, *Dialogue* 2.18; Tertullian, *Adv. Marc.* 4.5.

at the end of Romans (16.25–7), while unknown to Marcion, was added later by his followers.[29]

If Marcion and his followers added verses to their accepted texts, then they may just as well have added additional sources to their collection of scriptures. Marcion's followers, at least, appear to have easily added to his scriptures, suggesting that the boundaries of his collection may have been specific but were not fixed. The proscription of forged letters 'to the Laodiceans and Alexandrians and several others', as well as 'a new book of Psalms for Marcion' in the Fragment itself (ll. 64, 83), suggest that the Marcionite collection of Luke and ten Pauline epistles was later expanded and enlarged. Like the Fragment, Epiphanius at the end of the fourth century confirmed the presence among the Marcionite collection of an epistle to the Laodiceans (in addition to Ephesians).[30] Maruta bishop of Maipherkat in his work *De Sancta Synodo Nicaena*, confirmed that the Marcionites at the beginning of the fifth century had composed psalms of their own for use in worship instead of the Davidic psalms, and also in place of the book of Acts had one he called the 'Summa' (*sākā*).[31] This might be Marcion's *Antitheses* or perhaps another work. Marcion's *Antitheses* appears to have stood at the head of his collection, perhaps with equal authority to the 'Gospel and Apostle', for Tertullian in *Adversus Marcionem* responded to it first (books 1–3), then Marcion's version of Luke (book 4) and Paul's letters (book 5). That the Pastorals were at some time accepted by later Marcionites is suggested by a passage from Chrysostom which said that Marcionites used 2 Tim. 1:18 as evidence for their doctrine of two gods.[32] The so-called Marcionite Prologue to Titus may be suggestive of a Marcionite origin.[33] The Armenian Marcionites appear to have received the Diatessaron.[34] Finally, the *Fihrist al-ʿUlūm* of al-Nadīm (d. 995) recorded that Marcion wrote a book which he called the

[29] Cf. Harnack, *Studien zur Geschichte des Neuen Testaments und der Alten Kirche*, i: *Zur neutestamentlichen Textkritik* (Arbeiten zur Kirchengeschichte, 19; Berlin, 1931), 184–90.

[30] Epiphanius, *Haer.* 9–10.

[31] Maruta, *De Sancta Synodo Nicaena*; cf. Blackman, 64–5, Harnack, *Marcion*, 174–5.

[32] *PG* 62.615.

[33] Harnack, *Marcion*, 130.

[34] R. Casey, 'The Armenian Marcionites and the Diatessaron', *JBL* 57 (1938), 185–94.

'Gospel', and that his disciples composed a number of books 'which God alone is able to find'.[35]

Since there is no direct evidence that Marcion's collection was closed, it is something of a misnomer to refer to it as Marcion's 'canon'. Marcion may have been an early promoter of a collection of New Testament scriptures, but it is misleading to credit him with creating a New Testament canon.

## THE FOURFOLD GOSPEL CANON

The establishment of the Fourfold Gospel is another important milestone in the history of the New Testament Canon. It is the first definitive evidence of an attempt to limit the number of Christian scriptures even if only within a subcanonical group. As such, it is perhaps the initial step in 'closing' the New Testament collection. Edgar Goodspeed placed the establishing of the Fourfold Gospel at AD 115–25.[36] He arrived at this date by attempting to show the acquaintance with, and dependence upon, the Fourfold Gospel in the Preaching of Peter, 2 Peter, the Gospel of Peter, Papias of Hierapolis, the Epistle of the Apostles, and Justin Martyr. The attempt by Goodspeed to push the formation of the Fourfold Gospel back to 115–25 rests on particularly precarious grounds since four of his sources, namely 2 Peter, the Gospel of Peter, the Epistle of the Apostles, and the Preaching of Peter, are usually dated only from the middle of the second century.[37] Adolf von Harnack argued that the Fourfold Gospel could be traced back to Asia Minor to the time of Irenaeus' youth, 'just before the middle of the second century'.[38] John Knox suggested that Rome produced the Fourfold Gospel some time after 150 but before AD 175, by which time it was 'well established'.[39] Knox argued that there was 'no sufficient occasion for the formation' until the challenge of Marcion's 'Gospel'. Blackman argued that Montanism rather than Marcionism was the decisive factor in

[35] Quoted by Harnack, *Marcion*, 384, and Blackman, 49.

[36] E. Goodspeed, *The Formation of the New Testament* (Chicago, 1937), 37–8; id., *An Introduction to the New Testament* (hereafter *Introduction*) (Chicago, 1937), 314.

[37] K. L. Carroll, 'The Creation of the Fourfold Gospel', *JBRL* 37 (1954–5), 68–77.

[38] Harnack, *The Origin of the New Testament*, 71/2.

[39] Knox, *Marcion*, 150, 152.

producing the New Testament Canon, and declared that in principle the limits of the whole Canon were fixed by 180.[40] B. H. Streeter believed the Fourfold Gospel to be 'firmly established' *c.* 180 in Antioch, Ephesus, and Rome.[41]

There seems to be a confusion in the minds of many scholars between acquaintance with the four gospels and the Fourfold Gospel canon. The former does not imply the latter. Comments do not necessarily imply a collection, nor does a collection necessarily imply a canon. These scholars have not distinguished between the possession of gospel scriptures and a gospel canon. Thus it is essential to reconsider the formation of the Fourfold gospel canon with these considerations in mind.

The canonical gospels may have been among the earliest gospels to be written.[42] None the less, others continued to be composed through much of the second century, and Christian writers of the second century refer to many other gospels besides the canonical four.[43] This would seem unlikely if the Fourfold Gospel canon had already been established. The second century, therefore, possessed a multiplicity of written gospels besides the canonical four.

Papias is the first extant witness to mention or quote any known written gospel tradition.[44] In remarks preserved by Eusebius, Papias wrote of the gospel of Mark:

This also the presbyter [John?] said: Mark, having become Peter's interpreter, wrote down accurately all that he remembered, not indeed in order, of the things said or done by Christ. For he had not heard the Lord, nor had he followed him, but later on, as I said, followed Peter, who adapted his teaching to the needs of his hearers, but with no intention of giving a connected account of the Lord's discourses, so that Mark did nothing wrong in thus writing down single points as he remembered them. For to one thing he gave

[40] Blackman, 34.

[41] Streeter, *The Four Gospels: A Study of Origins*, 4th edn. (London, 1930), i, 7–15.

[42] Luke 1: 1–4 may suggest earlier written sources, just as Q may represent a written collection of sayings of Jesus.

[43] H. Koester, 'Apocryphal and Canonical Gospels', *HTR* 73 (1980), 105–30, at 107–12.

[44] The quotations from Matthew and Luke in Polycarp appear in the first chapters of the preserved letter, which is the part most probably composed much later than the covering letter to the Ignatian epistles; cf. P. N. Harrison, *Polycarp's Two Epistles to the Philippians* (Cambridge, 1936), 143–206.

attention, to leave out nothing of what he heard and to make no false statements. (*HE* 3.39.15.)

Immediately after this, Eusebius attached another quotation from Papias: 'So then, Matthew collected the oracles (*logia*) in the Hebrew language, and every one interpreted [translated?] as he was able' (*HE* 3.39.16). There is a certain defensiveness in Papias' remarks about Mark, perhaps implying that his gospel had been criticized as incomplete or lacking in proper arrangement. Papias' statements about Matthew are also of interest, since the canonical Matthew is not strictly a collection of *logia* nor was it most probably composed in Hebrew (or Aramaic). All that can be confidently concluded from these remarks is that Papias knew Mark and at least one other gospel-type document, possibly Matthew (or Q?).

Although Papias knew written gospels, he preferred the oral tradition:

If anyone ever came who had followed the presbyters, I questioned him in regard to the words of the presbyters, what Andrew or Peter or Philip or Thomas or James or John or Matthew, or any other of the Lord's disciples, had said, and what Aristion and the presbyter John, the disciples of the Lord, say. For I did not think that information from books would help so much as the word of a living and abiding voice. (*HE* 3.39.4.)

This preference for the oral tradition is also evident in other Christian literature of the early second century. H. Koester has shown that the citations of gospel traditions among the Apostolic Fathers are more likely to be drawn from oral tradition than to be free quotations from written gospels, to which no explicit appeals are made.[45]

Written gospels probably became increasingly used as oral tradition began to dissipate and grow unreliable. Originally they must have circulated individually and perhaps were used in isolation from each other, with only one such document being valued and used in any given Christian community. Marcion, it should be remembered, employed only the Gospel of Luke, and probably did not reject other gospel traditions but simply did not know them.[46] The only surviving gospel codices

[45] Koester (Köster), *Synoptische Überlieferung bei den apostolischen Vätern* (TU 65; Berlin, 1957).

[46] Cf. Knox, *Marcion*, 163–4; and discussion above.

of the first half of the second century appear to have contained only one work each, namely $\mathfrak{p}^{52}$ (John) and Pap. Egerton 2 (an unknown gospel). All but one of the extant late second- and early third-century gospel codices also included only one text, namely $\mathfrak{p}^{66}$ (John); $\mathfrak{p}^{64}$, $\mathfrak{p}^{67}$ (Matthew); Pap. Oxy. 1 (Thomas). Even in the third century, numerous single-gospel codices have survived, namely $\mathfrak{p}^{1}$, $\mathfrak{p}^{53}$, $\mathfrak{p}^{70}$ (Matthew); $\mathfrak{p}^{4}$, $\mathfrak{p}^{69}$ (Luke); $\mathfrak{p}^{5}$, $\mathfrak{p}^{9}$, $\mathfrak{p}^{22}$, $\mathfrak{p}^{28}$, $\mathfrak{p}^{39}$, $\mathfrak{p}^{80}$ (John); Pap. Oxy. 654, 655 (Thomas); Pap. Bodmer V (Protevangelium of James); Pap. Rainer (Fayyum) (an unknown gospel). $\mathfrak{p}^{75}$, which includes Luke and John, is the first multiple-gospel codex extant and is thus the first manuscript witness to a gospel collection; it was dated by the editors between 175 and 225.[47] The Egyptian codex, $\mathfrak{p}^{45}$, is the earliest manuscript to include the Fourfold Gospel (along with Acts) and thus is the first manuscript witness to the Fourfold Gospel collection. The codex was dated by its editor in the first half of the third century.[48]

Even when written gospels came into customary use, their authority was not absolute, as their texts were not beyond substantial alteration. Marcion altered Luke. Additional material was appended, probably in the first half of the second century, to the earliest manuscripts of Mark, which ended at 16:8: we find, for instance, (i) the traditional longer ending (16:9–20), (ii) the so-called 'shorter Marcan ending' inserted after 16:8, and (iii) the 'freer *logion*' inserted after 16:14. Similarly John 21 appears to have been added to the original text. The story of the woman taken in adultery (John 7:53–8:11) was certainly not original to John's gospel. Papias appears to have related this story, which, according to Eusebius, was contained in the Gospel according to the Hebrews (*HE* 3.39.16). The written gospels were thus first enlarged by adding material to their individual texts. Later, the gospel materials appear to have been enlarged by the addition of other written gospels.

Through the circulation of individual gospels, Christian communities must have gradually become acquainted with a variety of gospel documents, and gospel collections were estab-

[47] V. Martin and R. Kasser, *Papyrus Bodmer XIV* (Cologny-Geneva, 1961), 13.

[48] Kenyon, *The Chester Beatty Biblical Papyri: Description and Texts of Twelve Manuscripts on Papyrus of the Greek Bible* (hereafter, *Chester Beatty*), 8 fasciculi (London, 1933–58), Fasciculus II (Gospels and Acts), p. x.

lished. The first direct evidence of a knowledge and use of several gospels comes from the middle of the second century in the writings of Justin Martyr, who taught in Rome between 150 and 165.[49] In his *Dialogue* (49), Justin quoted directly from Matt. 17:10–13; for he included the words 'then the disciples understood that he spoke to them concerning John the Baptist', which are specifically Matthaean and are not found in Mark. There are good, if not quite so strong, reasons for supposing that Justin also knew Luke (cf. *Dial.* 76, 81, 95, 100, 103, 105; *1 Apol.* 17, 63, 66). That he knew Mark is more doubtful (cf. *1 Apol.* 16), and there is no firm evidence that he knew John.[50] The notion of the Logos, which is sometimes used as proof that Justin was acquainted with the Johannine gospel, was current throughout the ancient world at that time.

Because it is probable that Justin was acquainted with at least some of the canonical gospels, many scholars have thought that nearly all his quotations are derived from these, but that because he relied upon his memory he quoted them so inaccurately. As W. Sanday showed, the proportion of variation in Justin is more than three times as high for quotations from the gospels as for those from the Old Testament.[51] It is much more likely that Justin also relied upon other gospel sources similar to, but different from, the later canonical gospels. He seems at numerous points to have relied on oral tradition, or a compilation of sayings of Jesus, or perhaps on gospels not known, or variously on all of these. Evidently Justin did not invest any exclusive authority in the gospels which ultimately became canonical.[52] Thus while several gospels were known to Justin, it cannot confidently be said that he knew all four of the later canonical gospels, or that he relied solely upon them.[53]

[49] While Papias knew Mark and another gospel-type document (Matthew, Q?), he declared a preference for oral tradition. His defensiveness over Mark may suggest that he used that gospel, but there is no evidence that he relied upon his other gospel-type source.

[50] J. N. Sanders, *The Fourth Gospel in the Early Church: Its Origin and Influence* (Cambridge, 1943), 31.

[51] W. Sanday, *The Gospels in the Second Century* (London, 1876), 88–137.

[52] Grant, *The Earliest Lives of Jesus* (New York, 1961), 14–20.

[53] E. R. Buckley, 'Justin Martyr's Quotations from the Synoptic Tradition', *JTS* 36 (1935), 173–6.

The existence of gospel harmonies at the end of the second century suggests that the Fourfold Gospel canon was not yet established. In compiling the harmonies, the authors made use of the later canonical gospels in the same way that the writers of these four gospels utilized the materials in their hands. Each of these writers made use of the gospel materials available to him in compiling his works. No one would argue, for instance, that Mark's gospel was canonical simply because Matthew and Luke used parts of Mark in their own gospels.

Tatian, a Syrian Christian who had studied with Justin in Rome, is the best-known gospel harmonizer. He undertook (*c.* 170) to weave several separate gospels into one consecutive narrative, called in the East the Gospel of the Mixed, but in the West the Diatessaron. For his narrative Tatian employed all four of the later canonical gospels, and he is thus the earliest-known witness for the use of all four of them. But their position in his day was not so secure that they could not be displaced by the Diatessaron in the Syriac church. It is notable that Tatian apparently encountered no criticism for his work; on the contrary the Diatessaron enjoyed great popularity. This harmony actually established itself as the gospel for the Church in Syria, and was dislodged only at a late date, in the fifth and sixth centuries, and that with a great deal of difficulty. Some scholars have even argued that before the time of Tatian only the Gospel of Thomas had reached Edessa.[54]

There is also no consensus regarding the sources employed by Tatian. Eusebius seems to suggest that Tatian harmonized only the four canonical gospels, although he implies that he was unfamiliar with the work (*HE* 4.29.5–6). Rufinus' translation of Eusebius accentuated the implication ('conposuit euangelium unam *ex quattuor*'), and thereafter the opinion that Tatian quarried only the four later canonical Gospels became normative. Victor of Capua, on the other hand, reported in the preface to the Codex Fuldensis that Tatian named his Harmony *diapente*, perhaps suggesting that Tatian worked from five gospels. Epiphanius reported that the Diatessaron was sometimes called the 'Gospel according to the Hebrews'

[54] Koester, '*Γνῶμαι διάφοροι*: The Origin and Nature of Diversification in the History of Early Christianity', *HTR* 58 (1965), 279–318, at 304; Burkitt, 'Tatian's Harmony and the Dutch Harmonies', *JTS* 25 (1923–4), 113–30, at 128–30.

(*Haer.* 46.2.9). M. Black has therefore suggested that the Gospel according to the Hebrews was a fifth source.[55] There are also numerous parallels between the Diatessaron and the Coptic Gospel of Thomas.[56] Tatian probably employed several apocryphal works.[57] It is enough to recognize that Tatian apparently knew many gospel traditions, none of which was considered either canonical or non-canonical at the time of the Diatessaron's composition.

In the West a harmony closely akin to the Diatessaron exists. The Codex Fuldensis of Victor of Capua (546) contains a gospel in which verses from the canonical gospels of the Vulgate were harmonized. In a preface Victor explained that he found it anonymous, but that reading Eusebius he came to the conclusion that it was the work of Tatian. Burkitt suggested that this Latin harmony may have been the predecessor of Tatian's Diatessaron.[58] That Tatian had anything to do with a Latin ancestor of the Codex Fuldensis is nothing more than conjecture made by Victor of Capua on the strength of a passage in Eusebius. Eusebius acknowledged that he had never seen the work (*HE* 4.29.6). The manuscript found by Victor was anonymous, and all the tradition that connects Tatian with the Diatessaron relates to the Diatessaron in Syriac. Therefore another harmony, this time in Latin, may have existed some time in the second century in the West.

Other gospel harmonies are also known. No less a personage than Theophilus of Antioch is said to have 'combined the words of the four Evangelists in one work' (Jerome, *Ep.* 121.6). Although this information occurs only in Jerome, the harmony was mentioned by him again in *De Vir. Ill.* 25 and in the Prologue to his *Commentary on Matthew*. That Tatian cannot have been the only compiler of gospel harmonies is apparently confirmed by Ambrose, who noted in his *Commentary on Luke* (1.2): 'plerique etiam ex quattuor evangelii libris in unum ea quae venenatis putaverunt adsertionibus convenientia referserunt.' The 'Alexandrian Ammonius' is also said to have composed a

[55] M. Black, *An Aramaic Approach to the Gospels and Acts* (Oxford, 1967), 267–9.
[56] G. Quispel, 'The Gospel of Thomas and the New Testament', *VC* 11 (1957), 189–207.
[57] J. Charlesworth, 'Tatian's Dependence upon Apocryphal Traditions', *HeyJ* 15 (1974), 5–17.
[58] Burkitt, 'The Dura Fragment of Tatian', *JTS* 36 (1935), 255–9.

kind of synopsis of the four Gospels about 220 (Eusebius, *Ep. ad Carp.*). A fragment allegedly derived from Melito of Sardis' writings appears to suggest that he also combined John and the Synoptics (*PG* 89.229).

Besides the gospel harmonies, individual gospels other than the later canonical four were still being employed by Christians across a wide geographic area at the end of the second and beginning of the third centuries. The Valentinians in Rome (*c.* 180), for instance, availed themselves of the Gospel of Truth (Irenaeus, *Adv. Haer.* 3.11.8). Heracleon (fl. *c.* 145–80) made use of the Preaching of Peter (Origen, *Comm. on John* 13.17). The Valentinian Theodotus quoted the Gospel according to the Egyptians and the Gospel of Thomas (Clem. Alex. *Excep. ex Theo.*). Hegesippus (*c.* 180) quoted from the Gospel according to the Hebrews (Eusebius, *HE* 4.22.8). Julius Cassianus (*c.* 190) used the Gospel according to the Egyptians (Clem. Alex. *Strom.* 3.13). The church at Rhossos was reading the Gospel of Peter at the end of the second century, and what is more, with the explicit approval of Serapion, the then bishop of Antioch, permission which he only later withdrew on dogmatic grounds (Eusebius, *HE* 6.12.4, 6). Despite the bishop's later disapproval, the Syrian Didascalia was still using the Gospel of Peter in the third century.[59] Serapion's predecessor at Antioch, Theophilus, also appears to have recorded allusions to Petrine pseudepigrapha, specifically the Preaching of Peter and the Revelation of Peter.[60] The Nicolaitans used the Traditions of Matthias (Clem. Alex. *Strom.* 3.4). The Naasenes used the Gospel according to the Egyptians in the early third century (Hippolytus, *Haer.* 5.7) as did the Sabellians (Epiphanius, *Haer.* 62.4), and the Ebionites used the Gospel according to the Hebrews (Eusebius, *HE* 3.27.4). It is difficult therefore to acknowledge the claim that the Fourfold Gospel was 'firmly established' in the last quarter of the second century.

Nowhere before Irenaeus (*c.* 180–9) is there any specific mention of the Fourfold Gospel canon as such, a concept which entails a 'principle of exclusivity'. The earliest extant statement of that principle is Irenaeus, *Adv. Haer.* 3.11.11. The other extant evidence from that time suggests only that the later

[59] Campenhausen, 169–70.

[60] G. Quispel and R. Grant, 'Note on the Petrine Apocrypha', *VC* 6 (1952), 31–2.

canonical gospels were beginning to achieve growing significance and recognition as sources of tradition in the third quarter of the second century, but not that they were regarded as an exclusive and inviolable norm. None the less, Irenaeus stated that 'it is not possible that the Gospels can be either more or fewer in number than they are' (*Adv. Haer.* 3.11.8). He then continued with a long allegorical interpretation of why there could only be four gospels, noting, for instance, that there were four zones in the inhabited world, four principal winds, four faces to the cherubim, and four principal covenants (*Adv. Haer.* 3.11.8). Irenaeus' argument suggests that toward the end of the second century a fixed collection of four gospels was becoming current in at least the Western church. But his remarks also suggest that this must have been something of an innovation, for if a Fourfold Gospel had been established and generally acknowledged, then Irenaeus would not have offered such a tortured insistence on its numerical legitimacy.

The Gospel of John is certainly a surprising member of any orthodox gospel canon at the end of the second century. It appears not to have been known or used by most second-century Christian writers, and to all appearances was first employed among gnostic Christians.[61] Hippolytus reported that Basilides, a gnostic teacher in Alexandria (*c.* 130), used John in the time of Hadrian (*Haer.* 7.22). The Encratite Tatian (*c.* 160) is the earliest writer in whose works are found formal quotations from this gospel, and even then he did not name the book (cf. *Oratio* 13.1, 19.4).[62] The Valentinian gnostic teachers Ptolemaeus and Heracleon (160–70) both wrote expositions on it.[63] Theirs are the earliest known commentaries on John, or for that matter on any early Christian writing, and the fact that they considered it worthy of such detailed study shows that it had acquired considerable standing in gnostic Christianity by the middle of the second century. By contrast, outside gnostic circles there is scant knowledge of or interest in John, and prior to the late second century no broad recognition of its authority. John was also used by the so-called 'new prophecy' of

[61] J. N. Sanders, *The Fourth Gospel*, 47–66.

[62] Id., 'John, Gospel of', *IDB* ii (New York, 1962), 932–46, at 944.

[63] M. F. Wiles, *The Spiritual Gospel: The Interpretation of the Fourth Gospel in the Early Church* (Cambridge, 1960), 96–111.

Montanism, which flourished in the latter half of the second century. Its adherents claimed that the coming of the Paraclete promised there (e.g. 14:26, 15:26) had actually been fulfilled in the person of Montanus, the founder of the movement, and that the new Jerusalem foreseen in Revelation (21:2) would soon descend to earth. Thus the use of John by gnostics and Montanists may have militated against its more general acceptance. No orthodox theologian is known to have explicitly supported the gospel before Theophilus of Antioch (*c.* 180).

In Rome at the beginning of the third century, the theologian Gaius, who according to Eusebius was an orthodox churchman (*HE* 2.25.6), rejected John as a work of the heretic Cerinthus. Hippolytus (*c.* 212–*c.* 236) is the first known defender of the work in Rome, and the title of his lost work *Defence of the Revelation and Gospel of John* confirms that there were serious attacks on it. The polemic against Johannine writings may have first arisen in Asia Minor in the late second century, for Irenaeus also knew of a rejection of John by a group of orthodox Christians there (*Adv. Haer.* 3.11.9). These Alogi, as Epiphanius called them, may not have been a heretical group rejecting the long-accepted Gospel of John, but rather an orthodox element protesting against the introduction into the Church's usage of a gospel which heretics had long used.

Irenaeus is the earliest witness to suggest that there was an apostolic connection for the Fourth Gospel (*Adv. Haer.* 3.1.1). He appears to have believed that the John of whom his teacher Polycarp had been a disciple was the Apostle and author of the Fourth Gospel. This tradition is not known before Irenaeus, and is probably based upon a confusion of persons by him.[64] Whether or not the confusion was deliberate, the tradition that the Apostle John was the author of the Fourth Gospel gave the work apostolic authority and thus made it a more acceptable member of any orthodox gospel collection. From the beginning of the third century, the Gospel of John has been generally accepted in the churches.

In Irenaeus' defence of the Fourfold Gospel, there are also hints that the Gospel of Luke was not readily acceptable in

[64] Grant, 'The Fourth Gospel and the Church', *HTR* 35 (1942), 95–116, at 102–5.

orthodox circles at the end of the second century. After his famous argument for the Fourfold Gospel canon (*Adv. Haer.* 3.11.8, cf. 3.1.1), Irenaeus proceeded with a passage of special pleading for the status of Luke (ch. 13–15), which he saw as canonical, not in its own right, but by a dependence upon its special relationship to Paul and the other Apostles.[65] Irenaeus' argument included a defence of Paul's apostolicity: 'For neither can they contend that Paul was no apostle, when he was chosen for this purpose; nor can they prove Luke guilty of falsehood, when he proclaims the truth to us with all diligence . . . his [Luke's] testimony, therefore, is true, and the doctrine of the Apostles is open and steadfast, holding nothing in reserve; nor did they teach one set of doctrines in private, and another in public' (*Adv. Haer.* 3.15.1). The thrust of Irenaeus' argument here was not entirely directed against the followers of Marcion and Valentinus (*Adv. Haer.* 3.14.4), for Irenaeus would have no cause to defend Paul's apostleship to these groups. Therefore it appears that Irenaeus was not only refuting the Marcionite misuse of Luke, but that his greater concern was to give an apology for its use in the gospel collection of the Church.

One would expect to find in Irenaeus a similar apology for Mark as is found for Luke. Mark is a dependent gospel (upon Peter) and it was used by a group of an apparently docetic nature: 'Those who separate Jesus from Christ alleging that Christ remained impassible but it was Jesus who suffered, prefer the Gospel of Mark' (*Adv. Haer.* 3.11.7). Yet Irenaeus gave no apology for Mark's Gospel: his attention was focused primarily upon the status of Luke. If Irenaeus' account of the way each gospel was used by a particular heretical group is accepted (*Adv. Haer.* 3.11.7), namely that Ebionites used Matthew, Marcionites used Luke, Docetists preferred Mark, and Valentinians used John, then in view of the apologetic for Luke's gospel that followed, its purpose would seem to have been to support Luke by implying that, since the other three gospels were each used by a heretical group, Luke's gospel ought not to be eschewed because of its use by the Marcionites.

Despite Tertullian's implicit witness for the Fourfold Gospel canon (*Adv. Marc.* 4.2), the Gospel of Luke appears not to have

[65] Sundberg, 'Dependent Canonicity in Irenaeus and Tertullian', *StudEvan* 3/2 (1964), 403–9, at 403–5.

been readily appreciated by him. According to Tertullian, Luke was inferior to Paul as Paul was inferior to the other Apostles: 'Luke was not an apostle but apostolic, not a master but a pupil; in any case he was less than a master; certainly as inferior [to his master] as the inferiority of the apostle he followed, Paul without doubt, was [to the other apostles]' (*Porro, Lucas non apostolus, sed apostolicus; non magister, sed discipulus; utique magistro minor; certe tanto posterior, quanto posterioris apostoli sectator, Pauli sine dubio*). Tertullian went on: 'had Marcion even published his Gospel in the name of Paul himself, the single authority of the document, destitute of all support from preceding authorities, would not be a sufficient basis for our faith'. Since Luke's gospel agreed with the gospels written by the Apostles, then it too ought to be considered apostolic (4.3); that is to say, it is not apostolic on its own merit, but is dependent on this corroboration. It is clear from these passages that Tertullian did not regard Luke's gospel as authoritative in itself. 'Inasmuch, therefore, as the enlightener of St Luke himself desired the authority of his predecessors for both his own faith and preaching, how much more may not I require for Luke's gospel that which was necessary for the gospel of his master?' asked Tertullian (*Adv. Marc.* 4.2).

The arguments which Irenaeus and Tertullian give would certainly be odd if the Fourfold Gospel Canon was firmly established at that time, as so many scholars have suggested. The character of Tertullian's argument, with its strong depreciation of Luke, is more understandable if the Marcionite use of this gospel caused significant numbers in the churches to be averse to it. Both Irenaeus' and Tertullian's position suggest that Marcionism was of continuing strength in their day, with a consequent hesitation in the Church about full acceptance of that gospel which Marcion had abused. These passages put forward a view which Sundberg called 'dependent canonicity' and which was probably intended by their authors not only to defeat the Marcionites' claims about their gospel, but also to counter a hesitancy toward Luke in the Church.[66] Thus Irenaeus' explicit and Tertullian's implicit position on the Fourfold Gospel canon, far from proving its establishment,

[66] Sundberg, 'Dependent Canonicity', 406–9.

seems to be promoting it at a time when it is still not fully settled.

Although Clement (*Strom.* 3.93) and Origen (*Hom. on Luke* 1) explicitly affirmed in the East a principle of exclusivity for the Fourfold Gospel, they did not abide by that principle in practice. If the principle was one of long standing, then their use of other gospels would be particularly troublesome. However, their liberal usage may reflect the vestige of a previous practice to which this principle was being applied. Both of them continued to quote from non-canonical gospels. Clement, for instance, quoted passages from the Preaching of Peter on numerous occasions, e.g. *Strom.* 1.29 (cf. 2.15, *Eclog. Proph.* 58); 6.5 (*bis*); 6.6; 6.7 (?); 6.15—always with complete acceptance that it contained what Peter 'said' or 'wrote'.[67] Similarly Clement also quoted in several places from the Gospel according to the Egyptians, for example, *Strom.* 3.6 (cf. *Exc. Theo.* 67.2), 9, 13. In the first instance he took over a quotation from it without naming the book (*Strom.* 3.6). In the second instance he stated that he 'thinks' his reference is from it (*Strom.* 3.9). Clement emphasized, however, that the words quoted should be marked by those people who 'submit to anything rather than to the true rule of the Gospel' (*Strom.* 3.9). In the final instance Clement was sure that the quotation did come from the Gospel according to the Egyptians, which had been cited by the heretic Julius Cassianus; and he stopped there to point out that the Church accepted four Gospels and only four; Egyptians was not one of them (*Strom.* 3.13). Nevertheless, he went on carefully to allegorize the passage. In the *Stromateis* (2.9) Clement introduced a quotation with the words: 'It is written in the Gospel according to the Hebrews', without commenting upon its genuineness or spuriousness. When he later quoted from the same passage in *Strom.* 5.14, he did so without naming his source. The Traditions of Matthias was used by the Nicolaitans according to Clement (*Strom.* 3.4), but Clement quoted from it as well (*Strom.* 2.9; 7.13, cf. 7.17). Clement cited an unknown saying of Jesus as from 'Scripture' in *Strom.* 1.17 (cf. Epiphanius *Haer.* 44.2.6). In *Strom.* 5.63.7 he introduced another unknown quotation with the words, 'in

[67] J. Ruwet, 'Clément d'Alexandrie: Canon des Écritures et apocryphes', *Biblica*, 29 (1948), 391–408, at 402–3.

some gospel it says'. Other passages of unknown derivation were quoted elsewhere (*Strom.* 1.94.5, 2.70.5; 1.158.2; 3.97). So in spite of his statement about the four Gospels 'transmitted to us', Clement did not hesitate to make use of other gospel sources.

Like Clement, Origen occasionally quoted statements attributed to Jesus but not recorded in canonical sources (e.g. *Hom. on Pss.* 42; *Comm. on John* 19.2; *De orat.* 2.2; *Hom. on Num.* 23.4), one of which (*Hom. on Lev.* 10.2) he called 'apostolic'. It is significant, though, that Origen quoted non-canonical sources much less frequently than his predecessor. Origen cited the Gospel according to the Hebrews quite a few times, but expressed doubts about its authority on occasion (*Hom. on Jer.* 15.4; *Comm. on John* 2.12; *Comm. on Matt.* 15.4). When he made a list of condemned gospels (*Hom. on Luke* 1), he did not include the Gospel according to the Hebrews in the list, even though he was well aware that it lacked ecclesiastical authorization and authority. In a passage from the *Commentary on Matthew* (10.17) Origen mentioned the Gospel of Peter and seemed inclined to believe a story which he found in it. He described the Preaching of Peter in the *De Principiis* as 'not counted among the ecclesiastical books' (Preface, 7), though he took the trouble to explain away the argument based upon it on other grounds. In the *Commentary on John* (13.17) he mentioned the Preaching of Peter again and seemed uncertain about its genuineness. Finally he recorded a number of disconnected historical facts (or guesses) not found in the New Testament.[68] Although Origen regarded the Gospel Canon as closed in a more final sense than did Clement, his basic attitude was the same. In the words of Hanson: 'Fundamentally Origen's attitude to the Canon is the same as Clement's; he will accept as Christian evidence any material that he finds convincing or appealing'.[69]

Other sources which have been used to establish a second-century date for the Fourfold Gospel canon are now disputed. Many manuscripts of the Vulgate, for example, contain prologues to the different biblical books with information about the author of each, its importance and characteristics, and

[68] Hanson, 145–6. [69] Ibid. 143.

sometimes its occasion and history. There is a series of longer prologues to the gospels, the so-called Monarchian prologues, which used to be assigned to the first half of the third century. P. Corssen argued that they were Monarchian in character, coming from one and the same pen, and had been intended originally for an early edition of the four gospels, perhaps even the first.[70] Harnack suggested that Rome was the most likely place of origin, probably during the pontificate of Zephyrinus (198–217), and that they were afterwards worked over in an orthodox interest, and were of such high repute that they were incorporated in the Vulgate.[71] However, the idea of a Monarchian origin was abandoned after J. Chapman connected the prologues with Spain.[72] The prologues are now generally thought to have been composed at the end of the fourth or the beginning of the fifth century by some Priscillianist.[73] This point is of considerable importance since this set of prologues is clearly dependent upon the earlier 'Anti-Marcionite prologues'. If the so-called Monarchian collections could really have been assigned to the pontificate of Zephyrinus, then there would have been incontestable evidence for the primitive dating of the earlier set.

This other series of prologues to Mark, Luke, and John were believed to be anti-Marcionite in origin by D. De Bruyne and Harnack, and consequently assigned to a period shortly after the Marcionite crisis, *c.* 160–80.[74] They were thought to have been composed at Rome, originally in Greek, but translated in Africa at the end of the third century for a new edition of the Old Latin gospels. A copy of the prologue to Luke exists in both Greek and Latin. The arguments in favour of the original unity of the prologues were that they are united in two main branches of the manuscript tradition, that the prologues to Mark and Luke have similar phrases and are both used in the

[70] P. Corssen, *Monarchianische Prologe zu den vier Evangelien* (TU 15/1; Leipzig, 1896).

[71] Harnack, *Altchristliche Literatur*, ii. 2. 204–6.

[72] J. Chapman, *Notes on the Early History of the Vulgate Gospels* (Oxford, 1908), 217–88; cf. E. Ch. Babut, *Priscillien et le priscillianisme* (Bibliothèque de l'École des hautes études, 169; Paris, 1909), 294–308.

[73] F. L. Cross, 'The Priscillianist Prologues', *Expository Times* 48 (1937), 188–9.

[74] D. De Bruyne, 'Les plus anciens prologues latins des Évangiles', *RBén* 40 (1928), 193–214; Harnack, 'Die ältesten Evangelien-Prologe und die Bildung des Neuen Testamentes', *Sitzungsberichte der Preußichen Akademie der Wissenschaft*, phil.-hist. Klasse, 24 (1928), 322–41.

Monarchian prologues, and that those to Luke and John both show, the one implicitly, the other explicitly, an anti-Marcionite tendency.[75] However, these arguments have lost much of their impressiveness upon further examination.[76]

Harnack and De Bruyne took it for granted that all three prologues came from the same pen, but the disproportion in length and in content, and the difference in colouring and atmosphere, make it difficult to accept that assumption. Consequently the prologues were probably not originally united. Those to Mark and Luke may have been associated with each other before the later prologue to John was added to them. That to Mark reflects the tradition of the gospel much as it was known in the West towards the end of the second century. That to Luke, which in its present form is most clearly designed as a prologue for the gospel circulating independently, is not specifically anti-Marcionite, and probably dates from the third or early fourth century. The Prologue to John dates possibly from the fourth or fifth century. It is possible, though not certain, that all the prologues were originally composed in Greek. However, the very fact that these prologues were composed separately over several centuries militates against the assumption of an established Fourfold Gospel canon. This is seen especially in the independent character of the prologue to Luke. No unified set of prologues to all four later canonical gospels is evident until the fourth century. Yet within another century or so, the two gospel-prologue sets were widely circulating among the Vulgate manuscripts.

Campenhausen concluded that 'the restriction to four "Canonical" gospels must be seen as the result of a gradual, and at first quite limited, development which spread as a defence against the Marcionite and other heretical gospels, and finally prevailed'.[77] Previous attempts to suggest that the Fourfold Gospel canon was 'firmly established' in the last quarter of the second century must now be abandoned. Acquaintance with the four later canonical gospels does not necessarily imply

[75] W. F. Howard, 'The Anti-Marcionite Prologues to the Gospels', *Expository Times*, 47 (1935–6), 534–8.

[76] E. Gutwenger, 'The Anti-Marcionite Prologues', *TSt* 7 (1946), 393–409; R. G. Heard, 'The Old Gospel Prologues', *JTS*, NS 6 (1955), 1–16.

[77] Campenhausen, 174.

a Fourfold Gospel. Non-canonical gospel usage still abounded, even by some who promoted the Fourfold Gospel canon, such as Clement of Alexandria and Origen. Moreover, the prominence of gospel harmonies tends to suggest that the contents of the later canonical gospels were still not thought to be sacred at the end of the second century. Direct evidence for the Fourfold Gospel canon is really rather limited now that the gospel prologues are believed to be later. Irenaeus is the earliest witness for the Fourfold Gospel canon, and may have been the earliest promoter. His and Tertullian's polemic suggest some resistance to the acceptance of Luke in orthodox circles. The troubles in Rome and Asia Minor betray reluctance in accepting John at the end of the second and beginning of the third century. Even Clement of Alexandria's and Origen's 'firm' support of the Fourfold Gospel canon is questionable because of their liberal use of other gospel sources. Thus it was not widely accepted before the beginning of the third century, and was probably not 'firmly established' until the latter half of that century.

Consequently the presence of Fourfold Gospel in the Muratorian Fragment, as traditionally dated, would be surprising. While the Fragment's witness to it would not be impossible at the end of the second century and might take its place alongside those of Irenaeus, Tertullian, and Clement of Alexandria, this is unlikely because the Fragment bears none of the marks of recent development for the Fourfold Gospel.

The strongest evidence against a late second-century date for the Fragment's witness, however, is a realization that the Fragment represents more than just a gospel canon. It represents a New Testament canon. The presence of such a canon in the last quarter of the second century would be remarkable and completely anomalous beside the other sources of the formation of the Christian Bible. Such a date for the Fragment would require greater justification than it has thus far received. For the remaining elements of Christian Bible—the Old Testament, the *Corpus Paulinum*, and the catholic epistolary—all appear to be still in the early stages of development at the end of the second century. These other elements still appear as looser collections, which are generally continuing to expand and develop. But the Fragment represents the whole New Testament as closed, even on occasion specifying rejected works. A survey of the other elements will confirm that except for the gospel subcanon, the remaining subcanons of the Christian Bible are still at the stage of collections; that is to say, the concept of canon as applied to more than just the gospels is not evident with Christian scriptures before the fourth century.

## THE PAULINE LETTER COLLECTION

The history of the Pauline corpus up to and including the fourth century is one of continual expansion. The original letters of Paul were soon followed by pseudonymous additions. The Pauline authorship of 2 Thessalonians, Colossians, and Ephesians, for instance, is frequently disputed.[78] If any of these letters are not genuine, then they most probably represent pseudonymous Pauline literary activity of the generation after Paul's martyrdom (*c.* 65). The Pastoral Epistles (1–2 Timothy and Titus), similarly represent pseudonymous Pauline literary activity of the next generation, probably after the turn of the century.[79] Pseudonymous Pauline literary activity continued. The Acts of Paul (*c.* 185–95) contains apocryphal correspondence between Paul and the church at Corinth including a letter attributed to Paul, the so-called 3 Corinthians, which appears as a separate entity in a Coptic version, two Vulgate Latin manuscripts, and in the biblical canon of the Armenian church.[80] Ephraem Syrus (*c.* 360) treated 3 Corinthians as genuine, and included remarks on it in his Pauline Commentary. A spurious third-century correspondence of fourteen epistles between the philosopher Seneca (eight letters) and the apostle Paul (six letters) appears to have been accepted as genuine by Jerome, who noted that they were read by many (*De Vir. Ill.* 12), and by Augustine (*Ep.* 153. 14).[81] The so-called Latin epistle of Paul to the Laodiceans (4th c.) enjoyed considerable dissemination in Western manuscripts.[82] It is unlikely

[78] Fuller, *A Critical Introduction to the New Testament*, 57–68.

[79] Kümmel, 258–72.

[80] W. Schneemelcher, 'Acts of Paul', in id. (ed.), *New Testament Apocrypha*, trans. R. McL. Wilson, 2 vols. (Philadelphia, 1965), ii. 322–89.

[81] A. Kurfess, 'The Apocryphal Correspondence between Seneca and Paul', ibid. 133–40.

[82] Schneemelcher, 'The Epistle to the Laodiceans', ibid. 128–32.

that pseudonymous Pauline works would have continued to be composed into the fourth century if the *Corpus Paulinum* was closed. This continued literary activity in Paul's name suggests that there was no established Pauline canon, and that the Pauline collection remained open through the third and into the fourth century.

With the exception of the Fragment as traditionally dated, there is no evidence of a Pauline canon until the fourth century. Prior to that time there is ample attestation of a continually expanding Pauline Collection. The first indisputable evidence of a collection of Paul's letters is Marcion's *Apostolikon*. The contents are known from Tertullian's fifth book of his *Adversus Marcionem* (5.4) and Epiphanius' *Haereses* (1.42). According to Tertullian, the later canonical Ephesians was clearly referred to by Marcion as 'Laodiceans'. However, in Epiphanius' listing, Laodiceans is listed separately from Ephesians. Epiphanius might have been confused here, or else the collection may have been expanded by then to include a 'new' epistle to the Laodiceans.[83] The Fragment also attests to a Marcionite Laodiceans distinct from the canonical Ephesians (ll. 51, 64). It also suggests that at least one other epistle, 'to the Alexandrians', was added to the Marcionite Pauline collection (ll. 63–5). As mentioned previously, the Pastorals may also have been later accepted by the Marcionites.[84] Thus the Marcionite Pauline collection was clearly expanded in the third and into the fourth century.

Besides the testimony of Marcion's *Apostolikon*, a collection of Paul's epistles is also evidenced by the so-called Marcionite prologues.[85] N. A. Dahl has argued that the prologues presuppose an edition which was very similar to, but not identical with, Marcion's, and that the prologues represent an early non-Marcionite Pauline collection.[86] The order of the prologues

[83] See discussion below on the so-called Latin Epistle to the Laodiceans, Ch. 5.

[84] See discussion above on Marcion's collection.

[85] De Bruyne, 'Prologues bibliques d'origine marcionite', *RBén* 24 (1907), 1–16; cf. Corssen, 'Zur Überlieferungsgeschichte des Römerbriefes', *ZNW* 8 (1909), 1–45, 97–102; Harnack, 'Der marcionistische Ursprung der ältesten Vulgata-Prologe zu den Paulusbriefen', *ZNW* 24 (1925), 204–17; id., 'Die marcionitischen Prologe zu den Paulusbriefen, eine Quelle des Muratorischen Fragments', *ZNW* 25 (1926), 160–2.

[86] Dahl, 233–77.

appears to be due to chronological considerations. The early place of Romans within the chronological scheme, as well as the assignment of its composition to Athens rather than to Corinth, suggests that the author of the original prologue did not know Rom. 15–16, and this would confirm an early date for the prologue. Galatians is first, then, because it was thought to have been written first, and thus there is no need for a theory of a Marcionite substitution of Romans for Ephesians (Laodiceans) as Knox argued.[87] The address to the Laodiceans is often seen as peculiarly Marcionite. But the Ephesian address is only attested from Irenaeus onward. The Laodicean address need not be an invention of Marcion: the original set of prologues may have been composed before the title 'To the Ephesians' was generally accepted, in other words before the end of the second century. Perhaps the unfavourable comments of Rev. 3:14–22 about the church of Laodicea were a factor in the change. Ephesus, on the other hand, was treated far more kindly 2:1–11. That the original prologue might have treated Ephesians as a letter to the Laodiceans could suggest a pre-Marcion origin for the prologues and an earlier tradition.

Dahl disputed the common attribution of the prologues to Marcionites. If they are not Marcionite, then they constitute the earliest evidence of an orthodox Pauline collection and its expansion. From at least the fourth century onwards, commentators and editors took the repeated references to 'false apostles' in the prologues to represent heresy. De Bruyne and his followers argued that the 'false apostles' represent a Judaistic distortion of the gospel, whereas Paul as recovered by Marcion represents the true apostolic faith. The crucial question is which reading is more accurate. The prologue to Galatians states that the Galatians 'were tempted by false apostles to turn to the law and circumcision' (*temtati sunt a falsis apostolis ut in legem et circumcisionem verterentur*), a particularly Marcionite phrase. Yet the information could just as easily have been derived from the contents of the epistle itself. Most of the other prologues speak only in general terms about the false apostles.

The Corinthian prologue states that the Corinthians 'were

[87] Knox, *Philemon among the Letters of Paul* (hereafter *Philemon*) (Chicago, 1935), 40–1; id., *Marcion*, 53–73.

perverted variously by false apostles, some by the wordy eloquence of philosophy, others brought in by the sect of the Jewish Law' (*subversi multifarie a falsis apostolis, quidam a philosophial verbosa eloquentia, alii a secta legis Iudaicae inducti*). If nothing else, the false apostles appear here not to be a unified group, but are supposed to have taught several forms of heresy. The notion of two different heresies, one Judaizing and the other rhetorical and philosophical, corresponds more to what one might expect from an anti-heretical Catholic spokesman than a Marcionite. Moreover, Dahl noted textual variants of *ab apostolo* and *ab apostolis* in 'et his similiter ab apostolo audierunt verbum veritatis'. The plural is attested by many, diverse, and excellent manuscripts.[88] Thus it is probably original and not a correction. Such a reading would conflict with the Marcionite perception of Paul as the only true apostle and all the others as false apostles. The plural might refer to Paul, Silvanus, and Timothy (2 Cor. 1:19) or Paul and Cephas and Apollos (1 Cor. 1.11–12; 3.21–2).

While the prologue to the Corinthian letters makes difficulties for the conjectured Marcionite origin, that to Romans provides the strongest argument in its favour. A Catholic author would not be likely to say that false apostles introduced the Roman Christians to the Law and the Prophets, which sounds like a criticism of the Old Testament scriptures. Romans does not explicitly refer to false teachers except in 16:17–18, which the author of the prologue is thought not to have possessed. Consequently, he must have inferred what he says about the activity of the false apostles from those parts of Romans in which Paul explains how the Law and the Prophets are properly to be understood (Rom. 1.17b, 3.31–4.25, and most of chs. 9–11). Yet Dahl noted that these are exactly the parts of the letter which are not attested for Marcion. This suggests that the author of the prologue had the short version of Romans, without chs. 14–16, but *not* Marcion's revision of that text in front of him.

Dahl's proposed interpretation of this prologue may not be entirely satisfactory, but it is easier to ascribe the Roman prologue to a Catholic author than to ascribe the Corinthian

[88] Dahl, 244, 258.

prologue to a Marcionite. Finally, the prologue to Titus also hints at a rejection of the Old Testament. It says that the heretics, who are to be avoided, believed in 'Jewish scriptures' (*scripturis Iudaicis*) rather than in Jewish myths or fables (cf. Tit. 1: 14). Yet a Marcionite origin of the prologues to the Pastorals is unlikely if the original prologues are not Marcionite. If the Titus prologue is not considered Marcionite, then there is no reason to take the *scripturae Iudaicae* to be the later canonical Jewish scriptures. The author may have had in mind such Jewish writings of the pseudepigrapha as the Book of Jubilees or Enoch. It also seems unlikely that later Marcionites would have added secondary prologues which so soon became standard in Catholic manuscripts.

The prologue to Philemon also appears secondary. This may suggest a collection of Paul's letters which did not include Philemon. Ephraem did not comment upon the letter, probably because it was not in his collection. In their prefaces to Philemon, Jerome, Chrysostom, and more specifically Theodore of Mopsuestia all defend the canonicity and value of the letter. Apparently their opponents did not so much attack the letter as defend an ancient form of the Pauline collection which did not include it. If the original prologues presuppose a collection without Philemon, then they are probably not of Marcionite origin. However, there is another possibility. John Knox has argued that Marcion followed an ancient order which treated the letters to the Colossians and to Philemon as one, just as the two letters to the Corinthians or Thessalonians were treated as one.[89] Thus the prologue to Colossians could have been meant to cover both Colossians and Philemon. The probability of a lost prologue which treated Ephesians as a letter to the Laodiceans does not prove a Marcionite origin; neither does the possible lack of an original prologue to Philemon disprove it.

Dahl's summary of the history of the prologues' transmission suggested that a non-Marcionite author composed the original set, most likely in Greek, as an introduction to Paul's letters to the seven churches in the middle of the second century. At a later stage, probably in the middle of the third century when

[89] Knox, *Philemon*, 63–78.

the 'seven-church edition' was obsolete, the original prologues were translated into Latin and new prologues composed, to be used as prefaces to the individual letters in an edition of the thirteen letters of Paul.[90] A prologue to Hebrews was probably not added until the latter half of the fourth century.[91] In the fourth century the prologues became a common part of Pauline manuscripts, at least in Italy, and various types of texts emerged already before the prologues were incorporated into Vulgate manuscripts in the early fifth century. The striking similarities between Marcion's *Apostolikon* and the original prologues are easily explained on the assumption that in the second century a collection of Paul's letters similar to that of Marcion circulated even outside Marcionite circles. This collection did not contain the Pastorals, Hebrews, or perhaps Philemon. It did not distinguish between the two letters to the Corinthians and the Thessalonians, and it also probably called Ephesians 'Laodiceans' and contained the shortened form of Romans. Later in the third and fourth centuries both the Marcionite collection and the collection represented by the so-called Marcionite prologues were clearly expanded.

Another collection of Paul's epistles is found in the so-called Chester Beatty Papyrus ($\mathfrak{p}^{46}$), which confirms that the Pastorals were not part of the earliest Pauline collection and were only added in the third century.[92] The nine letters contained in this collection are in the order: Romans, Hebrews, 1 and 2 Corinthians, Ephesians, Galatians, Philippians, Colossians, 1 Thessalonians. There are some fourteen unaccounted-for pages missing from the end of the manuscript, the contents of which are uncertain. There is extant text until the end of 1 Thessaloninans (5:27). 2 Thessalonians, which would naturally follow, contains ninety-nine lines of text. As some fifteen lines with the title could appear on the remainder of the last fragmentary page, only three pages of twenty-seven lines per page would be needed to complete this epistle. Eleven pages would remain left in the codex. The first page of the manuscript

[90] Dahl, 257, 262–5.

[91] Souter, *The Text and Canon of the New Testament* (hereafter, *Text and Canon*) (London, 1913), 207; De Bruyne, 'Prologues bibliques', 7 n. 3.

[92] Kenyon, *Chester Beatty*, Fasciculus I (General Introduction), 6–7; Fasciculus III (Pauline Epistles and Revelation), p. ix; Fasciculus III (Supplement, Text), pp. xiv–xv; H. A. Sanders, *A Third-Century Papyrus Codex*, 12–15.

was not numbered and contained no text, so one might assume that the last page was also blank. The scribe averaged about nineteen lines of Oxford text per page for the first 140 pages. Then he began crowding an average of at least twenty-six Oxford lines to a page, perhaps realizing that the amount of text which he wished to include seemed larger than he first thought. If he was going to have ten (or eleven) pages unused at the end, he would have discovered that fact earlier and might have stopped crowding the lines some time before the end of the manuscript. The last five leaves (or ten pages) might have been left blank, just as the editors presume for an Old Testament codex in the same find.[93] If not, then these last ten (or eleven) pages could accommodate between 270 and 300 lines of Oxford text. Philemon contains only 40 lines, 1 Timothy 215 lines, 2 Timothy 156, and Titus 90, for a total of 501. Even assuming that all eleven pages were crowded to their very utmost, one page or more would need to be added to accommodate just 1 and 2 Timothy, without Philemon or Titus. Titus and Philemon could fit, but at least five pages would still remain blank. It is uncertain therefore what, if any, text(s) followed 2 Thessalonians. Perhaps some other work was meant to be included. It is not certain whether Philemon was originally present, but it seems most improbable that the Pastorals were included in 𝔭[46]. J. Quinn suggested that it represented only a collection of Pauline letters to the churches (including Hebrews), and that perhaps another collection of Pauline letters to individuals existed as well.[94]

There is no evidence that the Pastoral Epistles were part of the earliest Pauline collection(s). Tertullian stated that Marcion rejected (*recusaverit*) the Pastorals (*Adv. Marc.* 5.21), but there is really no proof that Marcion actually knew them. The so-called Marcionite prologues to the Pastorals are secondary and not part of the original collection. The pastorals are absent in 𝔭[46] (*c.* 200). Attestation of them before the end of the second century is very weak. The points of contact between Clement of Rome or Ignatius and the Pastorals concern only isolated expressions, for which no literary dependence can be proved.

[93] A. C. Johnson, H. S. Gehman, and E. H. Kase, *The John H. Scheide Biblical Papyri: Ezekiel* (Princeton, 1938), 2.

[94] Quinn, 379–85.

The linguistic agreements between the Pastorals and Polycarp (*c.* 135) suggest no more than that they both stand in the same ecclesiastical and cultural tradition. The author of the Acts of Paul mentioned various characters who appear elsewhere only in the Pastorals, namely Onesiphorus and Hermogenes, but no direct dependence can be established. No certain evidence of acquaintance with the Pastorals is extant before the third quarter of the second century, but from that time onwards the epistles are cited more regularly. Tatian (*c.* 172), according to Jerome (*Preface to Titus*), accepted Titus, but denied the authenticity of 1 Timothy. Theophilus (*c.* 177–80) alluded to 1 Tim. 2: 2 with 'that we may lead a quiet and peaceable life' (*Ad Autolyc.* 3. 14), while Irenaeus is the earliest witness to make allusions to all the Pastorals. Consequently the Pastoral epistles are generally believed to have been accepted in the churches later than the other Pauline epistles and not without some difficulty.[95]

The earliest Western Pauline collection appears to have been based upon a pattern of letters to seven churches. The particularity of Paul's letters may have been a problem in the ancient Church.[96] The idea that Paul, like John in Revelation (1–3), had written to seven churches, and thus to the whole Church, was frequently noted by early writers like Hippolytus, Cyprian, Victorinus of Pettau, Pseudo-Chrysostom, Jerome, and Isidore of Seville.[97] Through the mediation of Jerome and Isidore, the idea of Pauline epistles to seven churches found its way into the Vulgate preface to the Epistles. Knox argued that Marcion's *Apostolikon* consisted of letters to seven churches, although Marcion himself is nowhere known to have specifically numbered them so.[98] Scholars who have hypothesized about a

[95] P. N. Harrison, *The Problem of the Pastoral Epistles* (London, 1921), 67–86; A. T. Hanson, *The Pastoral Epistles* (London, 1982), 11–14.

[96] Dahl, 'The Particularity of the Pauline Epistles as a Problem in the Ancient Church', in *Neotestamentica et Patristica* (Novum Testamentum, suppl. 7; Leiden, 1962), 261–71; K. Stendahl, 'The Apocalypse of John and the Epistles of Paul in the Muratorian Fragment', in W. Klassen and G. F. Snyder (eds.), *Current Issues in New Testament Interpretation* (London, 1962), 239–45.

[97] Hippolytus, according to Dionysius Bar Salibi, cf. T. H. Robinson, 'Authorship', 488; Cyprian, *Test.* 1. 20, *Ad Fort.* 11; Victorinus of Pettau, *Comm. on Rev.* 1. 7, *De Fabr. Mundi* 11; P.-Chrysostom, *Opus Imperfectum in Matt.* 1; Jerome, *De Vir. Ill.*, 5; *Ep.* 53. 9; Isidore, *Prooem.* 92, 94, *De Num.* 38, 42.

[98] Knox argued that Philemon was counted with Colossians in *Marcion*, 39–76.

pre-Marcion Pauline collection have usually assumed that it took the shape of letters to seven churches.[99] Explicit citation of the seven-church scheme, however, is not found in the West until the third century.

The earliest Pauline collection, or collections, was, or were, expanded, probably in the third century, by the addition of the Pastorals. Eventually the Pauline collection changed from the pattern of letters to seven churches to a specifically thirteen-letter collection, with the Pastorals included. The addition of the secondary prologues among the so-called Marcionite prologues in the middle of the third century represented such a thirteen-letter collection. Eusebius noted that Gaius mentioned thirteen epistles of Paul, not counting the Epistle to the Hebrews with the others (*HE* 6.20.3). Whether this actual count was Gaius' or Eusebius' is not clear.[100] If it was Gaius' then he would be the earliest extant witness to the new thirteen-epistle collection of Paul. Otherwise Eusebius, and then Jerome, are reading back into his remarks a count which became well known in the West only later. A collection of specifically thirteen epistles was cited in the West during the fourth century, in the Mommsen Catalogue (*c.* 360), as well as in Filaster (*c.* 383), cf. *Haer.* 88/9. The African Council at Carthage (397), while accepting Hebrews, perhaps revealed an earlier pattern of enumeration with its listing: 'Pauli Ap. Epistolae XIII; eiusdem ad Hebraeos una'. Similarly Ambrosiaster (*c.* 380) and Pelagius (*c.* 400) in their Pauline commentaries dealt only with thirteen epistles of Paul, and so perhaps did Hilary (*c.* 315–67); but elsewhere Pelagius, *Comm. on Rom.* 1.17, and Hilary, *De Trin.*

[99] Goodspeed, *The Meaning of Ephesians* (Chicago, 1933); id., *New Solutions to New Testament Problems* (Chicago, 1927), 1–64; id., *Introduction*, 210–38. Goodspeed's theory has been variously adopted and adapted mainly by his students: Knox, *Marcion*, 39–76; A. E. Barnett, *Paul Becomes a Literary Influence* (Chicago, 1941); C. L. Mitton, *The Epistle to the Ephesians: Its Authorship, Origin, and Purpose* (Oxford, 1951); id., *The Formation of the Pauline Corpus of Letters* (London, 1955). W. Schmithals argued for a Collection of seven letters as opposed to letters to seven churches in 'On the Composition and Earliest Collection of the Major Epistles of Paul', *Paul and the Gnostics*, trans. J. E. Streely (Nashville, 1972), 239–74; id., 'Zur Abfassung und ältesten Sammlung der Paulinischen Hauptbriefe', *ZNW* 51 (1960), 225–45.

[100] Jerome's remarks that Gaius knew only thirteen epistles of Paul and rejected the Pauline authorship of Hebrews (*De Vir. Ill.* 59) would appear to be dependent upon Eusebius (*HE* 6.20.3).

4.11, both speak of *Hebrews* as a book of the Apostle. The new Collection of thirteen letters may have been suggested by the Platonic collection.

In the late fourth century, the Pauline collection in the West was enlarged again, this time by the addition of the epistle to the Hebrews. The epistle, however, was known in the West from an early date. Clement of Rome used it according to Eusebius (*HE* 3.38.1).[101] Irenaeus is also reported by Eusebius (*HE* 5.26) to have mentioned Hebrews and cited passages from it (cf. *Adv. Haer.* 2.30.9; 3.6.5; 4.17.1; 5.32.2). But until the end of the fourth century, there is no evidence in the West that Hebrews was considered Pauline. Marcion did not include it in his *Apostolikon* (cf. Jerome, preface to Titus). According to Photius, Hippolytus rejected Pauline authorship for it (*Biblio.* 121). Stephanus Gobarus said that neither Hippolytus nor Irenaeus thought Paul wrote it (Photius, *Biblio.* 232). Tertullian (*c.* 220) and the author of a Latin treatise wrongly attributed to Origen, *Tractatus Origenis de libris SS. Scripto*, ascribed Hebrews to Barnabas the Apostle. Gaius also rejected Pauline authorship, an opinion that Eusebius noted was 'still held by some Romans' (*HE* 6.20; cf. Jerome, *De Vir. Ill.* 59).

Later Western fathers, perhaps influenced by the East, persuaded the Western church to accept Hebrews into the Pauline collection. The prologue to Hebrews among the so-called Marcionite Prologues is obviously secondary and not added to the collection until *c.* 350–80. Hebrews was included in the New Testament Canon approved at the three African councils, namely Hippo (393) and Carthage (397, 419). That it was just being accepted into the Pauline collection at that time in the West is evident from the enumeration at the synods. At Hippo (393) and the first Carthaginian council (397), the enumeration, as already noted, read 'Pauli Ap. Epistolae XIII; eiusdem ad Hebraeos una'. By the second Carthaginian council (419), the clause had been altered to read 'Epist. Pauli Ap. numero XIV'. Rufinus also numbered the Pauline epistles fourteen (*Comm. in Symb. Apost.* 36), as apparently Pope

[101] The actual references to Hebrews by Clement of Rome are less direct, e.g. 1 Clem. 9, ~Heb. 6:5 (cf. Gen. 5:24); 10 ~Heb. 11:17 (cf. Gen. 21:22); 17 ~Heb. 11:37, 3:2 (cf. Num. 12:7); 21 ~Heb. 13:17 (cf. 1 Thess. 5:12–13), 23 ~Heb. 10:37 (cf. Hab. 2:3); 26 ~Heb. 6:18 (cf. Tit. 1:2); 43 ~Heb. 3:5 (cf. Num. 12:10).

Innocent did (*Ad Exsup. Tol.*),[102] though Jerome noted that 'the custom of the Latins does not receive it [Hebrews] among the canonical Scriptures' (*Ep. ad Dard.* 129.3; cf. *Comm. on Matt.* 26.8, 9; *Comm. on Is.* 6.2; 8.16), and that 'very many rejected the Epistle to the Hebrews' (*Ep. ad Paul.* 53.103; cf. *De Vir. Ill.* 5; *Comm. on Gal.* 1.1). Jerome also expressed doubts about the Pauline authorship (*Comm. on Amos* 8.7, 8; *Comm. on Jer.* 31.31). At times Augustine left the question of the canonicity of Hebrews uncertain (*Inchoat. Expos. Ep. ad Rom.* 11), while at other times he appears to have accepted it on the authority of 'the Eastern churches' (*De Pecc. Mer. et Remiss.* 1.27, 50; cf. *Serm.* 55.5). When listing the books of the New Testament, Augustine numbered Paul's letters 'fourteen' and included Hebrews (*De Doct. Christ.* 2.8.12). The late acceptance of Hebrews and a tentativeness about its authorship may be reflected in its position in most Western manuscripts. It was usually attached to the very end of the Pauline collection, after Philemon, e.g. in Old Latin codices, in manuscripts of the Latin Vulgate, and in Augustine's catalogue (*De Doct. Christ.* 2.8.12).

In the East, Hebrews was included in the Pauline collection at an early date, which may account for the absence of any early Eastern witnesses to the letters-to-seven-churches pattern. C. Anderson suggested that Hebrews was a part of the Pauline collection in the East from the very beginning.[103] In Alexandria, Hebrews was regarded as an epistle of Paul in every known ancient account. Clement clearly supported it as Pauline according to Eusebius (*HE* 6.14.2–4). Origen, according to Eusebius, acknowledged the linguistic difficulties of ascribing it to Paul (*HE* 6.25.11), but noted: that 'the thoughts of the epistle are admirable, and not inferior to the acknowledged apostolic writings, any one who carefully examines the apostolic text will admit' (ibid. 12–14). Dionysius, Theognostus, Peter Martyr, Alexander, and Athanasius of Alexandria all attest to the unanimous tradition of the church in Alex-

[102] Three MSS of Pope Innocent's letter, including the best of all (Vat. Reg. 1997), read 'XIII' for 'XIIII'; cf. C. H. Turner, 'Latin Lists of the Canonical Books: 3. From Pope Innocent's Epistle to Exsuperius of Toulouse (AD 405)', *JTS* 13 (1911–12), 77–82.

[103] C. P. Anderson, 'The Epistles to the Hebrews and the Pauline Letter Collection', *HTR* 59 (1966), 429–38.

andria, accepting Hebrews as Pauline.[104] The example of Alexandria was followed by Syria, for Eusebius of Caesarea stated: 'Paul's fourteen epistles are well known and undisputed (σαφεῖς)' (*HE* 3.3.5). Later, when cataloguing the books of the New Testament (3.25.2), Eusebius included after Acts and among the 'acknowledged' (ὁμολογούμενοι) books, the epistles of Paul, without either enumerating them or delineating their titles. The implication is that Hebrews was included since the Epistle was not mentioned among either the spurious or rejected works that follow. The Syriac fathers, from Ephraem onwards, made it clear that the canonicity and apostolicity of Hebrews was undisputed in their part of the world. The Peshitta New Testament, for instance, included it from the beginning. Thus there is no evidence of a Pauline collection in the East which excluded Hebrews.

The collection of fourteen Pauline epistles that won acceptance in the West late in the fourth century appears in the East perhaps as early as Origen. In a passage that is preserved only in the Latin translation of Rufinus, Origen apparently spoke of 'fourteen epistles of St Paul' (*Hom. on Jos.* 7). Eusebius, as noted above, when discussing the epistles of the Apostles, wrote that Paul's 'fourteen' epistles were 'well known' and 'undisputed'. However, in the very next sentence, Eusebius would appear to have introduced a qualification by declaring that as a matter of fact Hebrews had been disputed by the church of Rome and rejected by some (*HE* 3.3.5). Elsewhere, Eusebius appears to have ranked Hebrews among the 'disputed' works (ἀντιλεγόμεναι, *HE* 6.13.6). Later in the fourth century (*c.*396), Amphilochius revealed that a dispute about Hebrews was still known in the East, noting 'that some maintain that the Epistle to the Hebrews is spurious [νόθος]' (*Iambi ad Seleucum* 308–9). Amphilochius does not say who the 'some' are. Like Eusebius, he may be referring to Western objections.

Although Eusebius and Amphilochius acknowledged a dispute about Hebrews, it was generally accepted in the East. It was included in the Codices Vaticanus, Sinaiticus, and Alexandrinus, and in the Syrian New Testament catalogue, the list of Amphilochius, and probably in the catalogue of the

[104] Westcott, *The Epistle to the Hebrews* (London, 1892), lxii–lxxix.

Codex Claromontanus. Athanasius in his New Testament Catalogue (*Ep. Fest.* 39) numbered the epistles of Paul as 'fourteen' and included Hebrews among their titles. Other Eastern Fathers simply reckoned the Pauline letters as 'fourteen' without listing them, namely Cyril (*Catech.* 4.33), Epiphanius (*Haer.* 76.5), the Apostolic Canons (85), and Gregory of Nazianzus (*Carm.* 12.31). Thus the Eastern Fathers of the fourth century may have become aware of the Western disputes about Hebrews' Pauline authorship; but it was a dispute which they themselves seem never to have seriously entertained.

While Hebrews does not appear to have ever been seriously disputed by the Eastern churches, there was a change in its status in the fourth and fifth centuries.[105] Before then, in Egypt and Syria, Hebrews was generally listed among the letters of Paul to the churches. It was included among them in the Chester Beatty Collection ($\mathfrak{p}^{46}$), the archetype of Codex Vaticanus (B) (according to chapter-numeration), the Sahidic translation of Athanasius' thirty-ninth festal letter, a Syrian canon (*c.*400), and numerous minuscule manuscripts.[106] Hence it appears that, in Egypt in the third century and in Syria in the fourth, Hebrews stood among the letters of Paul to the churches. Yet for some reason in the fourth and fifth centuries, it was removed from among the letters to the churches in the East and placed elsewhere. In Syria, it appears to have been placed at the end of the Pauline Collection, after Philemon, as it was found in the West, perhaps because of Western influence. The numerous manuscripts of the Peshitta (*c.*400) and Harklean (616) versions placed Hebrews in that position, and this suggests that it was probably placed there in the lost translation made for Philoxenus of Mabbug (508).[107] According to Junilius, a high official at the court of Justinian, Hebrews followed Philemon in the canon of the church in Nisibis (*De Part. Div. Legis* 1.6). Elsewhere in the East, Hebrews was generally moved to stand after 2 Thessalonians, that is, after the letters to the churches and before those written to individuals. No Latin or Syriac manuscripts have the epistle

[105] W. H. P. Hatch, 'The Position of Hebrews in the Canon of the New Testament', *HTR* 29 (1936), 133–51.

[106] Ibid. 145.

[107] Zahn, *Geschichte*, iii. 171–2.

in this place. Yet Hebrews is clearly placed there in Codices Vaticanus (B), Sinaiticus (א), and Alexandrinus (A), as well as in six other uncial and at least sixty minuscule codices. It probably appeared there in the Catalogue found in the Codex Claromontanus.

The earliest patristic writer who bears witness to the placing of Hebrews after 2 Thessalonians is Athanasius (367). In the Euthalian prologue to the Pauline epistles (*c.* 350), Hebrews is mentioned between the two epistles to the Thessalonians and the two letters to Timothy. Epiphanius (d. 403) said that some manuscripts of the New Testament 'have the epistle to the Hebrews tenth, before the two to Timothy' (*Haer.* 76.5). Jerome (*c.* 394) spoke of Hebrews as the 'eighth' of Paul's epistles, just after the letters addressed to the churches and before Timothy, Titus, and Philemon (*Ep.* 53.8). Cyril of Alexandria (d. 444) has Hebrews before 1 Timothy. It also appears there among the Pauline commentaries of Theodoret of Cyrrhus (d. *c.* 466), and in the writings of Cosmas Indicopleustes (*c.* 547), John of Damascus (d. *c.* 749), the pseudo-Athanasian *Synopsis Scripturae Sacrae* (7th c.), and in the so-called Laodicean Canon number 60 (7th–9th c.).

The dispute about Hebrews reflected in the writings of Eusebius and Amphilochius appears never to have been so serious that the epistle was rejected by the Eastern Fathers, but it may account for the change in its placement among the Pauline letters in the East during the fourth and fifth centuries. If the dispute was about its Pauline authorship, then it might account for its transfer in the Syrian churches to the end of the Pauline Collection after Philemon, as was done in the West. However, such a dispute is a less likely explanation for the change of Hebrews' placement generally reflected in the rest of the East, namely after the letters to the churches but before the letters to the individuals.

There is no evidence that Western pattern of letters to seven churches in the early Pauline collection(s) was known in the East before the end of the fourth century, when it appears in Jerome (*Ep.* 53.8). The Eastern churches may have never considered the pattern of letters to seven churches before because Hebrews was a part of the Eastern Pauline collection from a very early point, if not from the beginning. The introduction in the East, at the end of the fourth century, of the pattern of letters to seven churches may have caused some confusion on the place of Hebrews, and may have resulted in its transfer from among the letters to the churches to either the end of the collection as in Syria, or after the letters to the seven churches as in the rest of the East. Jerome, writing from Bethlehem, referred to Hebrews as the 'eighth epistle', but noted that it 'is not generally counted in with the others [the other seven?]' (*Ep.* 53). Amphilochius also seems to be trying to introduce the seven-letter pattern into the larger established Eastern Pauline collection of fourteen epistles; he thus lists 'twice seven letters' sent to the churches, although some of those listed were not specifically written to churches. Hebrews is here listed last, and with some qualification. Thus the movement of Hebrews in the Eastern Pauline collection of the fourth and fifth century may have resulted from the introduction in the East of the Western pattern of Pauline letters to seven churches.

In any event, the various additions and adjustments to the *Corpus Paulinum* of both the East and West during the third and fourth centuries confirm that the Pauline collection remained open. A Pauline canon seems not to have been established until the fourth century. It is at that time that the first Pauline catalogues appear, and that the collection becomes so established that it can be referred to by number only. Thus the Fragment's inclusion of the Pastorals, and its witness to a closed Pauline canon (as reflected in the rejection of the letters to the Alexandrians and Laodiceans), would be extraordinary on the traditional dating.

The Fragmentist, if writing in the East and in the late fourth century, would provide another witness to the late introduction of the Western pattern of letters to seven churches. As with Amphilochius, this may also account for the Fragment's confused reproduction of the pattern. In his catalogue, the Fragmentist stressed the importance of the pattern of letters to seven churches several times (ll. 46–50, 57–9), but carelessly reversed the relationship between John's seven letters and Paul's.[108] His stress and confusion may suggest that the pattern was unfamiliar and needed explanation. Indeed the reason

108 T. H. Robinson, 488.

why the Fragmentist stopped delineating the epistles of Paul after Corinthians, Galatians, and Romans (ll. 42–6), and then started over again after introducing the pattern of letters to seven churches (ll. 46–54), may have been the presence of Hebrews among the letters to the churches in the East. It was after these letters delineated by the Fragmentist in the first instance, namely Corinthians, Galatians, and Romans, that Hebrews generally followed when it was included among the letters to the churches in the East.[109] Hebrews may either have been carelessly omitted in the Fragmentist's efforts to list the Western pattern of letters to seven churches and then the remaining letters to individuals (ll. 59–63), or else be absent from the Fragment as a result of the Western dispute about its authorship.

## THE CATHOLIC EPISTLE COLLECTION

The collection of catholic epistles was gradually enlarged in the Church in a similar way to that which has been shown in the case of the *Corpus Paulinum.* Eusebius is the first extant witness to the collection of 'seven' catholic epistles that eventually became part of the New Testament (*HE* 2.23.25). The collection of seven letters was probably established before the canon-forming process of the fourth century. However, not all seven catholic epistles were generally received until the latter half of that century. Eusebius accepted as undisputed only 1 John and 1 Peter (*HE* 3.25.2). James, Jude, 2 Peter, and 2 and 3 John were included by Eusebius among the 'disputed [ἀντιλεγομένων] which are known [γνωρίμων] by many' (*HE* 3.25.3; cf. 2.23.25; 3.3.1). Although Origen knew all seven, he too viewed only 1 Peter and 1 John as undisputed (cf. Eusebius, *HE* 6.25.10), and held 2 Peter, 2 and 3 John, Jude, and James as disputed. None the less, the seven catholic epistles were included in the probably Alexandrian catalogue found in the Codex Claromontanus. The festal letter of Athanasius (367) also contained all seven. Cyril of Jerusalem (d. 386) and Epiphanius (d. 403) both accepted all seven. Gregory of

[109] Hatch, 133–6.

Nazianzus (d. 391) recognized all seven epistles, as did Amphilochius of Iconium, though the latter acknowledged that some limited them to three. By the end of the fourth century in the East (excluding Syria), all seven letters were received by most Fathers.

In Syria, it appears that none of the catholic epistles was accepted until the fifth century. The *Doctrina Addai* (*c.* 390–430) reported that the founder of the church of Edessa, in his farewell speech to his follower Aggai, ordered that no writings other than the Old Testament, the Gospel (Diatessaron?), the epistles of Paul, and the Acts of the Twelve Apostles should be read in the churches.[110] From the period around 400, a Syrian catalogue is preserved which named in the New Testament the gospels, Acts, and Pauline epistles, but no catholic epistles.[111] By the early fifth century the Syrian collection of New Testament scriptures as reflected in the Peshitta had expanded to include James, 1 Peter, and 1 John. The Alexandrian merchant Cosmas Indicopleustes confirmed the new Syrian catholic epistle collection of three letters. After he became a monk (535×547), he defended himself from the charge of not making use of all the catholic epistles by appealing to the practice of the Syrian church, which accepted only the three epistles (*Top. Christ.* 7.265). The remaining catholic epistles (namely 2 and 3 John, 2 Peter, Jude) were added to the Syrian collection with the appearance of the so-called Philoxenian version in 508. Ephraem Syrus, however, appears to have accepted all seven catholic epistles earlier, according to translations of his works surviving only in Greek. If so, there is no other trace of the reception of 2 and 3 John, 2 Peter, and Jude in the Syrian church until the Philoxenian version.[112] John Chrysostom (*c.* 347–407) and Theodoret (*c.* 393–*c.* 466) used only the three (James, 1 John, 1 Peter), while Theodore of Mopsuestia (*c.* 350–428) and his followers, Junilius and Paul of Nisibis, appear to have accepted only two catholic epistles (1 John, 1 Peter).[113] Junilius, however, noted that 'very many add' the other five

[110] G. Phillips, *The Doctrine of Addai, the Apostle* (London, 1876), 44.

[111] A. S. Lewis, *Catalogue of the Syriac MSS. in the Convent of S. Catherine on Mount Sinai* (Studia Sinaitica, 1; London, 1894), 11–14.

[112] Westcott, *Canon of the New Testament*, 241 n. 2.

[113] Sanday, 'The Cheltenham List of Canonical Books, and the Writings of Cyprian' (hereafter, 'The Cheltenham List'), *StudBib* 3 (1891), 217–303, at 243–59.

epistles. Thus the catholic epistle collection of Syria expanded to seven letters slowly and probably not until the late fifth century.

In the West Irenaeus cited 1 Peter, and 1 and 2 John as Scripture. Tertullian knew 1 John, 1 Peter, and Jude. The Roman Novatian (*c.* 250) quoted 1 John. In North Africa in the works of Cyprian (d. 258) only 1 John and 1 Peter among the catholic epistles are cited; at the same time in Africa, Aurelius Chullabi quoted from 2 John.[114] The first catholic epistle collection can be established in the West with the African Mommsen catalogue (359), which named 'epistulae Johannis III *una sola*', 'epistulae Petri II *una sola*', but omitted Jude and James. The contradictory scribal note of 'una sola' suggests a protest and may imply an earlier catholic epistle collection in the West of only 1 Peter and 1 John. Hilary of Poitiers (d. 367) cited James and 2 Peter as scripture. Yet not until the end of the fourth century with Jerome (*c.* 342–420) and Augustine (354–430) and the African synods of Hippo (393) and Carthage (397, 419) is there any explicit evidence that all seven letters were contained in the catholic epistle collection of the West.

In summary, the catholic epistles as a subcanon were regularly grouped in specific combinations. These collections themselves expanded to the canonical seven, though sometimes with resistance. In Syria, for a significant period of time, none of the catholic epistles was received (e.g. *Doctrina Addai*, Syrian canon *c.* 400). A combination of only 1 John and 1 Peter received early and wide support (so Papias, Polycarp, Cyprian, Hilary, Pacian, Theodore of Mopsuestia, Paul of Nisibis), and was enlarged with some resistance (as in the Mommsen Catalogue and Eusebius). A collection of only James, 1 John, and 1 Peter also received wide support (as in Irenaeus, Peshitta, Chrysostom, Theodoret), and was also expanded with some resistance (e.g. Amphilochius of Iconium). The collection of all seven catholic epistles, however, eventually became the norm (e.g. Athanasius, Cyril of Jerusalem, Epiphanius, Apostolic Canons, Gregory of Nazianzus, Filaster, Ambrose, Rufinus, Jerome, Council of Carthage, Philoxenian Version, Priscillian). Beyond these collections, other combinations are rare and

[114] See above, Ch. 1 n. 33.

irregular (e.g. Tertullian and Origen mentioned Jude as well as 1 John and 1 Peter; Lucifer of Cagliari noted Jude as well as 1 John, 1 Peter, and James).

The collection of Jude and 1 and 2 (and 3?) John represented in the Muratorian Fragment is without parallel, and reflects none of the recognized patterns of expansion. The absence of 1 Peter especially, and perhaps James too, is suggestive that further entries in the Fragment are missing. Thus the Fragment may witness to a larger combination of catholic epistles, but such larger collections which included the minor catholic epistles of Jude and 2 (and 3?) John were not prominent until the early fourth century. Once again then, the Fragment, if traditionally dated, would be an anomaly.

## MISCELLANEOUS WORKS

The remaining New Testament books which were later deemed canonical, namely Acts and Revelation, appear to have entered the canon as individual works, and not as members of an earlier collection. Though Acts might be expected to be associated with Luke, or Revelation with the other Johannine works, there is little evidence of such groupings. The place of Acts and Revelation in most manuscripts further supports their independent acceptance. The idea of an apocalyptic collection, perhaps of the Shepherd and the Revelations of John and Peter, is no more than speculation,[115] just as is any notion of an earlier collection of Acts of various Apostles.[116]

Other works too, which like Acts and Revelation were held as Scripture prior to the fourth century, found themselves attached to the later New Testament catalogues and collections, e.g. the Shepherd, the Revelation of Peter, 1 and 2 Clement, the Wisdom of Solomon, Barnabas, and the Acts of Paul. The claims of these works to be considered canonical in the fourth century were like those of Acts and Revelation—not

[115] Campenhausen, 218–20.

[116] The Manichees did establish a collection of Acts containing five apocryphal Acts (of Paul, Peter, Andrew, Thomas, and John), but this collection probably did not appear until the middle of the 4th c., after the general process of canon-forming had begun in the churches; cf. Ch. 5.

as members of any earlier collection, but simply as works which had been appealed to as Scripture in the period before the formation of a canon. Thus the boundaries of the New Testament canon were settled in the fourth century in the process of canon-forming itself, the final expansion of the earlier collections of Pauline and catholic epistles was closed in the same process. After the fourth century, the entire Christian canon, namely the Old Testament, the Fourfold Gospel, the Pauline letter collection, the catholic epistle collection, and miscellaneous works, were generally perceived as closed, despite the occasional continuing dispute about one work or another, or the occasional appearance in a manuscript of an apocryphal writing.

## CONCLUSIONS

The formation of the Christian canon of scriptures was a gradual process that culminated in the fourth century. Prior to that time the churches gathered together and defined a number of different collections which were later incorporated into the New Testament, along with a number of singular works. In the case of Jewish scriptures, the Church inherited a large body of works which it apparently attempted to define and limit only later in the fourth century. With regard to specifically Christian scriptures, the Church began at an early stage to collect its valued works and accumulate a complement to the books of the Old Testament. However, not until the fourth century did the churches appear to define and restrict that New Testament collection. Thus the development of the New Testament collection was one of gradual accumulation and expansion into the fourth century. The Fourfold Gospel is the only subcanonical collection that appears closed before the actual activity of fourth-century canon-forming. It is only in that later process that the other collections appear to have been fixed and established.

The idea of a so-called 'core New Testament canon' at the end of the second century is now seen as misleading and unfounded. Once a distinction is made between scripture and canon, the idea of a New Testament canon does not appear applicable before the fourth century. Instead, a 'core New Testament collection' might be spoken of, which, while remaining open, contained a number of works which were regularly appealed to for religious authority as Scripture.

But even the elements of that 'core New Testament collection' are probably not as numerous as they were previously thought to be once a distinction between 'comments' and 'collections' is made. The four later canonical gospels enjoyed widespread usage, but there were disputes, and the Fourfold Gospel canon should perhaps be seen as only an innovation at the end of the second and beginning of the third century. A 'core' Pauline collection of perhaps the letters to seven churches in the West, plus Hebrews in the East, appears accepted in the second half of the second century. But the Pastorals should not be thought of as elements of that collection until later in the third century. Among the catholic epistle collection, a 'core' of 1 Peter and 1 John (and possibly James) might be postulated from the beginning of the third century. Thus there is a good case from the beginning of the third century for postulating a 'core New Testament collection' of perhaps the Fourfold Gospel, the Pauline letters to seven churches (and Hebrews in the East), and the major catholic epistles.

The Muratorian Fragment suggests a much larger New Testament collection than this 'core', including the pastorals, Jude, 2 and (?)3 John, the Wisdom of Solomon, the Revelations of John and Peter, and Acts. The Fragment, if traditionally dated, is thus an anomaly in terms of its contents. It would be one of the earliest, if not the earliest, witness to a Fourfold Gospel canon. It would be the earliest witness for the addition of the Pastorals to the Pauline collection. The Fragment's catholic epistle collection is unparalleled, especially with its absence of 1 Peter, and maybe James. If these works are simply missing from the Fragment, then the Fragment would represent the earliest larger such collection including minor catholic epistles. Therefore the hypothesis of a 'core New Testament collection' does not necessarily support the traditional dating of the Fragment, but serves to emphasize the extraordinary character of its contents, if it is dated at the end of the second century.

More significantly, the Muratorian Fragment clearly represents something more than a collection, however large. The Fragment represents a canon—a closed collection of scriptures. It delineates a specific group of works which the Fragmentist stated were accepted in the Catholic Church, namely (Matthew, Mark); Luke; John; Acts; 1 and 2 Corinthians; Ephesians; Philippians; Colossians; Galatians; 1 and 2 Thessalonians; Romans; Philemon; Titus; 1 and 2 Timothy; Jude; 1, 2, and (?)3 John; the Wisdom of Solomon; and the Revelations of John and Peter. The Fragmentist also clearly noted works which were rejected, namely Laodiceans, Alexandrians, and anything from Arsinous, Valentinus, and Miltiades, as well as works which were disputed (Revelation of Peter) or restricted to private reading (The Shepherd). The Fragment entails both conceptual elements and contents which are not elsewhere received in the churches until the fourth century. Thus the Fragment, on the traditional dating, is an anomaly in the development of the Christian canon both in the concepts it implies and the contents it suggests, and does not seem to have greatly influenced the development of the New Testament canon either conceptually or with regard to contents.

Finally the Fragment, on its traditional dating, is not only an anomaly in contents and concepts, but also in form. The Fragment is clearly a catalogue. It distinctly delineates the accepted, disputed, and rejected works, without significant narration. Boundaries are clearly established in the Fragment. Yet the catalogue as a New Testament form is nowhere else extant in surviving literature until the fourth century, more than one hundred years later. In the fourth century, numerous catalogues appeared in all parts of the Church. While some list has to be first, it is more than a question of just being the first. The Muratorian Fragment, if traditionally dated, is an extraordinary anomaly in the development of the Christian Bible on numerous counts.

# 4

# FOURTH-CENTURY CATALOGUES

EXCLUDING the Muratorian Fragment, there are no catalogues of the Christian canon until the fourth century. As Albert Sundberg noted in his argument for the redating of the Fragment:

during that century New Testament canonical lists came to appear in many parts of the church: in Syria/Palestine the list of Eusebius, *HE* 3.25 (303?–250); that of Cyril of Jerusalem (348), *Catech.* 4.33; of Epiphanius, *Haer.* 8.6 [*sic*]; and of Chrysostom (*c.*407), *Synopsis Sacr. Script.*; the list in Codex Claromontanus; and a Syrian canon of *c.*400; in Alexandria, the list of Athanasius, *Ep. Fest.* 39; an African canon of about 360; and the Carthaginian Catalogue (397); in Asia Minor, the list of Gregory Nazianzus, *Carm.* 12.31; of Amphilochius, *Iambi ad Seleucum*; and the Laodicene Catalogue (363); and in Rome, a canon dated about 400.[1]

The sudden and widespread appearance of New Testament catalogues confirms that the Fragment, if traditionally dated, is an anomaly in the formation of the canon. A consideration of the various catalogues of the fourth century is essential in understanding the place of the Fragment within the history of the canon.

## THE UNDISPUTED CATALOGUES

Sundberg acknowledged by footnote that his enumeration of fourth-century catalogues was drawn from the lists in Westcott and Souter.[2] His list included at least one work which by his own dating is not specifically fourth-century, namely that of

[1] Sundberg, 'Canon Muratori', 37–8.

[2] Ibid. 37 n. 167; Westcott, *Canon of the New Testament*, 531–71; Souter, *Text and Canon*, 205–37.

Chrysostom (*c.*407). Three of his entries, the Laodicene catalogue, the Roman canon (*c.*400), and Chrysostom, are disputed, and will be considered later. Sundberg, however, inexplicably failed to include several other important references which were also present in Westcott and Souter: Apostolic Canon 85 (380), Jerome, *Ep.* 53 (394); Augustine, *De Doctr. Christ.* 2.8.12 (*c.*396–7); Rufinus, *Comm. in Symb. Apost.* 36–7 (400); and Pope Innocent, *Ad Exsup. Tol.* (405).[3] With these items added, there appear to be fifteen undisputed catalogues from the fourth (and very first years of the fifth) century:

1. Eusebius, *HE* 3.25.1–7
2. Catalogue in Codex Claromontanus
3. Cyril of Jerusalem, *Catech.* 4.33
4. Athanasius, *Ep. Fest.* 39
5. Mommsen Catalogue
6. Epiphanius, *Pan.* 76:5
7. Apostolic Canon 85
8. Gregory of Nazianzus, *Carm.* 12.31
9. African Canons
10. Jerome, *Ep.* 53
11. Augustine, *De Doct. Christ.* 2.8.12
12. Amphilochius, *Iambi ad Seleucum* 289–319
13. Rufinus, *Comm. in Sym. Apost.* 36
14. Pope Innocent, *Ad Exsuper. Tol.*
15. Syrian catalogue of St Catherine's

For the sake of convenience, the contents of these catalogues are set out in columnar form in Table 4.1. In order to see how the Fragment is related to them, it is necessary to note the outstanding characteristics of each.

### 1. *Eusebius*

The canon of scriptures was a recurrent theme in Eusebius, since he acknowledged an interest in recording the usage of the ancient fathers (*HE* 3.3.3; 5.8.1).[4] Perhaps as a consequence, Eusebius created lists or catalogues of the New Testament from

[3] Sundberg obviously omitted several items from Westcott and Souter as clearly extraneous, either in date or in contents.

[4] Grant, *Eusebius*, 126–41.

TABLE 4.1. *Undisputed New Testament catalogues of the fourth century*

| 1 Eusebius | 2 Clermont | 3 Cyril of Jerusalem | 4 Athanasius |
|---|---|---|---|
| *Homologoumena* | Gospels 4 | *New Testament* | *New Testament* |
| Gospels 4 | Matthew | Gospels 4 | Gospels 4 |
| Acts | John | Acts | Matthew |
| Paul Epp. | Mark | Cath. Epp. 7 | Mark |
| 1 John | Luke | James | Luke |
| 1 Peter | Paul Epp. | Peter | John |
| Revelation (?) | Rom. | John | Acts |
| *Antilegomena* | 1, 2 Cor. | Paul Epp. 14 | Cath. Epp. 7 |
| 'Disputed' | Gal. | *Pseudepigrapha* | James |
| James | Eph. | Gosp. of Thomas | Peter Epp. 2 |
| Jude | (Phil.?) | | John Epp. 3 |
| 2 Peter | (1, 2 Thess.?) | | Jude |
| 2, 3 John | (Heb.?) | | Paul Epp. 14 |
| 'Spurious' | 1, 2 Tim. | | Rom. |
| Acts of Paul | Titus | | Cor. 2 |
| Shepherd | Col. | | Gal. |
| Rev. of Peter | Philemon | | Eph. |
| Barnabas | 1, 2 Peter | | Phil. |
| Didache | James | | Col. |
| Revelation (?) | 1, 2, 3 John | | Thess. 2 |
| Gosp. of Hebrews (?) | Jude | | Heb. |
| *Cited by heretics* | —Barnabas | | Tim. 2 |
| Gosp. of Peter | Revelation | | Titus |
| Gosp. of Thomas | Acts | | Philemon |
| Gosp. of Matthias | —Shepherd | | Revelation |
| Acts of Andrew | —Acts of Paul | | *Catechetical* |
| Acts of John | —Rev. of Peter | | Didache |
| | | | Shepherd |

| 5 Mommsen Catalogue | 6 Epiphanius | 7 Apostolic Canons | 8 Gregory of Nazianzus |
|---|---|---|---|
| Gospels 4 | Gospels 4 | Gospels 4 | Matthew |
| Matthew | Paul Epp. 14 | Matthew | Mark |
| Mark | Acts | Mark | Luke |
| John | Cath. Epp. | Luke | John |
| Luke | James | John | Acts |
| Paul Epp. 13 | Peter | Paul Epp. 14 | Paul Epp. 14 |
| Acts | John | Peter Epp. 2 | Cath. Epp. 7 |
| Revelation | Jude | John Epp. 3 | James |
| John Epp. 3 | Revelation | James | Peter 2 |
| (*una sola*) | Wisdom | Jude | John 3 |
| Peter Epp. 2 | Sirach | Clement Epp. 2 | Jude |
| (*una sola*) | | Apost. Const. | |
| | | Acts | |

| 9<br>African Canons | 10<br>Jerome | 11<br>Augustine | 12<br>Amphilochius |
|---|---|---|---|
| Gospels 4 | 'The Lord's Four' | Gospels 4 | Gospels 4 |
| Acts | Matthew | Matthew | Matthew |
| Paul Epp. 13 | Mark | Mark | Mark |
| + Heb. | Luke | Luke | Luke |
| Peter Epp. 2 | John | John | John |
| John Epp. 3 | Paul Epp. to 7 Chs. | Paul Epp. 14 | Acts |
| James | + Heb. 8th | Rom. | Paul Epp. to Chs. 14 |
| Jude | Tim. | Cor. 2 | Rom. |
| Revelation | Titus | Gal. | Cor. 2 |
| *Also read* | Philemon | Eph. | Gal. |
| Acts of Martyrs | Acts | Phil. | Eph. |
| | Epp. 7 | Thess. 2 | Phil. |
| | James | Col. | Col. |
| | Peter | Tim. 2 | Thess. 2 |
| | John | Titus | Tim. 2 |
| | Jude | Philemon | Titus |
| | Revelation | Heb. | Philemon |
| | | Peter Epp. 2 | Heb. (?) |
| | | John Epp. 3 | Cath. Epp. 7 (3?) |
| | | Jude | James |
| | | James | Peter |
| | | Acts | John |
| | | Revelation | Jude (?) |
| | | | Revelation (?) |

| 13<br>Rufinus | 14<br>Pope Innocent | 15<br>Syrian catalogue |
|---|---|---|
| *Canonical* | *New Testament* | Gospels 4 |
| Gospels 4 | Gospels 4 | Matthew |
| Matthew | Paul Epp. XIII(I) | Mark |
| Mark | John Epp. 3 | Luke |
| Luke | Peter Epp. 2 | John |
| John | (Jude Ep. 1) | Acts |
| Acts | James | Gal. |
| Paul Epp. 14 | Acts | 1, 2 Cor. |
| Peter Epp. 2 | Revelation | Rom. |
| James | *Repudiated* | Heb. |
| Jude | 'Matthias/James the | Col. |
| John Epp. 3 | Less' | Eph. |
| Revelation | 'Peter + John' = | Phil. |
| *Ecclesiastical* | Leucian | 1, 2 Thess. |
| Shepherd | ('Andrew' = | 1, 2 Tim. |
| Two Ways | Xenocharides and | Titus |
| Preaching of Peter | Leonidas) | Philemon |
| | 'Thomas' | |

the writings of his predecessors, namely Irenaeus (*HE* 5.8.1–15), Clement of Alexandria (*HE* 6.14.1–7), and Origen (*HE* 6.25.3–14). A reading of these passages reveals that Eusebius simply wove together various texts from their works in order to create the impression that each of these Church Fathers had a 'canon'. It was Eusebius who created the 'canon' from their comments, not the writers themselves, so that none of these lists are original catalogues. They are expressions of Eusebius' interest in the Canon, and not of his sources. The remarks of the earlier authors themselves reflect only the concept of Scripture. R. P. C. Hanson has confirmed that no list, not even the concept of a closed collection of New Testament Scriptures, was entertained by Origen and Clement of Alexandria.[5]

The absence of original New Testament catalogues in Eusebius' works, other than his own (*HE* 3.25.1–7), is a reliable indication that no such catalogues were known to him, and that probably none existed prior to his time. If Eusebius had known, or even heard of, any earlier catalogue he would surely have made a reference to it. That Eusebius created such catalogues for himself and others suggests that the interest in catalogues was his. The interest in defining the Canon by the use of catalogues, which was widely repeated in the fourth century, may be traced back no further than Eusebius.

Eusebius' own New Testament catalogue appears in the *Church History* (3.25.1–7). Its exact date is uncertain because the *History* went through several editions. In its present form it covers the period from the foundation of the Church to the victory of Constantine over Licinius in 324. The catalogue, therefore, is probably to be dated before 325. The earliest edition of the *History* may have appeared before the persecution of Diocletian in 303. In *HE* 5.8.1 Eusebius wrote that 'when beginning this work we made a promise to set forth from time to time quotations from the ancient ecclesiastical presbyters and authors in which they committed to writing the traditions that came down to them about the canonical [ἐνδιαθήκων] scriptures'.[6] The present introduction contains no such reference, but it was probably altered with later editions, and the reference may have been dropped or moved.

[5] Hanson, *Origen's Doctrine of Tradition*, 133, 137, 143, 182–3.

[6] English translation is derived from Grant, *Eusebius*, 126.

A promise of the sort mentioned does occur in *HE* 3.3.3. The interest in the canon may have been part of the earliest edition of the work. In any case the catalogue is to be dated some time between *c.* 303 and 325.

The motivation behind the catalogue is uncertain. During the Diocletianic persecution (303–11), Christians were forced to hand over their holy books to be burnt (Eusebius, *HE* 8.2.4–5; *Gesta apud Zenophilum*; Lactantius, *De Mort. Persec.* 11–13). A clarification as to which works were considered Scripture might have been helpful, but the persecution at Caesarea was very spasmodic, and was vigorously enforced during less than three out of the ten and a half years.[7] During the persecution's whole course, not one of the Palestinian bishops was put to death. Pamphilus' great library at Caesarea does not seem to have suffered either.[8] Moreover, the earliest edition of the *Church History* may have appeared with the catalogue before the persecution began. Thus the Diocletianic persecution was probably not a major factor in Eusebius' drawing up his catalogue.

The official recognition, and later sanction, of the Christian Church by Constantine (313–37) and his successors was also probably too late to be part of Eusebius' motivation, but it may have been a factor in the numerous other catalogues of the fourth century. Eusebius did not meet Constantine until they both attended the Council of Nicaea in 325, by which time the final edition of the *Church History* was probably completed.[9] In 331 Constantine commissioned Eusebius to prepare fifty copies of the sacred Scriptures for the church at Constantinople (Eusebius, *Life of Constantine* 4.36). In 340 Alexandrian scribes in Rome prepared copies of the Christian scriptures for the Emperor Constans (Athanasius, *Animadv.* 15). Such activities surely played a role in the development of the canon in the fourth century, but Eusebius' catalogue was earlier and thus not influenced by them.

Despite his renowned work as a biblical scholar, Eusebius was more concerned in his *Church History* with 'higher' criticism

[7] J. Stevenson, *Studies in Eusebius* (Cambridge, 1929), 50. [8] Ibid. 61.

[9] Eusebius probably did not meet Constantine when he saw him travelling through Palestine with Diocletian in 301 or 302; cf. T. D. Barnes, *Constantine and Eusebius* (London, 1981), 266.

than with 'lower'. There was more interest in the authorship and authenticity of the books of the New Testament than in a comparison of variant readings, such as Eusebius frequently made when quoting Jewish scriptures. What determined his attitude towards the 'canonicity' of a New Testament work was almost exclusively its use by the churches or by Christian writers such as Irenaeus, Clement of Alexandria, or Origen. It was his work as a historian more than anything else that may have led him to categorize his conclusions. The inconsistent usage of his predecessors may also account for his inability to place all of the works clearly. Therefore Eusebius' introduction of a New Testament catalogue in the *Church History* may have been motivated by nothing more than the simple wish to summarize his reading of history on this matter.

In many ways Eusebius' work on the Canon was a natural continuation of that of Origen. Origen also had a keen interest in determining the authenticity and authorship of the books to which the churches appealed. In his *Commentary on John* (13.17), Origen divided several works claiming to be inspired into three categories—genuine (*γνήσιος*), spurious (*νόθος*), and mixed (*μικτός*)—although elsewhere he did not often keep to this division and his vocabulary varied on other occasions.[10] Eusebius also employed a variety of terms to identify his categories. The lack of an established vocabulary and definite categories confirm that Eusebius' were innovative.

In discussing the works of the Apostles (*HE* 3.3.1–7), Eusebius appears to have employed different words or phrases to distinguish the works which were universally acknowledged from those which were disputed:

*acknowledged*: (§1) *ἀνωμολόγηται, ἀναμφιλέκτῳ*;
(§3) *τῶν ἐνδιαθήκων καὶ ὁμολογουμένων*;
(§4) *γνησίαν*;
(§5) *πρόδηλοι καὶ σαφεῖς*;
(§7) *ἀναντιρρήτων*.

*disputed*: (§1) *οὐκ ἐνδιάθηκον*;
(§2) *οὐδ' ὅλως ἐν καθολικοῖς*;
(§3) *τῶν ἀντιλεγομένων*;

[10] Hanson, *Origen*, 138; Campenhausen, 320–1.

(§6) ἀντιλέλεκται;
(§7) μὴ παρὰ πᾶσιν ὁμολογουμένων.

Eusebius refined his language somewhat within his New Testament catalogue (*HE* 3.26.1–7). The universally acknowledged works were simply called the ὁμολογούμενα and included the four gospels, Acts, the epistles of Paul, 1 John, 1 Peter, and possibly Revelation (§§1–2). Other works were called 'disputed' (ἀντιλεγόμενα), namely James, Jude, 2 Peter, 2 and 3 John (§3); and others still were spurious (νόθα), like the Acts of Paul, the Shepherd, the Revelation of Peter, Barnabas, the Didache, and possibly Revelation and the Gospel according to the Hebrews (§§4–5). However, the spurious works were really only a further division of the disputed category (ταῦτα δὲ πάντα τῶν ἀντιλεγομένων ἂν εἴη, §5); so that in actual fact Eusebius distinguished the 'true and genuine and commonly accepted writings from those that unlike them, although not canonical but disputed, are yet at the same time known to most ecclesiastical writers'(διακρίνοντες τάς τε κατὰ τὴν ἐκκλησιαστικὴν παράδοσιν ἀληθεῖς καὶ ἀπλάστους καὶ ἀνωμολογημένας γραφὰς καὶ τὰς ἄλλως παρὰ ταύτας οὐκ ἐνδιαθήκους μὲν ἀλλὰ καὶ ἀντιλεγομένας, ὅμως δὲ παρὰ πλείστοις τῶν ἐκκλησιατικῶν γιγνομένας, §6). Furthermore, all these writings were then distinguished from the 'fictions of heretics' (αἱρετικῶν ἀνδρῶν ἀναπλάσματα, §7), which 'are not to be placed even among the spurious (ἐν νόθοις), but are to be cast aside as utterly absurd (ἄτοπα) and impious (δυσσεβῆ)', such as the Gospels of Peter, Thomas, and Matthias, and the Acts of Andrew and John.

Eusebius, like Origen before him, could not simply distinguish between the canonical and non-canonical writings, but was forced to introduce a secondary class of works which were not strictly canonical nor completely rejected. This secondary class confirms that there was as yet no fixed Canon, and hence that there was no clear distinction between the accepted books and others. The employment of a secondary class suggests a transitional stage between undefined Scriptures and a finalized Canon.

However, even with a secondary category, which itself is subdivided, Eusebius is unsure where to place certain works, such as Revelation, and the Gospel to the Hebrews; perhaps too 1 Clement, cf. *HE* 3.16. This confusion suggests that the categories themselves are only just beginning to play a role in the formation of the Canon, and that its development is still in its creative stages.

The difference between Eusebius' activity and that of his predecessor Origen was comprehensiveness. Eusebius carried the procedure one step further than Origen. Rather than considering a few works one by one as Origen had done, he considered the categories one by one, fitting the individual books into each according to the usage of the Church Fathers. There is an important distinction between Origen's attempt to authenticate individual works and Eusebius' concern to categorize the complete collection of works. It is with this new concern that the concept of Canon, as opposed to a mere collection of accepted Scriptures, arises.

## 2. *The catalogue in the Codex Claromontanus*

Within the Codex Claromontanus ($D^p$) there is found a stichometrical catalogue of the books of the Old and New Testaments. The Codex itself, which contains the Pauline epistles and is generally assigned to the fifth or sixth century,[11] is a bilingual Greek and Latin manuscript, similar to the Codex Bezae (D), containing the Fourfold Gospel, Acts, and a small fragment of 3 John. The inclusion of a Latin text is sufficient to suggest that it was written in the West. Its exact place of origin is uncertain. The Latin belongs to the African type of the Old Latin version, suggesting Africa for its place of origin. However, the Latin text is almost identical with that used by Lucifer of Cagliari, and thus the manuscript may have been written in Sardinia.[12]

The catalogue within the Codex was probably not original to the manuscript. It is written in Latin only, and is found between the texts of Philemon and Hebrews. Zahn noted that the ink and handwriting of the catalogue differ from the

[11] Metzger, *The Text of the New Testament*, 51.

[12] Souter, 'The Original Home of Codex Claromontanus Paul', *JTS* 6 (1904–5), 240–3; H. J. Frede, *Altlateinische Paulus-Handschriften*, Vetus Latina (Freiburg i. B., 1964), 15–39; id., *Epistala ad Colossenses*, Vetus Latina (Freiburg i. B., 1969), 290–303.

preceding Pauline texts.[13] The catalogue, which does not contain Hebrews, differs in the order of Paul's letters from the Codex, which does contain Hebrews, and in the order of the gospels in Codex Bezae. Thus the origin of the catalogue is probably different from that of the biblical text.

The catalogue lists the books of the Old and New Testament. It numbers the gospels as four, and names them in the so-called Western order, Matthew, John, Mark, Luke. Then follow the Pauline epistles: Romans, 1 and 2 Corinthians, Galatians, Ephesians, 1 and 2 Timothy, Titus, Colossians, and Philemon. Philippians and 1 and 2 Thessalonians are absent from the list, probably by accidental omission. The confusing stichometry for 2 Corinthians and 1 Timothy may confirm a certain carelessness on the part of the scribe. Next are listed all the catholic epistles, followed by Barnabas, Revelation, Acts, the Shepherd, the Acts of Paul, and the Revelation of Peter. A horizontal line or bar, however, has been placed before four of the works, namely Barnabas, the Shepherd, the Acts of Paul, and the Revelation of Peter, perhaps suggesting some dispute about them.

Westcott and Jülicher suggested that following Tertullian's example (*De Pudicitia* 20), Hebrews was listed as 'Barnabas' in the catalogue.[14] Westcott pointed out that the stichometry for Barnabas in the catalogue, namely 850, differed significantly from Nicephorus' figure, 1,360 (or 1,206). C. F. Andry, however, compared the stichometry in the catalogue with the Pauline texts in the Codex and then compared the resulting numerical ratio with the texts of both Hebrews and Barnabas as found in Codex Sinaiticus. His results confirmed that the catalogue reference is clearly to Barnabas and not to Hebrews.[15]

Although the catalogue appears in Latin in a Western manuscript, it probably had an Eastern origin.[16] Harnack and Zahn both noted that the inclusion in the catalogue of all seven

[13] Zahn, *Geschichte*, ii. 157–72.

[14] Westcott, *Canon of the New Testament*, 557 n. 1; also id., *The Epistle to the Hebrews* (London, 1889), pp. xxviii f.; cf. Jülicher, 535–6.

[15] C. F. Andry, 'Barnabae Epist. ver. DCCCL', *JBL* 70 (1951), 233–8.

[16] Westcott and Jülicher argued that the catalogue was Western, but they both assumed that Barnabas in the catalogue was Hebrews and counted the Fragment as evidence of the use of the Revelation of Peter in the West.

catholic epistles would be remarkable in the West before the last third of the fourth century, *c.* 366–400,[17] and the appearance of the Acts of Paul, the Revelation of Peter, Barnabas, and the Shepherd at that time in the West would be most unlikely; it suggests an association with the school of Alexandria.[18] Yet it would be startling not to find Hebrews listed in a catalogue associated with Alexandria. Zahn suggested that a reference to Hebrews was accidentally dropped after Ephesians and before 1 Timothy along with the references to Philippians and 1 and 2 Thessalonians.[19] Hebrews would be most likely to follow 2 Thessalonians and precede 1 Timothy in a fourth-century Alexandrian list.[20] The similarity in the Greek titles of Ephesians, *ΠΡΟϹ Ε(ΦΕϹ)ΙΟΥϹ*, and Hebrews, *ΠΡΟϹ Ε(ΒΡΑ)ΙΟΥϹ*, would explain the omission.

The date of the catalogue is uncertain. This is the only catalogue, other than the Fragment, which has been dated prior to Eusebius. M. J. Lagrange dated it after Clement of Alexandria, declaring: 'Au temps d'Origène, et d'après ses écrits, on n'aurait pu obtenir une pareille liste.'[21] Yet this is a misleading statement since there are no 'such lists' with which to compare. The very formation of a list or catalogue suggests a time after Origen. Harnack noted a similarity between this catalogue and Eusebius', where the four works marked by the scribe are also grouped together by Eusebius, along with the Didache (*HE* 3.25.4).[22] However, this catalogue does not reflect the reservations expressed by Eusebius with regard to James, Jude, 2 Peter, 2 and 3 John, and Revelation (*HE* 3.25.3). The lack of these reservations may suggest a date after Eusebius (*c.* 303–25). The presence in the catalogue of Barnabas, the Shepherd, the Acts of Paul, and the Revelation of Peter, even with the scribal marks, may suggest a period before Athanasius (367), where Barnabas, the Acts of Paul, and the Revelation of Peter were omitted together, and the Shepherd (with the Didache) was clearly placed in a secondary class outside the canon (*Fest. Ep.* 39). Didymus the Blind (*c.* 313–98), however, seems still to have considered the Shepherd, Barnabas, the Didache (and 1

[17] Harnack, *Altchristliche Literatur*, ii. 2, 84–8; Zahn, *Geschichte*, iii. 168–72.

[18] Lagrange, *Introduction à l'étude du Nouveau Testament*, i (Paris, 1933), 92–3.

[19] Zahn, *Geschichte*, ii. 171–2.

[20] Hatch, 136–42.

[21] Lagrange, loc. cit.

[22] Harnack, loc. cit.

Clement) as Scripture.[23] Some time in the second quarter of the fourth century is perhaps the most probable date for the catalogue in the Codex Claromontanus, with a provenance in the East, perhaps in Alexandria.

## 3. *Cyril of Jerusalem* (c.*315–86*)

Cyril of Jerusalem's most famous work is the twenty-four *Catecheses*, which he delivered mostly in the Church of the Holy Sepulchre in Jerusalem in 348 (or 350).[24] A note preserved in several of the manuscripts recorded that they were taken down in shorthand, which suggests that the texts are transcripts made by one of his listeners, not by Cyril himself. In the fourth Catechetical Lecture, Cyril outlined the Christian faith, concluding with comments on the divine scriptures. Within these remarks, Cyril warned the catechumens 'to read none of the apocryphal (*ἀποκρύφων*, §33; cf. §35) writings' which were 'disputed' (*ἀμφιβαλλόμενα*, §33), but only those from the Church. He then listed the books of the Old and New Testaments. He counselled that there are only four Gospels, for the rest have 'false titles and are mischievous' (*ψευδεπίγραφα καὶ βλαβερά*, §36). Of the latter he explicitly mentioned only the Gospel of Thomas. Then Cyril listed 'the Acts of the Twelve Apostles', and 'the seven catholic epistles of James, Peter, John, and Jude.' Finally, he mentioned without delineation the 'last work of the disciples, the fourteen epistles of Paul'.

Cyril's catalogue is notable for the absence of Revelation.[25] This book appears to have been generally accepted in the East until the second half of the fourth century. Dionysius may have introduced an element of doubt about the work, perhaps reflected in Eusebius' confusion in placing it (*HE* 3.25.2, 4). Yet Cyril is the earliest witness to the rejection of Revelation in an Eastern list.

In Cyril's catalogue, there is no class of secondary works, of books that while not universally accepted are approvingly used

[23] B. D. Ehrman, 'The New Testament Canon of Didymus the Blind', *VC* 37 (1983), 1–21.

[24] A. Piedagnel, *Catéchèses mystagogiques* (SCh 126; Paris, 1966), 18–40; cf. W. Telfer, 'Cyril of Jerusalem and Nemesius of Emesa', *LCC* 4 (1955), 30–43.

[25] See discussion in Ch. 1.

by many (Eusebius, *HE* 3.25.3). Although much of Cyril's language is similar to Eusebius', like 'those acknowledged among all' (ὁμολογούμενα, §33), 'apocryphal writings' which are 'disputed' (ibid.), those of 'secondary rank' (§36), and those 'with false titles' (ψευδεπίγραφα, ibid.), only the 'acknowledged' works are received by Cyril. After the catalogue, there follows in Cyril the warning to 'let all the rest be put aside in a secondary (ἐν δευτέρῳ, §36) rank' and 'whatever books are not read in Churches, these read not even by thyself'. Cyril's several references to what ought to be read by his listeners in §§33–6 may suggest that some were reading other works. The intent of Cyril's catalogue was to limit reading to the universally accepted writings, the *homologoumena.*

### 4. *Athanasius* (c.*296–373)*

During the third century it became customary for the bishops of Alexandria to announce each year, by a letter to the suffragan sees usually issued shortly after Epiphany, the beginning of Lent and the correct date of Easter. These pastoral letters would also contain a discussion of current ecclesiastical affairs or problems. In 367 Athanasius issued his thirty-ninth festal letter as bishop of Alexandria, which was specifically concerned with the fact that apocryphal (ἀπόκρυφα) books were leading the simple 'astray by the similarity of their names with the true books' (*Ep. Fest.* 39.1).[26] Athanasius then set forth 'in order the writings that are in the list and handed down and believed divine', by cataloguing the books of the Old and New Testament. His New Testament list is the first which is identical with the traditional twenty-seven-book New Testament Canon.

There is a distinctive secondary class in Athanasius, for following his list he mentioned 'other books apart from these, not indeed in the list, but produced by our ancestors to be read by those who are just coming forward to receive oral instruction in the word of true religion [catechumens]' (§7). The approval of non-canonical catechetical reading contrasts sharply with Cyril's warnings, and may confirm a common practice to

[26] *PG* 26.1436.

which Cyril was responding. Athanasius included among the New Testament catechetical reading the Didache and the Shepherd. Mention of Barnabas, the Revelation of Peter, and the Acts of Paul, on the other hand, is noticeably absent.

### 5. *The Mommsen Catalogue*

In 1885 Theodor Mommsen discovered a stichometrical catalogue of Old and New Testament books in a tenth-century manuscript (no. 12266) in the Phillipps Collection at Cheltenham (thus sometimes called the Cheltenham list),[27] now Rome, Biblioteca Nazionale, Fondo Vittorio Emanuele 1235. Another copy of the catalogue has turned up in a ninth-century manuscript (no. 133) at Sankt-Gallen.

The contents of the codex in which the Cheltenham list was found can be dated by two references. At the end of the *Liber Generationis*, which was included in the codex, is a chronological calculation brought down to the consulship of the two brothers Eusebius and Hypatius in the year 359. There is an interval of five pages between this note and the biblical catalogue, but the text which connects them was not all taken from the same work. At the beginning of the table of contents of the *Liber Generationis* is another note which would bring the date down to the consulship of Valentinian and Valens in 365.[28] These two chronological notations of 359 and 365 are near enough to each other to suggest that the compiler or compilers of the manuscript were active about that period, or shortly thereafter.

The New Testament catalogue names in Latin the four gospels followed by the thirteen, unnamed epistles of Paul. Next is listed Acts, Revelation, three epistles of John and two of Peter. There is no mention of James, Jude, or Hebrews. Moreover, in the Cheltenham list, following the listing of the Johannine and Petrine epistolary there follows on each occasion the phrase 'una sola', suggesting a protest by the scribe at including among the catholic epistles anything more than 1 John and 1 Peter.

[27] First printed in Th. Mommsen, 'Zur lateinischen Stichometrie', *Hermes*, 21 (1886), 142–56.

[28] Sanday, 'The Cheltenham List', 217–61.

A number of the Old Testament books in the catalogue are found in a peculiar order; some of the patterns have a parallel in Augustine.[29] The order of the Gospels, however, Matthew, Mark, John, Luke, is paralleled only in the Old Syriac versions and in the so-called Commentary of Theophilus of Antioch, where in the preface the symbols of the gospels are described in that order. It is possible that these coincidences are accidental. The usual Western order of the Gospels was Matthew, John, Luke, Mark. After the catalogue is a short note on the stichometry:

> Quoniam indiculum versuum in urbe Roma non ad liquidum, sed et alibi avariciae causa non habent integrum, per singulos libros computatis syllabis posui numero XVI versum Virgilianum omnibus libris numerum adscribsi.

It may be assumed from this note that the author of the catalogue was not writing in Rome, but that he knew well the custom of trading there. The stichometry is that of the Vulgate (382+), and was perhaps the source for it, since none of the Vulgate manuscripts has any stichometries for Ezra–Nehemiah, of which both parts are wanting in the Mommsen Catalogue.[30] The absence of Hebrews supports a date before 393 for the catalogue, since the epistle was only tentatively accepted as Pauline in the Hippo Breviary. There is also little evidence for the acceptance of 3 John and 2 Peter in the West prior to the Councils in North Africa at the end of the fourth and beginning of the fifth century, namely Hippo (393), Carthage (397, 419). The presence of Revelation in the list may further support a Western provenance. The catalogue may be seen as possibly dated between 365 and the later Councils of North Africa, beginning in 393. Zahn favoured a later rather than an earlier dating (*c.* 379–90) because of the use of the word *canonicus* in the interpolation between the Old and New Testament lists.[31] In either case, this catalogue would represent the earliest known list of North Africa, and the Western church.

[29] Sanday, 'The Cheltenham List', 226–43.
[30] Ibid. 261–73.
[31] Zahn, *Geschichte*, ii. 153–6.

### 6. *Epiphanius of Salamis (*c.*315–403)*

There is no single catalogue of Old and New Testament books in Epiphanius. In his *Panarion*, completed about 377, he included both Old and New Testament lists, but they are not placed together. The *Panarion* is Epiphanius' most voluminous and valuable work, refuting a series of eighty heresies. After dealing with the philosophical heresies of the pagan schools and just before confronting the heresies of the Jewish sects, Epiphanius included a catalogue of the Old Testament (*Pan.* 8.6). In the midst of a long discussion about Aetius the Anomoean, Epiphanius listed a catalogue of New Testament works (*Pan.* 76.5). In another work, *De Mensuris et Ponderibus* (4.23), complete in 392, Epiphanius included two other Old Testament lists.

The four gospels are numbered but not named in the New Testament catalogue, just as the fourteen epistles of Paul are numbered but not named. The catholic epistles, however, were not numbered seven as they were by most writers in the East, such as Eusebius, Cyril, Athanasius, Gregory of Nazianzus, Jerome (in Bethlehem), and Amphilochius. Epiphanius' New Testament catalogue is most remarkable for its inclusion of the Wisdom of Solomon and Sirach as New Testament works. The catalogue is also unusual for its inclusion of Revelation (cf. *Pan.* 51.3, 35), which in the last half of the fourth century was absent from many Eastern sources (e.g. Cyril, the 'Apostolic Canons', Gregory of Nazianzus, Amphilochius, the Peshitta).

### 7. *The 'Apostolic Canons'*

In the eighth book of the so-called Apostolic Constitutions (8.47), there is a collection of 85 so-called 'Apostolic Canons', apparently compiled by the redactor of the Constitutions: they deal almost exclusively with the election, ordination, and duties of the clergy, and are entirely in the form of council canons. Their contents are similar to the decisions of Antioch (341) and Laodicea (*c.* 360), and are probably later in date. The absence of any hint of the Nestorian controversy would suggest a date earlier than the beginning of the fifth century. Canon 85 enumerates the books of the Old and New Testaments.

The eight books of the *Constitutions* represent the largest collection of legislative and liturgical material of the early church. The compiler drew from a number of earlier sources, such as the Didascalia, the Didache, and the *Apostolic Traditions* of Hippolytus. A Syrian provenance for the Constitutions is suggested by the celebration of Christmas on 25 December and the equation of the Sabbath with Sunday as an ecclesiastical holiday. The Antiochene liturgy and the Syrian calculation of the months confirm a Syrian origin. All eight books, including the 'Apostolic Canons', were probably compiled by the same author and originated *c.* 380 in Syria.[32]

The four gospels are named in the catalogue in the Eastern order of Matthew, Mark, Luke, John. The fourteen epistles of Paul are numbered but not named. The catholic epistles are in a remarkable order for the East: Peter, John, James, Jude. They are surprisingly followed by the two epistles of Clement and the Apostolic Constitutions themselves. Acts is listed last. Revelation is missing.

### 8. *Gregory of Nazianzus (329–89)*

Two catalogues of books of the Old and New Testament have been preserved among the works of Gregory of Nazianzus, both in verse. The second catalogue, though it bears the name of Gregory, is now commonly attributed to his contemporary Amphilochius of Iconium.[33] It was at the end of his life, during his retirement at Arianzum, that Gregory composed his poems. He retired around 384 and died a few years later in 389–90. His catalogue is dated some time in this last period of his life, 384–90.

There are about 400 extant poems attributed to Gregory, and in one of them, *In Suos versus*, he explained how he turned to poetry at the end of his life to prove that the new Christian culture was not inferior to the old pagan one, and how, since certain heresies spread their teachings in verse, it was necessary to refute them in verse. Thus almost forty of his poems are dogmatic in nature on a variety of themes, including the short poem entitled *De Veris Scripturae Libris*, which consists of a catalogue of accepted scriptures (*Carm.* 12.30–9).

[32] M. Metzger, *Les Constitutions apostoliques* (SCh 320; Paris, 1985), 57–60; cf. F. X. Funk, *Didascalia et Constitutiones Apostolorum*, i (Paderborn, 1906), 564–93.

[33] See below, Ch. 5.

The gospels are listed first among the New Testament works and named in the Eastern order: Matthew, Mark, Luke, John. Remarkably, they are not numbered as they are in all the other fourth-century catalogues. This may be because of the demands of poetry. Gregory then listed the 'Catholic Acts of the wise Apostles' and the fourteen epistles of Paul, without naming them. Then he mentioned the seven catholic epistles in the order James, Peter, John, Jude. Gregory concluded with the words: 'In these you have all the inspired books; if there be any book besides these, it is not among the genuine [scriptures].'

Though he admitted the canonicity of the seven catholic epistles, Gregory does not appear to have ever quoted them by name elsewhere in his extant writings. There are, however, two possible allusions to James, both unattributed (*Orat.* 26.5, 40.45). Although he omitted Revelation from his catalogue, Gregory once made an obvious allusion to it (*Orat.* 29) and in another place he referred to it expressly with marked respect (*Orat.* 40.45).

## 9. *The African canons*

There were three African synods in the late fourth and early fifth centuries at which catalogues of the Old and New Testaments were approved. According to the *Codex Canonum Ecclesiae Africanae*, the first of these synods was held in the Secretarium of the Basilica at Hippo on 8 October 393.[34] The complete acts of this synod have been lost. An abridgement of the canons of Hippo, however, was read out and renewed at a synod in Carthage held on 28 August 397, and it is from this Hippo Breviary that the acts of Hippo are known. A copy of the Hippo Breviary is found in the canons of Carthage (397) and in the works of Leo. On 25 May 419 Aurelius presided over another synod at Carthage at which he decided that a copy of the acts of Nicaea, together with the canons of the former African councils, should be added to the acts of that synod. Thus all the canons of the previous Carthaginian synods, along with those from Milevis and Hippo, were read, approved, and received a new sanction from this synod of 419. This collection became

[34] C. J. Hefele, *A History of the Councils of the Church*, trans. by H. N. Oxenham, ii (Edinburgh, 1876), 394–402.

known as the *Codex Canonum Ecclesiae Africanae.* Unfortunately Dionysius Exiguus (*c.* 500–50), who incorporated these African canons in his collection, inserted only the headings of the acts of Hippo, and not the canons themselves.

Augustine appears to have been a principal figure behind the synod at Hippo in 393 and may have been an important influence on the contents of the catalogue adopted there. In 392 Augustine propounded the importance of synods in a letter to Aurelius, archbishop of Carthage since 391 (*Ep.* 22.1.4). The choice of location of this synod the next year confirms that Augustine played a part in its organization, especially since he was allowed to deliver an address to the assembly while still only a priest (Possidius, *Life of Augustine*, 50.7). The catalogue accepted does not substantially differ from Augustine's own and is remarkable for its acceptance of Hebrews, 2 Peter, and 3 John (cf. the Mommsen Catalogue).

The New Testament list of Hippo (393) and Carthage (397) was straightforward and reads: 'the four gospels, the Acts of the Apostles, thirteen epistles of Paul, one epistle of Paul to the Hebrews, two epistles of Peter, three epistles of John, the epistle of James, the epistle of Jude, the Revelation of John.' The canon was followed by the statement: 'Concerning the confirmation of this canon, the transmarine Church shall be consulted.' The catalogue concluded with a note that on the anniversaries of the martyrs, their acts would also be read, thus allowing the public reading of non-canonical works. The separation of Hebrews from the other Pauline letters suggests that the acceptance of the book was tentative. If so, that tentativeness had been overcome by the time of the Council of Carthage (419) whose catalogue numbered the Pauline epistles as fourteen, without any separate mention of Hebrews.[35] This catalogue also omitted any mention of the reading of the acts of the martyrs.

## 10. *Jerome (c.342–420)*

Jerome, in a letter written from Bethlehem in 394, urged his friend Paulinus of Nola to make a diligent study of the Scriptures and to devote himself to God (*Ep.* 53). Within the context

[35] C. J. Hefele, *A History of the Councils of the Church*, 407–18.

of this letter, Jerome enumerated the books of both the Old and New Testaments.[36] There is a short description of each book accompanying the list of the Old Testament (53.8), but the letter went on for such length that Jerome, by his own admission, cut short the description of the books of the New Testament (53.9).

He named Matthew, Mark, Luke, and John as 'the Lord's four-in-hand' (*quadriga Domini*). Next he related that Paul wrote to seven churches, which went unnamed, although he added, 'for the eighth epistle—that to the Hebrews—is not generally counted in with the others'. He wrote that Paul 'instructs Timothy and Titus; he intercedes with Philemon for his runaway slave'. Acts was then mentioned, followed by 'The apostles James, Peter, John, and Jude, [who] have published seven epistles.' Lastly Revelation was added, which is remarkable for a catalogue originating from the East at the end of the fourth century.

### 11. *Augustine (354–430)*

Augustine's *De Doctrina Christiana* was written for the most part (1–3.25, 36) in 396–7, but not completed until 426–7. Books 1 and 2 commented upon the training necessary for a successful study of Scripture. In book 2, ch. 8, Augustine listed the books of the Old and New Testaments, 'those of them, at least, that are called canonical [*canonicae*]' (2.12). He wrote:

> That of the New Testament, again, is contained within the following: four books of the Gospel, according to Matthew, according to Mark, according to Luke, according to John; fourteen epistles of the Apostle Paul, one to the Romans, two to the Corinthians, one to the Galatians, to the Ephesians, to the Philippians, two to the Thessalonians, one to the Colossians, two to Timothy, one to Titus, to Philemon, to the Hebrews; two of Peter; three of John; one of Jude; and one of James; one of the book of the Acts of the Apostles; and one of the Revelation of John. (*De Doct. Christ.* 2.13.)

Augustine's enumeration of the Old and New Testament works is almost identical with that of the Synod of Hippo (393)

[36] Jerome has another Old Testament catalogue paralleling the Jewish canon in the *Prologus Galeatus* (*c.* 391), where he named as *apocrypha*: the Wisdom of Solomon, Sirach, Judith, Tobias, the Shepherd, and the books of the Maccabees.

as preserved in the canons of the Synod of Carthage (397). Augustine was present at those councils and was probably influential in the decisions. Even the tentativeness in accepting Hebrews as Pauline, reflected in the contrasting statements of Hippos and Carthage, is apparent in the works of Augustine. Although his catalogue appears to have unhesitatingly accepted Hebrews as Pauline, Augustine himself seems to have wavered on the issue.[37]

### 12. *Amphilochius (*c.*340–*c.*396)*

Cosmas Indicopleustes (*c.* 547) referred to Amphilochius as the author of the *Iambi ad Seleucum* (*Top. Christ.* 7.265), although the work has come down among those of his cousin Gregory of Nazianzus. It seems probable that the work is Amphilochius', although it is his only known composition in verse.[38] Amphilochius, who became bishop of Iconium in 373, admonished Seleucus through the poem in the devout life and in the study of Scripture, adding a complete list of the Old and New Testaments in vv. 251–319.

K. Bone argued that the date of the *Iambi ad Seleucum* could not be before 396, although Amphilochius is last mentioned in 394, when he attended the Synod of Constantinople.[39] The year of Amphilochius' death is unknown, and if this catalogue was written after 396, then it was probably not much later and shortly before his death.

The catalogue (vv. 289–31) is similar to that of Gregory of Nazianzus, but more detailed. The New Testament catalogue begins with the four Gospels in the order Matthew, Mark, Luke, John. Then Amphilochius listed Acts and the epistles of Paul to the 'twice seven churches', after which he added (vv. 308–13, 316–19):

But some maintain that the Epistle to the Hebrews is spurious [νόθον], not speaking well; for the grace (it shews) is genuine. To

[37] O. Rottenmanner, 'S. Augustin sur l'auteur de l'épître aux Hébreux', *RBén* 18 (1901), 257–61.

[38] J. Quasten, *Patrology*, 3 vols. (Westminster, Md., 1953), iii. 298; B. Altaner, *Patrology*, tr. H. C. Graef (London, 1960), 357–8.

[39] K. G. Bone, *Περὶ τῆς μητρὸς τῆς ἁγίας Ὀλυμπιάδος*, *Studi bizantini e neoellenici*, 8/2 (1953), 3–10.

proceed: what remains? Of the Catholic epistles some maintain that we ought to receive seven, and others three only, one of James, and one of Peter, and one of John . . . The Apocalypse of John again some reckon among (the Scriptures); but still the majority say that it is spurious [νόθον]. This will be the most truthful Canon of the inspired Scriptures.[40]

## 13. *Rufinus (c.345–410)*

Tyrannius Rufinus returned to Rome in 397 and to his native Aquileia in 399, after spending about seventeen years (371/2–397/8) in the East. It was only after his return to the West that he embarked upon writing and translating, including his translation of, and additions to, Eusebius' *Church History* in 402–3. Rufinus' most important original work, *Commentary on the Apostles' Creed*, was written in 400.

In his translation of Eusebius' *Church History*, Rufinus revealed his concerns about the Canon by the alterations he made to Eusebius' statements. Rufinus weakened many remarks by Eusebius that tended to cast doubt on the canonicity of any New Testament work: James and Jude (*HE* 2.23.25), 2 Peter (*HE* 3.3.1–4; 6.25.7–14), Revelation (*HE* 3.25; 7.25.8–9), Hebrews (*HE* 3.3.5; 6.20.3).[41]

Rufinus' exposition on the Apostles' Creed was made at the request of an otherwise unknown Bishop Laurentius (*Comm. in Symb. Apost.* 1). Rufinus introduced his catalogue of the Old and New Testaments among reflections upon the Holy Spirit and the Holy Church:

And therefore it seems proper in this place to enumerate, as we have learnt from the tradition of the Fathers, the books of the New and of the Old Testament, which, according to the tradition of our forefathers, are believed to have been inspired by the Holy Ghost, and have been handed down to the Churches of Christ. (*Comm. in Symb. Apost.* 36.)

The New Testament list is straightforward and without elaboration:

[40] Translation quoted from Westcott, *Canon of the New Testament*, 441–2.

[41] J. E. L. Oulton, 'Rufinus's Translation of the Church History of Eusebius', *JTS* 30 (1928–9), 130–74, at 150–3, 156–9.

Of the New there are four Gospels, those of Matthew, Mark, Luke, John; the Acts of the Apostles, composed by Luke; fourteen epistles by the Apostle Paul; two by the Apostle Peter; one by James, brother of the Lord and Apostle; one by Jude; three by John; and the Apocalypse of John. (§37.)[42]

Rufinus' stress on the fact that Paul, Peter, and James were all Apostles may be an indication that for Rufinus canonicity depended on apostolic authorship.[43]

The commentary was partly based upon the catechetical lectures of Cyril of Jerusalem, so that Rufinus was probably familiar with Cyril's catalogue (*Catech.* 4.33). Rufinus may have known Athanasius' catalogue (*Ep. Fest.* 39) as well, since he not only studied in Alexandria (*c.*372) but was also baptized and received his early training in a monastery which Athanasius had founded in Aquileia during one of his exiles.[44]

In addition to the 'canonical' books Rufinus introduced a secondary class of works which were not strictly canonical, but which he designated as 'ecclesiastical' (*ecclesiastici*). The distinctive characteristic of these books was that they could be read freely in the churches, but could not be invoked as authoritative for doctrine (*Comm. in Symb. Apost.* 38). This secondary class included in the New Testament: the Shepherd, the Two Ways, and the Preaching of Peter. This position is similar to Jerome's, who declared in one passage that Tobias, Judith, and the books of the Maccabees 'are not among the canonical Scriptures', but that 'the Church reads them for the edification of the people and not for the support of ecclesiastical doctrine' (preface to the books of Solomon). Rufinus also mentioned a third category of works, the 'apocryphal' (*apocryphas*), which could not be read out in the churches (38).

## 14. *Pope Innocent I (d. 417)*

A gathering of the letters of Pope Innocent I (402–17) is reflected in an epistle (*Ep.* 4.5) of Leo the Great (443) and formed the principal part of the first collection of papal decretals. Of the thirty-six surviving letters of Innocent, one to

[42] Trans. J. N. D. Kelly, *Rufinus: A Commentary on the Apostles' Creed* (Ancient Christian Writers, 20; London, 1955), 73.

[43] Ibid. 23.

[44] Ibid. 20–6.

Bishop Exsuperius of Toulouse (405) contains a list of the books of the Old and New Testaments (*Ep.* 6). C. H. Turner provided a critical text for the letter based upon the evidence of thirteen manuscripts ranging in date from the end of the sixth century to the end of the ninth.[45] The number of manuscripts suggests that the list of canonical books must have been very widely known. If the disputed Damasine Decree is not authentic, then Pope Innocent's letter is the earliest extant copy of a New Testament catalogue from the city of Rome.

The catalogue is introduced with the words: 'Qui uero libri recipiantur in canone breuis adnexus ostendit. haec sunt quae desiderata moneri uoce uoluisti' (*Ad Exsup. Tol.*, ll. 1–2). There follows an unadorned list of the Old Testament books, immediately followed by the New Testament catalogue: 'euangeliorum IIII; apostoli Pauli epistulae XIII(I); epistulae Iohannis III; epistulae Petri II; (epistulae Iudae I); epistula Iacobi I; actus apostolorum; apocalypsis Iohannis' (ll. 24–31). The catalogue concludes with the warning: 'cetera autem quae uel sub nomine Mathiae siue Iacobi minoris; uel sub nomine Petri et Iohannis, quae a quodam Leucio scripta sunt; (uel sub nomine Andreae, quae a Xenocaride et Leonida philosophis); uel sub nomine Thomae; et si qua sunt alia; non solum repudianda uerum etiam noueris esse damnanda.'

There are several notable differences among the manuscripts. The absence of Jude in the Chieti manuscript is presumably a mere omission by homoeoarcton. Three manuscripts, including the best of all (Vaticanus Reginensis 1997), read for the epistles of Paul 'XIII' instead of 'XIIII'. This divergence may be explained by an accidental confusion between these two numbers, but it must also be remembered that the church at Rome was very slow in accepting Hebrews as Pauline. Pope Innocent did not in fact cite Hebrews elsewhere in his extant decretals. Eight manuscripts, again including the *codex optimus*, omit the mention of 'writings published under the name of Andrew, and in fact, composed by the philosophers Xenocharides and Leonidas'. M. R. James suggested that the work in question was the 'Leucian' Acts of Andrew and that the philosophers named were characters in whose name

[45] See Ch. 3 n. 102.

the book was written.[46] The omission is probably accidental since it is difficult to account for its insertion.

### 15. *A Syrian catalogue*

Among the Syriac manuscripts from the Convent of St Catherine on Mount Sinai published by A. S. Lewis,[47] there is a Syrian stichometrical catalogue of the books of the Old and New Testaments. It derives from a ninth-century manuscript attributed to Irenaeus.[48] According to J. Rendel Harris, the catalogue appears Edessan in origin and dependent upon the Peshitta, and must therefore be dated later, *c.* 400.[49]

The Gospels are numbered four in the Catalogue and named in the Eastern order, Matthew, Mark, Luke, John. Acts follows, after which are listed without enumeration the Pauline epistles, including Hebrews. The most notable feature of the catalogue is the absence in the New Testament list of the catholic epistles and Revelation. The latter is often absent from Eastern lists of the second half of the fourth century; the former are also absent in the Doctrine of Addai.[50] Likewise neither in Aphraates nor in the genuine works of Ephraem, both fourth-century Syriac authors, is there any reference to any catholic epistle.[51]

## DISPUTED CATALOGUES

Before considering the relationship between the Muratorian Fragment and these fifteen undisputed catalogues, it is important to review four catalogues traditionally assigned to this period, namely Laodicene Canon 60, the Damasine Decree, the Roman Canon (*c.* 400), and the *Synopsis Veteris et Novi Testamenti* ascribed to John Chrysostom. The authenticity of each of these catalogues has been questioned.

[46] Quoted in Turner, 'Latin Lists, 3', 79–80.

[47] See Ch. 3 n. 110.

[48] Zahn, *Grundriß der Geschichte des neutestamentlichen Kanons* (hereafter *Grundriß*) (Leipzig, 1904), 86.

[49] Quoted in Lewis, 15–16.

[50] See Ch. 3 n. 110.

[51] Souter, *Text and Canon*, 209 n.

### 1. *Laodicene Canon 60*

In many old collections of the councils, which have their origins in the sixth century and later, there are found the acts of the Synod of Laodicea, placed after those of Antioch of 341, but before those of the second Ecumenical Council of 381. Canon 59 of the Synod in most manuscripts reads: 'No psalms composed by private individuals or uncanonical [ἀκανόνιστα] books may be read in the church, but only the canonical [κανονικά] books of the Old and New Testaments.' The last canon, usually numbered 60 but sometimes added to 59, names the books of the Christian Bible.

The gospels are listed in the Eastern order; Matthew, Mark, Luke, John. Acts follows, then the seven catholic epistles are listed, namely James; 1 and 2 Peter; 1, 2, and 3 John; Jude. These are followed by the fourteen epistles of Paul, which are named, with Hebrews after the Thessalonian correspondence and before the epistles to Timothy. Revelation is not listed. The list as given closely resembles that of the Apostolic Canons 85 (84), and Cyril of Jerusalem (*Catech.* 4.33).

There are questions about the authenticity of the sixtieth canon. The oldest copy of the canons of Laodicea is found in a Syrian translation of an early Greek collection of canons (*c.* 501). Canon 60 is not present there. It is also not present in the oldest Latin translation extant, that of Dionysius Exiguus (*c.* 500–50). It might be argued that he omitted it because in Rome, where he composed his work, the catalogue of Pope Innocent took precedence.[52] Canon 60 is also missing in the collection of John Scholasticus (d. 577) and Martin of Braga (*c.* 520–80) and the African Cresconius (*c.* 690).[53] Since the last indisputable canon of Laodicea might lead one to imagine a list of 'canonical' books, it would be easy to understand the motivation of some later compiler of canons to include a catalogue to 'complete' Canon 59. The absence of Canon 60 from the earliest sources of the council suggests that the Catalogue was not original to the Synod of Laodicea.

[52] Hefele, ii. 295–8.

[53] Zahn, *Geschichte*, ii. 195.

## 2. *The Damasine Decree*

A catalogue of the Old and New Testaments is found in a decree attributed in several manuscript to Pope Damasus (366–84). In other and more numerous manuscripts the same decree occurs in an enlarged form assigned within the documents in some cases to Pope Gelasius (492–6), in others to Pope Hormisdas (514–23), and in a few cases the documents are simply anonymous. The copies of the decree attributed to Damasus are contained in four manuscripts, two dated in the eighth century and two in the ninth.[54] Each decree is headed 'Incipit concilium urbis Romae sub Damaso Papa de explanatione Fidei'. Each consists of three short chapters, the second of which treated 'de scripturis divinis agendis est quid universalis catholica recipiat ecclesia et quid vitare debeat'. There follows a catalogue of Old and New Testament books. The later editions appended a list of apocryphal books and retitled the second chapter 'De libris recipiendis et non recipiendis'.

The Damasine documents are not dated nor is the year or number of the council given. Conjecture has assigned the document to a known Roman council in 382.[55] Very little is really known about this synod. No official acts have been preserved, and the only surviving conciliar pronouncement may be this Damasine Decree, for which there is no known reference until the end of the eighth or the beginning of the ninth century. The three brief contemporary references to the synod do not refer to any decree. Jerome mentioned the synod twice, but only in passing. In his letter to Eustochium he wrote:

> It so happened that at that time the bishops of the East and West had been summoned to Rome by letter from the emperors [Theodosius and Valentinian] to deal with certain dissensions between the churches, and in this way she [Paula] saw two most admirable men and Christian prelates, Paulinus bishop of Antioch and Epiphanius bishop of Salamis, or, as it is now called, Constantia, in Cyprus. (*Ep.* 108.6.)

In a letter to Ageruchia (*Ep.* 123.10), Jerome related a story about a married couple he saw 'a great many years ago while I

[54] Turner, 'Latin Lists of the Canonical Books: 1. The Roman Council under Damasus, AD. 382', *JTS* 1 (1899–1900), 554–60, at 555.

[55] Ibid. 554–5.

was helping Damasus bishop of Rome with his ecclesiastical correspondence, and writing his answers to the questions referred to him by the councils of the east and west.' The only other contemporary reference to the synod is from Theodoret, when he reported that a synodal letter which was sent from the Council of Constantinople was replied to by the Fathers who met at Rome in the following year.[56] Apart from these three references there is no other information about the Council of Rome in 382.

It seems highly improbable that, if Jerome, who was probably present at the council and was certainly at Rome, had ever heard of such a pronouncement about canonical books, he should nowhere have mentioned it, or that it should not have qualified his own statements on the Canon. For instance, why should Jerome write in his preface to the books of Solomon: 'Sicut ergo Iudith, et Tobi, et Macchabeorum libros legit quidem Ecclesia, sed inter canonicas scripturas non recipit', when the Damasine Decree contained all these books in its Old Testament list? Again, in the preface to the books of Kings (the *Prologus Galeatus*) Jerome writes: 'Igitur Sapientia, quae vulgo Salomonis inscribitur, et Iesu filii Sirach liber et Iudith et Tobias et Pastor non sunt in canone', yet all these works except the Shepherd are accepted as canonical in the Damasine Decree. If the Damasine Decree is authentic, then Jerome must have changed his views and must have done so almost immediately after an official pronouncement from a synod which he probably attended and by a pope whom he greatly regarded and by whom he was patronized.[57] Yet there is no mention or evidence of a change of position in the works of Jerome. The authenticity of at least the catalogue in the Damasine Decree is thus called into question.

Nicholas I (858–67), when writing about the Canon to the church of Gaul, wrote:

Sed reponsuri sunt isti qui non ad obediendum potius quam ad resistendum sunt parati aientes, Quod inter Canones inveniatur Capitulum S. Papae Innocentii; cuius autoritate doceatur a nobis

[56] Quoted in H. H. Howorth, 'The Decretal of Damasus' (hereafter 'Damasus'), *JTS* 14 (1912–13), 321–37, at 326.

[57] Id., 'The Influence of St. Jerome on the Canon of the Western Church', *JTS* 10 (1908–9), 481–96; 11 (1909–10), 321–47; 13 (1911–12), 1–19.

utrumque Testamentum esse recipiendum, quanquam in ipsis paternis Canonibus nullum eorum ex toto contineatur insertum.[58]

It is noteworthy that Pope Nicholas referred to the Decree of Innocent I issued in 405 and completely ignored the supposed earlier and thus more important decree of Damasus. It is also noteworthy that the later writers of the ninth century, who refer to the decree under the name of Gelasius or Hormisdas, should have entirely omitted any reference to the Damasine decree upon which it supposedly depended.

If the Damasine Decree were genuine, then it would represent the earliest known official catalogue of canonical books in the Western church. Yet the work is not mentioned in any independent document before the year 840, nor was it named by any of the ecclesiastical historians such as Gennadius, Ildefonsus, Isidore of Seville, Sigebert of Gembloux, or Honorius of Autun. The earliest collection of Latin conciliar canons and decretals, namely that of Dionysius Exiguus, began with those of Siricius, the successor of Damasus. The fact that Dionysius began at that particular date with the decretals of an obscure pope implies that Siricius was the first pope who issued decretals. If so, this fact could explain the false attribution to Damasus, in that there would be no means later of verifying it and no appeal to an earlier genuine work on decretals and canons. There are also difficulties in identifying the Decretum Gelasianum with a suppositious Roman synod in 494.[59] Dionysius Exiguus, for instance, did not mention the Decree among those of Gelasius in his collection. Consequently it appears that both the decrees were written after the time of Gelasius, and only later attributed to these early bishops of Rome.

Those who sustained the authenticity of the Decree argued that the enlarged Decretals were really later editions of a primitive Damasine text. The treatment of the second and third epistles of John as by John 'the presbyter' was suggested by Turner as evidence of Jerome's influence.[60] Similarly the description of Jeremiah in the Decree with the phrase 'cum Cinoth id est Lamentationibus suis' may be related to Jerome,

[58] Howorth, 'Damasus', 327–8. [59] Ibid. 329–35.
[60] Turner, 'Roman Council', 554.

who used the same phrase word for word in the *Prologus Galeatus.* The third part of the decree, according to Turner, is similar to the preface of the 'Isidorian' translation of the Nicene canons.[61] Howorth, however, disputed that there was any dependence between the third part of the decree and the 'Isidorian' preface.[62] The phrases from Jerome could have been borrowed at any later time. Therefore a serious doubt about the authenticity of the Damasine Decree remains.

### 3. *A Roman canon (*c.400)

Sundberg listed among his fourth-century catalogues a Roman canon dated about 400, which he derived from Souter.[63] The Roman catalogue, first published in 1901 by C. H. Turner,[64] is a stichometrical list from Munich, Clm 6243 (*olim* Freising 43). A copy of the Damasine Decree is also found in the MS (fo. $1^{v}$). The Roman Catalogue, which occupies fos. $189^{v}$–$191^{v}$, was attributed to Jerome, just as the catalogue of the Damasine Decree was attributed to Pope Damasus.

Turner dated the Roman catalogue around 400 because he noted nothing in the manuscript to indicate that its original material was later than the first half of the fifth century.[65] The term *theotokos* in l. 45 of an anti-Arian creed found in the manuscript militated against a date earlier than *c.*400. Other documents there, however, were thought by Turner to be fourth-century, namely the law of Constantine against Arius, the Damasine Decree, and a very primitive version of some of the canons of Nicaea and Sardica.

The dating of the Roman catalogue was also dependent upon similarities with other documents. In particular, Turner compared the Roman catalogue with one in a Vatican manuscript (Reginensis 199, fo. $84^{r}$: saec. xii) attributed to Pope Gelasius (492–6). The principal point of contact between the Roman catalogue and the Decretum Gelasianum was their possession of a common stichometry which, according to

61 Ibid. 555.

62 Howorth, 'Damasus', 322–5.

63 Souter, *Text and Canon*, 206–8.

64 Turner, 'Latin Lists of the Canonical Books: 2. An Unpublished Stichometrical List from the Freisingen MS of Canons', *JTS* 2 (1900–1), 236–53.

65 Ibid. 236–7, 252–3.

Turner, was quite independent of anything else known in Latin. The epithet 'canonical' for the catholic Epistles in the Roman catalogue appeared in both the Damasine Decree and the Decretum Gelasianum, and the title 'Zealot' applied to Jude was again common with the Damasine list. The phrase 'Actus apostolorum quos descripsit Lucas' recurs in Rufinus. Turner concluded that the author of the Roman Catalogue depended for the stichometry of his biblical list on an earlier Greek original possibly associated with the library of Pamphilus at Caesarea, *c.* 300–50.[66]

Turner's dating depended entirely upon the authenticity of the Damasine Decree and the Decretum Gelasianum. E. von Dobschütz, however, carefully analysed both the Freising and Vatican manuscripts presented by Turner, and clearly included them in the Gelasian family, thus confirming a date for them of no earlier than the sixth century.[67] If the Damasine Decree and Decretum Gelasianum are seen as inauthentic, then this Roman catalogue cannot reliably be dated around 400, but is apparently related to much later documents.

### 4. *John Chrysostom (*c.*347–407)*

Sundberg also included a catalogue found in Westcott from a work entitled *Synopsis Veteris et Novi Testamenti*,[68] which Montfaucon published as among the works of John Chrysostom.[69] The *Synopsis Veteris et Novi Testamenti* is an introduction to Scripture, in which the content of each biblical book is briefly described, and its importance and place in the history of revelation made clear. Thus the work is very similar to the *Synopsis Scripturae Sacrae* which was falsely attributed to Athanasius and is to be dated much later, perhaps in the sixth century.[70] The texts of the *Synopsis Veteris et Novi Testamenti* are incomplete, with quite a number of chapters lost, especially on the books of the New Testament. Moreover, the oldest manuscripts go back only to the eleventh century.

[66] Turner, 'Unpublished Stichometrical List', 246–7, 252–3.
[67] E. von Dobschütz, *Das Decretum Gelasianum* (Leipzig, 1912), 147, 191, cf. 338–57.
[68] Westcott, *Canon of the New Testament*, 535–6.
[69] Repr. *PG* 56. 313–86.
[70] Zahn, *Geschichte*, iii. 302–18.

It is from the introduction to the *Synopsis Veteris et Novi Testamenti* that Westcott derived his catalogue. The New Testament works were listed there in a single paragraph and included in this order: the fourteen epistles of Paul; four Gospels, two by the disciples of Christ, John, and Matthew, and two by Luke and Mark, disciples of Peter and Paul; Acts; and three unspecified catholic epistles, presumably 1 John, 1 Peter, and James. According to Westcott this catalogue of New Testament works agreed exactly with Chrysostom's usage, except for one very doubtful quotation from 2 Peter (*Hom. in Joan.* 34).[71] While the *Synopsis Veteris et Novi Testamenti* does show some agreement with the distinctive exegetical characteristics of Chrysostom, it contrasts strongly with his other works with regards to language and style.[72] Thus it is now generally believed to be spurious.[73]

The authenticity of all four of these catalogues is seriously disputed. None of them will be considered in the conclusions of this chapter, since all probably derive from a period significantly removed from the fourth century.

## COLLECTIONS OF THE FOURTH CENTURY

Before any conclusions are drawn, one further piece of evidence needs to be cited. Just as there are no catalogues of the Christian canon until the fourth century, so there are no extant manuscripts which are thought to have contained a complete Christian Bible before the fourth and early fifth century. Though the number of surviving manuscripts is small, the appearance of codices and versions of the entire Christian Bible may also be reflective of a conceptual transition from Scriptures to Canon in the fourth century. Consequently the contents and order of these collections are relevant to the questions of the formation of the catalogues.

[71] Westcott, *Canon of the New Testament*, 437–8.

[72] C. Baur, *John Chrysostom and His Time*, trans. by M. Gonzaga, i (London, 1959), 288.

[73] O. Bardenhewer, *Patrology*, tr. T. S. Shahan (Freiburg i. B., 1908), 337; Quasten, iii. 472. Altaner, 381.

TABLE 4.2. *Collections of the fourth and early fifth centuries*

| Vaticanus | Sinaiticus | Peshitta | Alexandrinus |
|---|---|---|---|
| Matthew | Matthew | Matthew | Matthew |
| Mark | Mark | Mark | Mark |
| Luke | Luke | Luke | Luke |
| John | John | John | John |
| Acts | Romans | Acts | Acts |
| James | 1 Corinthians | James | James |
| 1 Peter | 2 Corinthians | 1 Peter | 1 Peter |
| 2 Peter | Galatians | 1 John | 2 Peter |
| 1 John | Ephesians | Romans | 1 John |
| 2 John | Philippians | 1 Corinthians | 2 John |
| 3 John | Colossians | 2 Corinthians | 3 John |
| Jude | 1 Thessalonians | Galatians | Jude |
| Romans | 2 Thessalonians | Ephesians | Romans |
| 1 Corinthians | Hebrews | Philippians | 1 Corinthians |
| 2 Corinthians | 1 Timothy | Colossians | 2 Corinthians |
| Galatians | 2 Timothy | 1 Thessalonians | Galatians |
| Ephesians | Titus | 2 Thessalonians | Ephesians |
| Philippians | Philemon | 1 Timothy | Philippians |
| Colossians | Acts | 2 Timothy | Colossians |
| 1 Thessalonians | James | Titus | 1 Thessalonians |
| 2 Thessalonians | 1 Peter | Philemon | 2 Thessalonians |
| Hebrews | 2 Peter | Hebrews | Hebrews |
| (1 Timothy) | 1 John | | 1 Timothy |
| (2 Timothy) | 2 John | | 2 Timothy |
| (Titus) | 3 John | | Titus |
| (Revelation) | Jude | | Philemon |
| | Revelation | | Revelation |
| | Barnabas | | 1 Clement |
| | Hermas . . . | | 2 Clement |
| | | | Psalms of Solomon |

## 1. *Codex Vaticanus*

Codex Vaticanus contains the Old and New Testaments in Greek.[74] The beginning of the Codex is lost as far as Gen. 46:28; in the middle Pss. 106–38 have fallen out; and the ending is mutilated after Heb. 9:14. 1 and 2 Timothy, Titus,

[74] See Ch. 3 n. 16.

Philemon, and Revelation are believed to have been lost. Whether other works were also included is uncertain.

The Pauline epistles in Vaticanus have 'chapter' numbers which do not start again with each work but continue in one series from Romans onwards. In the manuscript Hebrews follows 2 Thessalonians, but the sequence of the chapter numbers reveals that previously Hebrews had followed Galatians. The 'chapter' divisions in the other epistles do not include 2 Peter, suggesting an origin for the divisions predating the general acceptance of this work as canonical.

Palaeographic and textual evidence suggest Alexandria as the likely provenance of Codex Vaticanus,[75] though the manuscript appears to have been corrected in the seventh century in Caesarea.[76] Certain resemblances in style with the Codex Sinaiticus suggest that both works may have come from the same scriptorium, but the similarities are not sufficient for C. Tischendorf's assertion that the same scribe copied both.[77] The writing in Vaticanus is in small and delicate uncials, perfectly simple and unadorned. There are no enlarged initials, no periods or accents, and this complete absence of ornamentation in Vaticanus has led to its being generally regarded as slightly older than Sinaiticus.

Codex Vaticanus is identical with Athanasius' Catalogue (*Fest. Ep.* 39) in content and in the sequence of biblical books of both the Old and New Testaments as far as they can be compared (since Vaticanus ends in the midst of Hebrews). It has been suggested that Vaticanus may represent the copy prepared for the Emperor Constans by Alexandrian scribes in 340 at Rome while Athanasius lived there in exile (Athanasius, *Animadv.* 15).

## 2. *Codex Sinaiticus*

The story of the discovery of the Codex Sinaiticus by Tischendorf is well known.[78] The manuscript originally contained the

[75] K. Lake, *The Text of the New Testament* (London, 1928), 13–16.

[76] Souter, *Text and Canon*, 21.

[77] H. J. M. Milne and T. C. Skeat, *Scribes and Correctors of the Codex Sinaiticus* (London, 1938), 89–90.

[78] C. Tischendorf, 'Discovery of the Sinaiticus Manuscript', *Codex Sinaiticus* (London, 1934), 15–32.

whole Greek Bible, but in the case of the Old Testament only pieces escaped the waste-paper basket of the Sinai monastery; the surviving contents are listed in Table 3.2. The canonical New Testament is complete, and at the end of the manuscript are added Barnabas and part of the Shepherd.[79] Whether other works followed is unknown.[80]

The provenance of the Codex Sinaiticus is not certain. K. Lake argued for Alexandria as the most likely, since the spelling in the manuscript bears a distinct resemblance to that of papyri from Egypt dated considerably earlier.[81] In addition, the text of the Psalms in Sinaiticus is remarkably like the text in the early Coptic version found in the Pistis Sophia. However, Harris, followed by Lagrange, argued for a Caesarean origin.[82] Sinaiticus almost certainly was in the library of Pamphilus at Caesarea during the sixth or seventh century, since it is likely that the corrector (ℵ$^{C}$) worked on it there. The Eusebian Canons are indicated in the margin of the gospels, in a hand evidently contemporaneous with the text.

Comparison with other hands of the fourth century, which are now more numerous, seems to indicate that the manuscript cannot be dated appreciably later than the middle of the fourth century.[83] As previously noted, the Emperor Constantine commissioned Eusebius in 331 to prepare fifty copies of sacred Scripture for the church at Constantinople (Eusebius, *Life of Constantine*, 4.36). In describing the execution of the Emperor's request, Eusebius wrote: *ταῦτα μὲν οὖν βασιλεὺς διεκελεύετο, αὐτίκα δ' ἔργον ἐπηκολούθει τῷ λόγῳ, ἐν πολυτελῶς ἠσκημένοις τεύχεσιν τρισσὰ καὶ τετρασσὰ διαπεμψάντων ἡμῶν* (§37). The meaning of *τρισσὰ καὶ τετρασσὰ* is uncertain. It has usually been taken to mean 'in gatherings of three or four sheets', but two alternative suggestions have been made. It may mean that the completed codices were sent 'by threes and

[79] H. and K. Lake, *Codex Sinaiticus Petropolitanus. The New Testament, the Epistle of Barnabas and the Shepherd of Hermas*, 2 vols. (Oxford, 1911–23).

[80] Milne–Skeat, 17.

[81] K. Lake, 'The Sinaitic and Vatican Manuscripts and the Copies sent by Eusebius to Constantine', *HTR* 11 (1918), 32–5.

[82] J. Rendel Harris, 'Appendix: On the Common Origin of Codices ℵ and B', *Stichometry* (London, 1893), 69–89; M. J. Lagrange, 'Le manuscrit sinaïtique: II. L'Origine médiate et immédiate du ms. sinaïtique', *RBib* 35 (1926), 91–3.

[83] Milne–Skeat, 60–5.

fours'. Lake, however, argued for another alternative, that the codices were 'written in three and four columns to the page'.[84] There are four narrow columns to each page in the Codex Sinaiticus (except in the poetical books, where there are only two), and there are three columns to a page in the Codex Vaticanus. These are the only known manuscripts of exactly this type. Therefore some scholars have suggested that both Vaticanus and Sinaiticus were originally among the fifty copies of Scripture that Constantine ordered.[85] Whether the suggestion is correct or not, the parallel does insinuate that at the time of Eusebius calligraphic fashion consisted of manuscripts written in three or four columns. The column divisions of Vaticanus and Sinaiticus support a date for both of these codices in the early part of the fourth century.

### 3. *The Peshitta*

The Peshitta is not the name of a single manuscript like Vaticanus and Sinaiticus, but of a Syriac version of the Old and New Testaments which though frequently reproduced represents an ancient original source. *Peshitta* literally means 'simple'; this version has been so named since the ninth century to distinguish it from the more elaborate forms of the Syriac text, such as the Hexaplaric version of the Old Testament or the Harklean version of the New Testament, both of which have marginal variants and other critical apparatus. There are over 350 manuscripts of the Peshitta, two of the fifth century, more than a dozen not later than the sixth, and three bearing precise dates, namely 530–9, 534, 548.[86] The New Testament of the Peshitta appears to have contained only twenty-two books; 2 Peter, 2 and 3 John, Jude, and Revelation are usually absent from the manuscripts.

The date of the New Testament Peshitta is disputed. Scholars in the early nineteenth century generally believed the Peshitta originated in the first half of the second century.[87] In

[84] K. Lake, 'Sinaitic and Vatican Manuscripts', 34–5.

[85] B. M. Metzger, *The Text of the New Testament*, 7–8, 47–8.

[86] G. H. Gwilliam, 'The Materials for the Criticism of the Peshitto New Testament, with Specimens of the Syriac Massorah', *StudBib* 3 (1891), 47–104.

[87] e.g. Westcott, *Canon of the New Testament*, 233–44; Bleek, 233–89.

1858 and 1910, manuscripts were published of an Old Syriac version which served as the basis of the New Testament Peshitta revision, just as the Old Latin version was the basis of the Vulgate revision.[88] The form of the text which the Old Syriac version preserves dates from the close of the second century or the beginning of the third.[89] The Peshitta must therefore be later.

Since both the Monophysite and the Nestorian churches used the Peshitta, it must have been generally accepted before 431, when the Nestorian secession took place. Copious quotations from the Old Testament Peshitta are found in the writings of Ephraem (d. 373) and Aphraates (mid-4th c.). It was formerly supposed that Ephraem also used the New Testament Peshitta, but F. C. Burkitt disputed such contentions since there is no other evidence of its use before the fifth century, to which the earliest extant manuscripts of it belong.[90] Burkitt argued instead that Rabbula bishop of Edessa (412–35) translated the Peshitta New Testament.

Recent studies have challenged Burkitt's thesis. It is unlikely that either the Monophysite or Nestorian party would have knowingly adopted a text revised by Rabbula. On the basis of a careful examination of the gospel quotations in Rabbula's translation of Cyril of Alexandria's *De Recta Fide*, made towards the end of his life, M. Black revealed that Rabbula's revision contained a considerable Old Syriac element.[91] Moreover, some remnants of the Peshitta have emerged in a manuscript in the British Library (Add. MS 12150) copied in 411 in Edessa.[92] Thus the last decades of the fourth century appear as the most probable date for the origin of the Peshitta, although it may not have enjoyed widespread recognition until the second half of the fifth century.[93]

88 W. Cureton, *Remains of a Very Ancient Recension of the Four Gospels in Syriac* (London, 1858); A. S. Smith, *The Old Syriac Gospels* (London, 1910).

89 B. M. Metzger, *The Text of the New Testament*, 69.

90 Burkitt, *S. Ephraim's Quotations from the Gospel* (TxSt 7.2; Cambridge, 1901); cf. id., *Evangelion da-Mepharreshe* (London, 1904).

91 M. Black, 'Rabbula of Edessa and the Peshitta', *BJRL* 33 (1950–1), 203–10.

92 A. Vööbus, *Studies in the History of the Gospel Text in Syriac* (Louvain, 1951), 50–1; cf. id., *Researches on the Circulation of the Peshitta in the Middle of the Fifth Century* (Pinneberg, 1948); id., *Early Versions of the New Testament: Manuscript Studies* (Stockholm, 1954), 88–102.

93 Kenyon, 229–31; B. M. Metzger, *The Text of the New Testament*, 69–70.

## 4. *The Codex Alexandrinus*

Codex Alexandrinus is the name given to the Greek Bible which Cyril Lucar, then Patriarch of Constantinople, offered to James I of England, where it was received in 1627. The manuscript contains almost the whole Bible, except for certain accidental mutilations.[94] The two epistles of Clement of Rome are included after the New Testament, after which, according to the table of contents, the Psalms of Solomon followed. This title, however, is separated from the others in the table of contents in such a way as to suggest that it stood on a different footing from those preceding.[95] The leaves containing the Psalms of Solomon have been lost. The whole of Matthew as far as 25:6 is lost, as is a section of John (6:50–8:52), a substantial portion of 2 Corinthians (4:13–12:6), one leaf of 1 Clement and the greater part of 2 Clement.

The early history of the Codex is obscure. Cyril Lucar, according to contemporary accounts, brought the manuscript to Constantinople from Alexandria, of which see he had previously been patriarch. An Arabic note at the beginning of the manuscript signed by 'Athanasius the humble', now known as Athanasius II, patriarch of Alexandria (d. 1316), states that the manuscript was a gift to the patriarchal cell in that city. But similar notes in two other volumes still in the Patriarchal Library at Alexandria suggest that Athanasius acquired the manuscript in Constantinople, where he spent many years in the service of the emperor.

Another Arabic note, written in the thirteenth or fourteenth century, states that the manuscript was written by Thecla the Martyr. Cyril Lucar himself repeated this statement, adding that Thecla was a noble lady of Egypt, and that she transcribed the manuscript shortly after the Council of Nicaea (325), and that her name was originally written at the end.[96] The authority for this tradition is unknown, and such an early date is hardly possible. The appearance in the manuscript before the Psalms of a summary of their contents by Eusebius (d. *c.* 340), and an

94 E. M. Thompson, *Facsimile of the Codex Alexandrinus: New Testament and Clementine Epistles* (London, 1879).

95 Ibid.: *The Old Testament*, i: *Genesis–2 Chronicles* (London, 1881), 6.

96 Kenyon, 198–9.

epistle of Athanasius to Marcellinus on the Psalter, make a date before the middle of the fourth century unlikely. The Eusebian Canons are also found in the margin of the gospels. The style of writing, with its enlargement of initial letters and similar elementary ornamentation, suggests that Alexandrinus is somewhat later, perhaps in the first half of the fifth century.[97] Alexandrinus is the earliest example of a division into chapters of the Gospels, but the absence of a similar division of Acts and the epistles, ascribed to Euthalius of Alexandria (*c.* 458), supports a date not later than the middle of the fifth century.

## CHRONOLOGY

Thus there appear to be fifteen undisputed catalogues and four collections of the Christian Canon belonging to the fourth and early years of the fifth centuries. None of the catalogues or collections seems to predate Eusebius. Eusebius' own writings seem to confirm an absence of earlier lists in his creation of catalogues for Irenaeus, Clement, and Origen, and in his ambiguous and inconsistent use of terminology. Only one of these catalogues other than Eusebius' own, namely the catalogue in the Codex Claromontanus, is likely to be earlier than the middle of the fourth century. The earliest extant catalogues are derived from Caesarea and Alexandria.

The reasons for the introduction of catalogues are uncertain. It seems clear that the catalogues are, in part at least, a natural development of the biblical scholarship inherited from the schools at Alexandria and Caesarea, but a more specific element in their formation may also have been a systematic attempt to limit and combat the writings used by heretics. The establishment of the Church under the Roman Emperor Constantine seems also to have contributed to their proliferation. But the introduction of catalogues is not a particularly surprising development and can readily be understood as an attempt by the churches to get their affairs in order. Whatever the reasons, however, the activity of cataloguing the books of the Christian Bible is most evident from the middle of the fourth century onwards.

[97] B. M. Metzger, *The Text of the New Testament*, 46–7.

TABLE 4.3. *Chronology of fourth-century catalogues*

| | | |
|---|---|---|
| 1 | 303–25 | Eusebius, HE 3.25.1–7 |
| 2 | 303–67 | Catalogue in Codex Claromontanus |
| | (331–50 | Codex Vaticanus) |
| | (331–50 | Codex Sinaiticus) |
| 3 | 350 | Cyril of Jerusalem, *Catech.* 4.33 |
| 4 | 367 | Athanasius, *Ep. Fest.* 39 |
| 5 | 365–90 | Mommsen catalogue |
| 6 | 374–77 | Epiphanius, *Haer.* 76.5 |
| 7 | *c.*380 | Apostolic Canon, 85 |
| 8 | 383–90 | Gregory of Nazianzus, *Carm.* 12.31 |
| 9 | 393–419 | African Canons |
| 10 | 394 | Jerome, *Ep.* 53 |
| 11 | 396–7 | Augustine, *De Doct. Christ.* 2.8.12 |
| 12 | 396+ | Amphilochius, *Iambi ad Seleucum* 289–319 |
| | (*c.*400 | Peshitta) |
| 13 | *c.*400 | Rufinus, *Comm. in Symb. Apost.* 36 |
| 14 | *c.*405 | Pope Innocent, *Ad Exup. Tol.* |
| 15 | *c.*400 | Syrian catalogue of St Catherine's |
| | (*c.*425 | Codex Alexandrinus) |

## PROVENANCE

Although Sundberg's list of New Testament catalogues needed some modification, his conclusion that numerous lists appeared during the fourth century throughout the Church remains accurate. The geographical provenance of the undisputed catalogues and collections is indeed widespread.

The impetus for the development of the Christian canon appears to be located in the first half of the fourth century in the regions of Alexandria/Egypt and Palestine/Western Syria, perhaps from the schools at Alexandria and Caesarea. From there it seems to have spread northward to Asia Minor and westward to North Africa. Finally the development spread to Eastern Syria, and across the Mediterranean to Rome/Italy.

TABLE 4.4. *The provenance of fourth-century catalogues*

| | |
|---|---|
| *Palestine/Western Syria* | |
| 303–25 | Eusebius |
| 350 | Cyril |
| 374–77 | Epiphanius |
| 380 | Apostolic Canons |
| 394 | Jerome |
| *Alexandria/Egypt* | |
| 303–67 | Claromontanus |
| (331–50 | Codex Vaticanus) |
| (331–50 | Codex Sinaiticus) |
| 367 | Athanasius |
| *Asia Minor* | |
| 390 | Gregory Nazianzus |
| 396+ | Amphilochius |
| (*c.* 425 | Codex Alexandrinus) |
| *Northern Africa* | |
| 365–90 | Mommsen Catalogue |
| 393–419 | African Canons |
| 396–7 | Augustine |
| *Rome/Italy* | |
| 404 | Rufinus |
| 405 | Pope Innocent |
| *Eastern Syria* | |
| (*c.* 400 | Peshitta) |
| *c.* 400 | Syrian catalogue |

## A 'CANON' OF SCRIPTURE

The conceptual shift from scriptures to canon exemplified by the appearance of catalogues may also be implied in the late employment by the Church of the Greek word *κανών* for a list of books counted as accepted Scripture. Prior to the fourth century, the word 'canon' had a long history of being applied both to metaphorical ideals and fixed lists.

Metaphorically the word *κανών* referred to any 'norm' or 'measure', and so it was applied to Aristotle's ethics, Epicurean philosophy, and Pliny's description of the sculpture of Polyclitus.[98] From the time of Irenaeus 'canon' was used in the Church in a variety of ways to depict the normative ideals of Christian teachings, in phrases like the 'canon of truth', the 'canon of faith', or the 'ecclesiastical canon'. But although early Christianity in the first three centuries employed the word in this metaphorical sense, it apparently never did so in connection with specific written materials.[99]

Besides the metaphorical usage, 'canon' had also been applied to fixed lists. The word κανών was used for a 'list' or 'table' in astronomical, mathematical, and chronological writings. Eusebius employed the term in his *Chronicle* in reference to the second part of the work, which consisted of synchronous tables arranged in parallel columns. Similarly, the system of lists devised by Eusebius on the basis of the Ammonian Sections indexing parallel Gospel passages was called the Eusebian Canons (κανόνες). After the Council of Nicaea (325), the resolutions of Church synods were regularly called κανόνες. An official list of the clergy also became known in the fourth century as a 'canon'.[100]

The word 'canon' was not applied by the Church to Christian writings until the fourth century. Eusebius (*c.* 303–25) used the term κανών in *HE* (6.25.3), but the reference is to the Fourfold Gospel canon and not the New Testament in general.[101] Athanasius (*c.* 350) provides the earliest extant use of κανών in reference to the Scriptures in general, when he wrote that the Shepherd was not 'part of the Canon' (ἐκ τοῦ κανόνος, *De Decretis Nicaenae Synodi* 18.3). Somewhat later (367), Athanasius provided a catalogue of accepted Christian writings and described them as 'canonical' (κανονιζόμενα, *Fest. Ep.* 39). At about the same time the Council of Laodicea (*c.* 360) referred to the 'canonical' (κανονικά) and 'uncanonical'

[98] H. W. Beyer, *Κανών*, *TDNT* iii (1965), 596–602; Westcott, *Canon of the New Testament*, 499–506; Zahn, *Grundriß*, i–14.

[99] From about this time and up to the middle of the 4th c. the idea of a collection of Scripture appears to have generally been expressed by διαθήκη; cf. W. C. van Unnik, 'Ἡ καινὴ διαθήκη: A Problem in the Early History of the Canon', *StudPat* 4 (1961), 212–27.

[100] Council of Nicaea (325), canon 16, 17, 19; Cyril of Jerusalem (348–50), *Procatechesis*, 4; Council of Laodicea (*c.* 360), canon 15.

[101] Cf. R. Pfeiffer, *History of Classical Scholarship from the Beginnings to the End of the Hellenistic Age* (Oxford, 1968), 207 n. 4.

(ἀκανόνιστα) books of the old and new covenants (canon 59). The adjectival form 'canonical' (*canonicus*), is also found in translations of Origen (*De Princ.* 4.1.33; *Prol. Cantic.*; *Comm. on Matt.* 117.28) and may possibly suggest an Alexandrian origin for Athanasius' usage. However, all Origen's references are extant only in the Latin translation of Rufinus and it is more probable that their presence there is due to Rufinus, who frequently introduced the Latin word into his translation of Eusebius' *Church History* where it was not present in the Greek. The Greek κανών, however, quickly found entry among the Latins, occurring in the Mommsen Catalogue (*c.* 360), and later in Priscillian, Filaster, Rufinus, and Augustine.[102] In Latin *canon* became used synonymously with *biblia*.

After the middle of the fourth century, 'canon' was regularly used in both the East and West for the accepted collection of Scripture. While such usage may be dependent upon the earlier sense of a metaphorical norm, the evidence suggests that here 'canon' primarily had the simple sense of 'list',[103] and thus that its appearance in this sense in the fourth century coincided with the proliferation of Christian catalogues.

## OBSERVATIONS

The contents of the undisputed fourth-century catalogues (and collections) reveal certain patterns which support the conclusions drawn in the previous chapter regarding the formation of the Christian canon in the fourth century.

### 1. *The Old Testament*

The endorsement of an Old Testament for the Christian Church appears interwoven with the fixing of the New Testament canon in the fourth century. Almost all the New Testament catalogues of that time (and all the New Testament collections) are preceded by an Old Testament. Melito's and

[102] A. Blaise, *Dictionnaire latin-français des auteurs chrétiens* (Turnhout, 1954), 128.

[103] F. Ch. Bauer, 'Bemerkungen über die Bedeutung des Wortes κανών', *ZWT* 1 (1858), 141–50.

Origen's earlier Old Testament catalogues (*HE* 4.26.14; 6.25.2, respectively) appear to be only Christian lists of the Jewish Canon. The first extant Christian recensions of the Old Testament canon are dated to the fourth century, and during that period there are seventeen undisputed Old Testament catalogues, all but one of which was associated with a New Testament list. The exception is Hilary's Old Testament catalogue (*Prol. in Lib. Ps.* 15) which was probably derived from Origen. Eusebius is the only New Testament cataloguer without an original Old Testament list. This absence in Eusebius may be contextual, since his New Testament list appeared after a discussion of the apostles, and since he provided Melito's and Origen's Old Testament lists later in the work (*HE* 4.26.14; 6.25.2, respectively). Epiphanius too did not immediately precede his New Testament list (*Pan.* 76.5) with one from the Old, but an Old Testament list is present earlier in the source where the New Testament catalogue is found (*Pan.* 8.6). Moreover, Epiphanius provided two other Old Testament catalogues elsewhere in his writings (*De Mens. et Pond.* 4, 23). Thus the action of cataloguing Christian scripture not only appears to have originated in the fourth century, but also to have been a matter related generally to the whole Christian canon, and not simply to the Old or New Testament independently. New Testament catalogues always appear in the context of the formation of the whole Christian canon, and not in response to a previously established Old Testament.

## 2. *The Fourfold Gospel*

The Fourfold Gospel canon appears to be established before the activity of fourth-century cataloguing. The fact that the gospel canon is numbered, often unnamed, and usually in the same order in the fourth-century catalogues confirms that it was a well-known and independent entity. The gospels are specifically numbered four in all but one of the catalogues (and in the table of contents of the Codex Alexandrinus). The exception is the catalogue of Gregory of Nazianzus, where poetry may have dictated the absence of numbering the gospels. In numerous catalogues the gospels are numbered four without even being individually named; among them

Eusebius (the earliest list), Cyril of Jerusalem, Epiphanius, the African Canons, and Pope Innocent's letter (possibly the latest). Thus the Fourfold Gospel canon, as suggested in Ch. 3, appears established before and independently of the remaining New Testament scriptures.

## 3. *The* Corpus Paulinum

A Pauline collection of fourteen epistles appears established in the East before the fourth-century cataloguing. The Pauline epistles are specifically numbered fourteen in all the Eastern lists except the Syrian catalogue, Amphilochius' catalogue, and the catalogue in the Codex Claromontanus (for Eusebius, see *HE* 3.3.5). And only in Athanasius' list, the catalogue in the Codex Claromontanus, Amphilochius' catalogue, and the Syrian catalogue are the letters individually named. The fact that the lists in the Codex Claromontanus and the Syrian catalogue are stichometrical may account for their delineation. However, the order of the Pauline collection does not appear to have been previously established. This is especially evident in the shift of Hebrews (cf. Athanasius, Amphilochius, Syrian canon) from among the letters to the churches, but is also apparent in the varying place of Colossians (see the catalogue in the Codex Claromontanus, Athanasius, and the Syrian Canon).

A Pauline collection of thirteen epistles was probably established in the West before the fourth century. In the earliest Western list, the Mommsen catalogue, Paul's epistles are specifically numbered thirteen and unnamed. The African canons testify to the expansion of the collection, in that the catalogue from the Hippo breviary (393) reads 'Epistolae Pauli Apostoli XIII, *eiusdem ad Hebraeos una*', while the Canon is altered in Carthage (419) to read: 'Epistolae Pauli Apostoli XIIII'. Jerome's comments (*Ep.* 53.9) may suggest that Hebrews was not counted in the West and some manuscripts suggest that Pope Innocent I counted only thirteen epistles for Paul. Yet Augustine and Rufinus specifically number Paul's epistles as fourteen, with Rufinus, like Innocent, not bothering to name them individually. In the West at least, the fourteen-epistle Pauline collection appears to have been established only well on in the process of fourth-century cataloguing.

## 4. *Catholic epistles*

The seven-letter collection of catholic epistles was known in the East before the fourth century, but was not entirely received. Eusebius numbered the collection as seven (*HE* 2.23.25), and all were named in his catalogue but all were not accepted (*HE* 3.25.2–3). All seven were named and accepted in the next surviving Eastern list, the catalogue of the Codex Claromontanus, but they were not specifically numbered there as seven. The catholic epistles were specifically numbered seven in all the remaining Greek catalogues—Cyril, Athanasius, Epiphanius, Gregory of Nazianzus, and Amphilochius (and in Jerome writing from Bethlehem)—and in the table of contents of Codex Alexandrinus, with one exception, namely the Apostolic Canons. The failure of canon 85 to enumerate the epistles as seven may be due to the inclusion of the Clementine epistles or to Syrian influence, where the minor catholic epistles were accepted only later. In his catalogue Amphilochius acknowledged that there was some dispute about their number. The order is the same in all the Eastern lists, namely James, Peter, John, Jude, except again for Apostolic Canon 85, which may reflect Syrian influence, and in the catalogue in the Codex Claromontanus, where the Latin translator may have altered the order to put Peter first. That the catholic epistle collection was an independent unit established before the fourth century is reflected in the fact that it was generally numbered, unnamed, and in the same order throughout the Eastern lists, except in Syria. The entire collection would not appear to have been commonly accepted in the East until the cataloguing of the fourth century (cf. Eusebius).

None of the Western catalogues (the Mommsen catalogue, the African canons, Augustine, Rufinus, and Pope Innocent I) states that there are seven catholic epistles. The Mommsen catalogue included only the Johannine and Petrine letters, and apparently with a scribal protest. The remaining Western lists, however, included all seven epistles. Yet in no two of these lists do the letters appear in the same order. Thus while a seven-letter collection probably existed before the fourth century, it was only in the process of cataloguing that the complete collection was accepted as part of the Canon, first in the East, and then later in the West.

### 5. *Spurious works*

Throughout the fourth century, in the catalogues of both the East and West, there is evidence that the contents of the Canon were still disputed. The fact that certain works were neither universally accepted nor completely rejected, but placed in a secondary class of disputed items, suggests a period of formation, where tradition had not clearly decided the issue, and which had to be worked out among the churches themselves.

In the East, Eusebius' secondary class of works was itself divided, between those writings which were recognized by many (James, Jude, 2 Peter, and 2 and 3 John) and those which were rejected (Acts of Paul, Shepherd, Revelation of Peter, Barnabas, Didache, Revelation?, Gospel of the Hebrews). The scribal marks in the catalogue of the Codex Claromontanus suggest a dispute about Barnabas, the Shepherd, the Acts of Paul, and the Revelation of Peter.

After the middle of the fourth century, the debate appears to have expanded to consider not only what works were spurious, but also what place the spurious works should have in the Church. On several occasions Cyril of Jerusalem clearly rejected even the private reading of what he called the 'apocrypha': 'And, pray, read none of the apocryphal writings: for why dost thou, who knowest not those which are acknowledged among all, trouble thyself in vain about those which are disputed?' 'And whatever books are not read in Churches, these read not even by thyself, as thou hast heard me say.' In contrast, Athanasius allowed the reading of the spurious works by the catechumens:

> But for greater exactness I add this also, writing of necessity; that there are other books besides these not indeed included in the Canon, but appointed by the Fathers to be read by those who newly join us, and who wish instruction in the word of godliness, the Wisdom of Solomon, and the Wisdom of Sirach, and Esther, and Judith, and Tobit, and that which is called the Teaching of the

Apostles, and the Shepherd. But the former, my brethren, are included in the Canon, the latter being [merely] read; nor is there in any place a mention of apocryphal writings. (*Ep. Fest.* 39.)

Epiphanius did not explicitly name a class of spurious works, but he did amend his various lists and seemed unsure where to place certain writings. In one of his Old Testament lists (*De Mens. et Pond.* 23) he added Lamentations at the end, while in another Old Testament list in the same work (*De Mens. et Pond.* 4) he attached the Wisdom of Solomon and Sirach to the end. In his New Testament list (*Pan.* 76.5) Epiphanius again appended the Wisdom of Solomon and Sirach to the conclusion. In the Apostolic Canons, Sirach appears after the Old Testament list with the instruction: 'And besides these, take care that your young persons learn the Wisdom of the very learned Sirach.' The New Testament list that follows included the Apostolic Constitutions themselves, about which it noted: 'dedicated to you the bishops by me Clement, in eight books; which it is not fit to publish before all, because of the mysteries contained in them.' Amphilochius acknowledged that four of the catholic epistles were still disputed; and that Hebrews and Revelation were considered spurious, by some in the first case and by the majority in the latter. The Psalms of Solomon were separated in the table of contents of the Codex Alexandrinus suggesting a secondary position. Thus throughout the fourth century in the East, certain works were disputed and considered spurious. Some among the New Testament scriptures, like the minor catholic epistles and Revelation, were eventually accepted as canonical, while others, e.g. the Acts of Paul, the Shepherd, the Revelation of Peter, Barnabas, the Teaching of the Apostles, Didache, and the Gospel of the Hebrews, were eventually rejected and forgotten.

The situation was similar in the West. The *una sola* of the Mommsen catalogue suggests a scribal dispute about the minor catholic epistles. The counting of the Pauline letters in the canons of the Hippo breviary at Carthage (397) suggests a controversy about Hebrews. Jerome acknowledged that it was not counted with the others, and was not accepted by many. Yet both Hebrews and the minor catholic epistles were later accepted in the West as canonical. The contents of Rufinus' clearly defined class of spurious works, which he called 'ecclesiastical', were later completely rejected. After listing the books of the Old and New Testaments, he wrote:

At the same time we should appreciate that there are certain other books which our predecessors designated 'ecclesiastical' rather than 'canonical' . . . In the New Testament we have the little work known as the Book of the Shepherd, or Hermas, and the book which is named the Two Ways, and the Preaching of Peter. They desired that all these should be read in the churches, but that appeal should not be made to them on points of faith. The other writings they designated 'apocryphal', refusing to allow them to be read out in church. (*Comm. in Symb. Apost.* 38.)

### 6. *Rejected works*

The concept of a class of rejected writings is inherent in the formation of a Canon. Occasionally within a catalogue some mention of this class, or even some members of it may be found. Eusebius named several of the 'fictions of heretics', namely 'the Gospels of Peter, of Thomas, of Matthias, or of any others besides them, and the Acts of Andrew and John and the other Apostles' (*HE* 3.25.6). These he declared 'are not to be placed even among the rejected writings, but are all of them to be cast aside as absurd and impious'. Cyril named only the Gospel of Thomas among those which 'have false titles and are mischievous.' Athanasius and Rufinus both mentioned the 'apocrypha' without delineating any particular works. Pope Innocent mentioned several apocryphal Acts. Jerome in *Prologus Galectus* named the Shepherd along with several Old Testament apocrypha. Long lists of apocrypha, however, did not appear until later; for instance in the so-called *Decretum Gelasanium* (6th c.), the catalogue of the sixty canonical books (7th c.) and the stichometry of Nicephorus (9th c.).

## THE MURATORIAN FRAGMENT

The Muratorian Fragment does not differ in form from the undisputed catalogues of the fourth century and could easily find a place among them. A supposed Greek original for the

Fragment would, however, necessitate that, if dated at this time, the Fragment should be Eastern in origin.

The beginning of the Muratorian Fragment is missing so that it is not known whether an Old Testament catalogue preceded it. An Old Testament list is perhaps probable since the only New Testament catalogues which were not preceded by Old Testament lists were those of Eusebius and Epiphanius, both of whom included Old Testament catalogues elsewhere in their works. The reference in the Fragment to 'the prophets, whose number is settled' (l. 79) may be a reference to the Old Testament canon.

Because the beginning is mutilated, it cannot be determined whether the gospels were specifically numbered at the start of the New Testament list. However, the fact that Luke is called 'the third gospel book' (*tertio evangelii librum*, l. 2) and John is named as the 'fourth of the gospels' (*quarti evangeliorum*, l. 9) suggests that the Fragmentist recognized the Fourfold Gospel canon and ordered them in the so-called Eastern order.

The Fragment lists thirteen Pauline letters, although they were not specifically so numbered. The delineation of the Pauline epistles in the Fragment is, however, somewhat confusing, since the Fragmentist started (ll. 39–46), stopped (ll. 46–50), and started over again (ll. 50–63) in the midst of introducing the scheme of letters to seven churches (ll. 46–50, 57–9). Hebrews may have been lost in the confusion.

The catholic epistles mentioned in the Fragment are idiosyncratic in terms of both contents and order. The absence of 1 Peter (and James) is extraordinary, and most probably implies omissions in the Fragment. The letters found in the Fragment, namely 2 (and 3?) John and Jude, are elsewhere found only in larger collections of the catholic epistles, which were accepted as canonical only in the fourth century. Jude, which is listed before the letters of John in the Fragment, was usually listed last among the catholic epistles both in the East, where the order James, Peter, John, Jude was standard, and in the West, where the order varied.

The Fragment clearly lists certain spurious works. The private reading of the Shepherd, for instance, was encouraged by the Fragmentist, but the public reading disallowed (ll. 77–80). The Revelation of Peter was accepted by the Fragmentist, although he noted that some people opposed its public reading (ll. 72–3).

Certain works are completely rejected in the Fragment, specifically Pauline forgeries by the Marcionites to the Laodiceans and the Alexandrians and several others (ll. 63–6), and anything from Arsinous, Valentinus, Miltiades, or the new psalm-book of Marcion (ll. 81–5).

The Fragment, if traditionally dated, is an anomaly in the development of the New Testament as regards not only the concept of the Canon and its contents, but also its format as a catalogue. There is nothing about the form of the Fragment which distinguishes it from the fifteen undisputed catalogues of the fourth and early fifth centuries, and nothing that suggests that it was earlier than the others, or that it influenced their development. Rather, the Fragment appears as simply another New Testament list which ought to find its place among the others of that time.

# 5

# PECULIARITIES IN THE FRAGMENT

THERE are a number of peculiarities in the Muratorian Fragment which are often attributed to its barbarous Latin, omissions in the text, incorrect translation, poor transcription, or confusion on the part of the Fragmentist. In a number of these instances, however, the irregularity is removed with the supposition of a fourth-century Eastern origin for the Fragment. While none of these instances in itself is sufficient to demand redating of the Fragment, the cumulative effect is a substantial refutation of the traditional date, and corroborates the findings of the earlier chapters in favour of a later fourth-century date and an Eastern provenance.

## THE GOSPEL ORDER

The assumed order of the Gospels in the Muratorian Fragment would be extraordinary if the Fragment were Western and dated, as traditionally held, from the late second century.

The beginning of the Fragment is lost. As we have seen, some leaves may be missing in the Codex Muratorianus, for the page now preceding the Fragment, fo. 9$^{v}$, ends abruptly in the middle of a quotation from Eucherius and the Fragment begins in the middle of a sentence at the top of the next extant page, fo. 10$^{r}$. There is no vacant space either at the bottom of fo. 9$^{v}$ or at the top of fo. 10$^{r}$. It is assumed that four gospels were originally mentioned in the Fragment since the Gospel of Luke is called the 'third gospel-book' (*tertio euangelii librum sec(a)undo Lucan*, l. 2) and shortly afterwards the Gospel of John is styled the 'fourth gospel' (*quarti euangeliorum Iohannis ex decipolis*, l. 9).

Since no collection of four gospels other than of Matthew, Mark, Luke, and John is known in the Church, it is supposed that Matthew and Mark were the first two gospels mentioned, in the missing portion of the Fragment. The first surviving line of the Fragment reads '. . . quibus tamen Interfuit et ita posuit' ('. . . at which, however, he was present and so he has set it down') (l. 1). This line of the Fragment would appear to refer to either Matthew or Mark. Matthew seems an unlikely choice since the order of Mark, Matthew, Luke, John for the gospels is without precedent in biblical manuscripts and patristic texts.[1] Mark, for that matter, is not found at the beginning of any ordering of the Fourfold Gospel. Thus the first line of the Fragment, presumably regarding the second gospel, is usually understood to refer to the evangelist Mark. The 'quibus tamen Interfuit' in this first line may suggest that the Fragmentist thought Mark had been present at some event of Jesus' ministry and had faithfully recorded it (e.g. Mark 16:9–20, cf. 14:51–2).[2]

The phrase may indeed have referred to someone else, for in mentioning Luke the Fragmentist wrote 'dñm tamen nec Ipse (d)uidit in carne' (ll. 6–7). This phrase seems to suggest that someone previously mentioned in the Fragment had also not seen the Lord in the flesh. If this is meant to refer to either Matthew or Mark, clearly Mark would be favoured. However, such a conclusion would then conflict with the previous interpretation of 'quibus tamen Interfuit'. The remark in ll. 6–7 may not be meant to refer to someone else at all, or perhaps the other person was mentioned in narrative material about Mark or Matthew. Paul was mentioned in the narrative material about Luke (l. 3), and Andrew in that about John (l. 14). Perhaps in a similar fashion Peter was mentioned in the narrative material about Mark, and 'quibus tamen Interfuit' may then have referred to him. Alternatively, Mark may have been present ('quibus tamen Interfuit') at Peter's preaching, though he had not seen Jesus ('dñm tamen nec Ipse (d)uidit in carne'), and Mark wrote down what he heard ('et ita posuit'). Papias (*c.* 60–*c.* 130), as preserved in Eusebius (*HE* 3.39.15), recorded that Mark, though he had neither heard nor followed

[1] The Gospel of Matthew does follow Mark in Codex Bobiensis (κ), but only after John and Luke; cf. E. Nestle, *Introduction to the Textual Criticism of the Greek New Testament*, trans. W. Edie (London, 1901), 161–2.

[2] Zahn, *Geschichte*, ii. 14–20.

Jesus, was the interpreter of Peter (Acts 12: 12; 1 Pet. 5: 13). A similar association between Mark and Peter is found in the writings of Justin (*Dial.* 106), Irenaeus (*Adv. Haer.* 3.1.1), Tertullian (*Adv. Marc.* 4.5), Origen (in Eusebius, *HE* 6.25.5), Eusebius (*HE* 2.15), and Jerome (*De Vir. Ill.* 8). Westcott therefore read *et ita* as καὶ οὕτως, i.e. 'even so (as Mark had heard from Peter)'.[3] Various other constructions to complete the sentence have been proposed by scholars,[4] but it is enough for present concerns to acknowledge that the gospel referred to in l. 1 was probably Mark's, and that the order of the four gospels in the Fragment appears to have been: Matthew, Mark, Luke, John.

This is the so-called Eastern order. When it became generally received is not certain. Clement of Alexandria (*c.* 150–*c.* 215) accepted the Fourfold Gospel (*Strom.* 3.93.1), but the manner in which he ordered the gospels is not clear. Eusebius (*HE* 6.14.5) reported that Clement in the *Hypotyposes* declared 'the tradition of the earliest presbyters' was that the gospels containing genealogies were written first. Rufinus clarified this statement in his translation of Eusebius' *Church History* by interpolating here: 'id est Matthaei et Lucae'. After this statement Eusebius related the occasion which Clement gave for the composition of the gospel of Mark (*HE* 6.14.6), and then noted that Clement considered John's gospel 'last of all' (*HE* 6.14.7). These remarks would suggest a chronological order of either Matthew, Luke, Mark, John or Luke, Matthew, Mark, John. Since there is no precedent for the latter it is probable that Clement believed the chronological order of the Gospels to be Matthew, Luke, Mark, John.[5] In either case Mark was thought by Clement to have been written after Matthew and Luke.

Thereafter in the East, the order of Matthew, Mark, Luke, John was generally considered to be the correct chronological order of the Gospels. Origen (*c.* 185–*c.* 254) in the first book of his *Commentary on Matthew*, as quoted by Eusebius (*HE* 6.25.4–6), acknowledged the Fourfold Gospel as written in the

[3] Westcott, *Canon of the New Testament*, 527, n. 1.

[4] Tregelles, *Canon Muratorianus*, 30.

[5] Zahn, *Geschichte*, ii. 364–75; Nestle, 161–2; the supposed Clementine order of Matthew, Luke, Mark, and John is thrice found in Irenaeus (*Adv. Haer.* 3.9.1–11.6, 3.11.7, 4.6.1).

Eastern order, for 'I have learned by tradition that the first [of the four Gospels] was written by Matthew . . . The second is by Mark . . . And the third by Luke . . . Last of all that by John.'[6] This same order is found in 𝔭⁴⁵, an Egyptian codex dated by its editor in the first half of the third century.[7] The Eastern order was also given by Eusebius (*HE* 3.24.6–7, 9–12) and was utilized by him in his *Canons*. It is found in nearly all Greek and Syriac manuscripts,[8] including all the earliest extant Greek MSS before the fifth century, namely 𝔭⁴⁵, Codex Vaticanus (B), Codex Sinaiticus (א), Codex Alexandrinus (A), as well as the Sinaitic Old Syriac manuscript and the Peshitta versions. The same order is also found in all but one of the fourth-century Eastern New Testament catalogues where the Gospels are named: in Athanasius, the Apostolic Canons, Gregory of Nazianzus, Amphilochius, Jerome (writing from Bethlehem), and the Syrian catalogue. The exception is the catalogue in the Codex Claromontanus, whose order may have been corrupted by Western influence when translated into Latin.

In the West a different order for the gospels initially obtained, which placed first the Gospels of the two apostles. Most existing manuscripts of the Western church before the fifth century testify to the order Matthew, John, Luke, Mark. So the gospels stand in the manuscripts of the Old Latin versions of the second and third centuries,[9] in the Gothic versions of Ulphilas (*c.* 311–83), and in the uncial Codex Bezae (D). In other Western sources, the Apostles are also predominantly listed first. Tertullian (*c.* 200) in one place gave the order John, Matthew, Luke, Mark (*Adv. Marc.* 4.2), and in another John, Matthew, Mark, Luke (*Adv. Marc.* 4.5). The Latin catalogue of the Codex Claromontanus has the order of Matthew, John, Mark, Luke. The Mommsen catalogue departed from the Western pattern with the unusual sequence

[6] Origen gave the order John, Matthew, Mark, and Luke in his *Commentary on John* (1.6), but the context probably accounted for the precedence and reordering of John.

[7] Kenyon, *Chester Beatty*, Fasciculus II (Gospels and Acts), pp. x–xi.

[8] The Curetonian Old Syriac MS is the principal exception to the Eastern order among Syriac MSS with its unusual order of Matthew, Mark, John, and Luke, also found in the Mommsen Catalogue.

[9] The principal exception to the Western order among the Old Latin versions is Codex Bobiensis (see n. 1).

of Matthew, Mark, John, Luke, perhaps in order to list Luke just before the evangelist's other work, Acts.

When the Western preference for listing the gospels of the apostles first became generally accepted is not clear. Irenaeus (*c.* 180), the first extant witness to the Fourfold Gospel, ordered the gospels in several different ways, but never in the Western order. On three occasions Irenaeus ordered them Matthew, Luke, Mark, John (*Adv. Haer.* 3.9.1–11.6, 3.11.7, 4.6.1), as perhaps Clement of Alexandria had done. In the famous passage where Irenaeus insisted that 'it is not possible that the Gospels should be either more or fewer in number than they are', he listed them in the order John, Luke, Matthew, Mark (*Adv. Haer.* 3.11.8). On another occasion he listed the Gospels in the Eastern order (*Adv. Haer.* 3.1.1; cf. Eusebius, *HE* 5.8.2–4), apparently as their chronological sequence. The appearance of the Eastern order in Irenaeus, however, seems to be an exception, especially since it does not reappear in Western sources for 200 years. But at the end of the fourth century the Eastern order became widely accepted by Western writers. Jerome adapted the Old Latin versions to the Eastern order in the Vulgate (384) and it became the standard sequence for the Western church. At about the same time the Eastern order is also attested to in the writings of Augustine (*De Doctr. Christ.* 11.12.8) and Rufinus (*Comm. in Symb. Apost.* 37).

The gospel order of Matthew, Mark, Luke, John in the Muratorian Fragment, if considered Western and traditionally dated, would be remarkable. While a precedent can be found in one of Irenaeus' references, it is a precedent which is itself exceptional—exceptional even in Irenaeus. The common Western tradition was to place the gospels of the two apostles first. However, the gospel order of the Fragment would not be in the least extraordinary if a fourth-century date and an Eastern provenance for the Fragment were supposed.

## THE JOHANNINE LEGEND

A Johannine legend recorded in the Muratorian Fragment suggests an Eastern origin for the Fragment and a later date than has been traditionally assigned. In the narrative material about the gospel of John, the Fragmentist recorded a curious legend about its origin (ll. 9–16).

**quarti euangeliorum Iohannis ex decipolis**
cohortantibus condescipulis et ep̃s suis
dixit coieiunate mihi·odie triduo et quid
cuique fuerit reuelatum alterutrum
nobis ennarremus eadem nocte reue
latum andreae ex apostolis ut recognis
centibus cuntis Iohannis suo nomine
cun*c*ta discrib*e*ret . . .

There are three elements to be particularly noted in this legend.[10] The first element to be noted is the account of who compelled John to write his gospel. In the Fragment, John is 'urged by his fellow-disciples and bishops' (*cohortantibus condescipulis et ep̃s suis*, l. 10). Clement of Alexandria appears to have been making an allusion to a similar tradition when he wrote:

But last of all, John, perceiving that the physical things were made known in the Gospels, *being urged by his pupils* (προτραπέντα ὑπὸ τῶν γνωρίμων) and taken up in the Spirit to God, composed a spiritual gospel. (Eusebius, *HE* 6.14.7.)

Victorinus of Pettau recorded a similar story:

Johannes evangelium postea conscripsit. cum essent Valentinus et Cerinthus et Ebion et cetera scola Satanae sparsa per orbem, convenerunt ad illum [sc. *Johannem*] *de finitimis civitatibus episcopi et compulerunt eum*, ut ipse testimonium conscriberet in Dominum. (*Comm. Rev.* 11.1.)

Jerome also related the tradition:

Johannes apostolus quem Jesus amabat plurimum, filius Zebedaei et frater Jacobi apostoli . . . novissimus omnium scripsit evangelium,

[10] There is an obvious difference in the Fragment between the description of 'John' as 'one of the disciples' (*Iohannes ex decipolis*, l. 9), on the one hand, and 'Andrew' as 'one of the apostles' (*andreae ex aposotolis*, l. 14) on the other. However, it is the description of Andrew as an 'apostle' which is remarkable, for in two other places John is among 'disciples' (ll. 10, 22). This may confirm the suggestion that the Andrew story is an interpolation into the Johannine legend of the Fragment. If so this refutes a dependence upon Irenaeus suggested by A. A. T. Ehrhardt, 'The Gospels in the Muratorian Fragment', *Ostleirchliche Studien*, 2 (1953), 123–4. In any case Irenaeus always referred to John as 'the disciple', and used the singular for no one else, while the Fragmentist merely refers to John, as 'one of the disciples' (*Iohannis ex decipolis*, l. 9).

*rogatus ab Asiae episcopis*, adversus Cerinthum aliosque haereticos et maxime tunc Ebionitarum dogma, qui adserunt Christum ante Mariam non fuisse. (*De Vir. Ill.* 9.)

... ultimus Iohannes apostolus et euangelista, quem Iesus amauit plurimum, qui super pectus Domini, recumbens purissima doctrinarum fluenta potauit, et qui solus de cruce meruit audire: 'Ecce mater tua'; is cum esset in Asia et iam tunc hereticorum semina pullularent Cerinti, Hebionis et ceterorum qui negant Christum in carne uenisse, quos et ipse in epistula sua antichristos uocat et apostolus Paulus requenter percutit, *coactus est ab omnibus paene tunc Asiae episcopis et multarum ecclessiarum legationbus* de diuinitate Saluatoris altius scribere et ad ipsum ut ita dicam Dei uerbum non tam audaci quam felici temeritate prorumpere. Unde et ecclesiastica narrat historia cum *a fratribus cogeretur* ut scriberet, ita facturum se respondisse si indicto ieiunio in commune omnes Dominum precarentur; quo explete reuelatione saturatus in illud proemium caelo ueniens eructauit: 'In principio erat Verbum ...'. (*Praef. Comm. in Matt.*, ll. 39–54.)

All these references agree that John was somehow prevailed upon to write his Gospel although they differ in their depiction of who it was that compelled him. In Clement of Alexandria (*c.* 150–*c.* 215) it was John's γνώριμοι. Lampe suggests a meaning of either 'pupil' or 'disciple' for γνώριμος.[11] Clement used the word elsewhere for the followers of Christ (*Paed.* 1.5) and for the converts of Paul (*Strom.* 7.9.53).[12] Rufinus translated Clement's account in Eusebius with *discipuli* (*HE* 6.14.7). The original intent of the story may well be that converts of John, his pupils and disciples, urged him to write the gospel.

In the account Jerome derives from *ecclesiastica historia* those who urged John were the *fratres* (*Praef. Comm. in Matt.* l. 50).[13] Vagueness as to the identity both of Clement's γνώριμοι and of the *fratres* of *ecclesiastica historia* probably accounts for the later elaboration. With the passage of time the identity of those who

[11] Lampe, 318.

[12] Cf. Justin, *I Apol.* 50.12; Eusebius, *DE* 3.4.

[13] The referent of Jerome's *ecclesiastica historia* is uncertain. If he is referring to a specific work, Eusebius' *Church History* would seem to be the likely choice, but the exact details mentioned by Jerome, like the general fast, are not found in extant editions of Eusebius (cf. *HE* 3.24.11–14, 6.14.7), so that Jerome was either mistaken in his source or quoting very loosely. Bunsen's suggestion (*Analecta Ante-Nicaena*, i. 126) that *ecclesiastica historia* was Hegesippus' 'memoirs' is disputed by Donaldson, 208–10. *Ecclesiastica historia* may simply mean 'a church tradition' in an indefinite way.

urged John to write his gospel became more important, as did the gospel itself. In Jerome's retelling and in Victorinus' story those who urged John are *episcopi*; this introduction of bishops into the tradition is probably a later element. In Victorinus of Pettau (d. *c.* 304) John is 'compelled by the bishops from neighbouring provinces'. Victorinus may have intended these bishops to be identified with those whom John went off to appoint in a tale handed down by Clement of Alexandria (*Quis Dives Salv.* 42) and repeated by Eusebius (*HE* 3.23.5–6). Jerome identified the bishops more specifically as *Asiae episcopi*. Victorinus' and Jerome's accounts are also similar in mentioning, as a factor in John's writing, certain heresies, especially of Cerinthus and Ebion. Jerome knew Victorinus' *Commentary on Revelation*, and his description of the *Asiae episcopi* in the Johannine legend appears to be a clarification of Victorinus' *de finitimis civitatibus episcopi*.

The Fragment named those who urged John to write his gospel as 'condescipulis et eps̃ suis' (l. 10). *Condescipulis* is similar to Clement's γνώριμοι and the *fratres* of the *ecclesiastica historia*, but the inclusion of *episcopi* in the Fragment suggests a later development. This element of the legend would seem to imply that the Fragment's version is later than that in Clement and the *ecclesiastica historia* cited by Jerome.

The second element to be particularly noted in the Johannine legend is the mention of a fast. The procedure of forcing a vision by means of a fast is an ancient one (cf. Apocalypse of Ezra 1.5). Clement of Alexandria remarked that John was 'taken up by the Spirit to God' (πνεύματι θεοφορηθέντα) in the writing of his gospel (Eusebius, *HE* 6.14.7). The introduction into the legend of a fast may represent an attempt to explain the circumstances and occasion of John's 'inspiration'. As such it would represent a later development. The length of the fast in the *ecclesiastica historia* is not recorded by Jerome, nor is there any mention of an intended sharing of revelations by the participants in the fast. These two elaborations found in the Fragment strongly suggest that its version of the legend is later than that of the *ecclesiastica historia*.

While John called for a three-day fast in the Fragment's account, the decisive vision was seen by Andrew in the first night, right at the beginning of the fast. No further visions are recorded, and neither is it known whether John and his companions continued their fast or began immediately to compile their analects. Thus the legend in the Fragment appears defective: the introduction of Andrew's vision interrupts the flow of the story, and is probably an interpolation.

The mention of the apostle Andrew is the third element to be particularly noted in the legend and may be the most revealing because few early traditions about him are known. He appears inconsequentially in a couple of stories in Mark (1:29–31; 13:3–4); however, he is not mentioned when these stories are retold by Matthew (8:14–7, 24:4) and Luke (4:38–41; cf. 21:8–36). None the less, Andrew was included among the twelve apostles in all the synoptic lists (Matt. 10:2–4; Mark 3:16–19; Luke 6:14–16) and also in Acts (1:13). He played a more prominent role in the gospel of John, being portrayed as a follower of John the Baptist, who brought his brother Simon Peter to Jesus (John 1:35–44). At the feeding of the five thousand, it was he who called attention to the boy with five loaves and two fishes (John 6:5–14). Finally, when certain Greeks wished to see Jesus, Philip referred the request to Andrew (John 12:20–34). The association of Andrew with John in the legend of the Muratorian Fragment may be based upon nothing more substantial than the prominence given to Andrew in the gospel of John.

Early legends about Andrew are found almost exclusively in Eastern sources and materials.[14] According to Origen, Andrew's field of labour was Scythia (Eusebius, *HE* 3.1) and stories about him circulated in the East as early as the second century. The Acts of Andrew (Eusebius, *HE* 3.25.6) is dated by W. Schneemelcher between *c.* 120 and *c.* 200.[15] Stories of Andrew are also found in the Gospel of Peter (*c.* 150), the Acts of John (*c.* 150), the Epistle of the Apostles (*c.* 160), Origen, Pistis Sophia, Eusebius, Gregory of Nazianzus, Epiphanius, John Chrysostom, Jerome, and Theodoret of Cyrrhus.[16] The Byzantine Church promoted Andrew as the 'First-Called' of

[14] P. M. Peterson, *Andrew, Brother of Simon Peter: His History and His Legends* (*Novum Testamentum*, suppl. 1; Leiden, 1958), 6–13; cf. F. Dvornik, *The Idea of Apostolicity and the Legend of the Apostle Andrew* (Cambridge, Mass., 1958), 138–299.

[15] M. Hornschuh, 'Acts of Andrew', trans. E. Best, in W. Schneemelcher (ed.), *New Testament Apocrypha*, ii. 396–7.

[16] Peterson, 6–13.

the Apostles (cf. John 1:40–2; also Papias, in Eusebius, *HE* 3.39.4), probably in opposition to Rome's claims concerning Peter (cf. Matt. 16:18–19). In the West, on the other hand, Andrew received little attention until the late fourth century, when he is found, for example, in the Gothic Calendar of Ulphilas, Filaster (d. *c.* 397), Pacian (d. 390), and Evodius of Uzala (d. 424).

The incorporation of Andrew so prominently into the Fragment's legend about John's gospel suggests an Eastern origin. Similarly the introduction of *episcopi* among those who urged John to write his gospel and of a three-day fast as the means of inspiration probably derive from a time after Clement of Alexandria and the *ecclesiastica historia* known to Jerome. Each of these elements is extraordinary within the Fragment if composed in the West at the end of the second century. However, none of these elements would be particularly remarkable if the Fragment were a fourth-century Eastern document.

## THE ACTS OF ALL THE APOSTLES

After the gospels in the Muratorian Fragment, there is a short description of the book of Acts (ll. 34–9).

> Acta autẽ omniu apostolorum
> sub uno libro scribta sunt Lucas obtime theofi
> le conprindit quia sub praesentia eius singula
> gerebantur sicut(e) et semote passionẽ Petri
> euidenter declarat Sed (&) profectionẽ pauli a(d)*b* ur
> be(s) ad spaniã proficescentis

The presence of Acts in a catalogue of the early Church is not surprising, for it appears in almost all known lists of New Testament scripture. There are possible allusions to it in early works, for instance in Clement of Rome, Ignatius, Barnabas, the Didache, the Shepherd, and Polycarp, and more probably in Justin Martyr (150–60).[17] Marcion seems not to have known the work,[18] although the author of the Gospel of Truth (*c.* 180) appears to have been acquainted with it.[19] Irenaeus provides

[17] E. Haenchen, *The Acts of the Apostles: A Commentary* (Oxford, 1971), 3–14.
[18] Knox, *Marcion*, 121.
[19] W. C. van Unnik, in F. L. Cross (ed.), *The Jung Codex* (London, 1955), 122.

the earliest known explicit quotations (e.g. *Adv. Haer.* 3.12–14.2).

If the author of Acts did provide a title for the work, it has not been preserved. Irenaeus quoted from or referred to Acts frequently, but without ever naming it.[20] Tertullian, on the other hand, mentioned the title on numerous occasions.[21] From the beginning of the third century it has been called 'Acts' or 'Acts of the Apostles' by Greek, Latin, and Syriac writers. If the Muratorian Fragment is late second century, its mention of Acts would be the earliest explicit reference extant and the first to provide a title for the work.

The description in the Fragment 'the Acts of *all* the Apostles' (*Acta autẽ omniu apostolorum*, l. 34) is something of an overstatement, since Acts really does not contain a history of 'all' the apostles, but only a few. Some scholars—for example Knox and Campenhausen[22]—believed that such an exaggeration revealed an anti-Marcionite concern for apostolicity. If so, it is perhaps remarkable that the Fragment's title is nowhere paralleled in the anti-Marcionite polemics of any other writer.

The title in the Fragment is similar to Cyril of Jerusalem's description (*c.* 349) of the book as 'The Acts of the Twelve Apostles' (*Catech.* 4.36). Similarly the *Doctrina Addai* (*c.* 390–430) referred to it as 'The Acts of the Twelve Apostles' (p. 44 Phillips). Gregory of Nazianzus listed it in his New Testament catalogue as the 'catholic Acts of the wise apostles' (*Carm.* 12.13) and Amphilochius described it as 'the catholic Acts of the apostles' (*Iambi ad Seleucum* 296–7). Thus there was in the East from the middle of the fourth century a tendency to amplify the title of Acts.

These amplifications may have been in response to the Manichaean collection of five apocryphal Acts, of Paul, Peter, Andrew, Thomas, and John.[23] Photius (*c.* 810–*c.* 895) in his *Bibliotheca* described this collection in some detail and said that it was written by one Leucius Charinus. The Manichaean

[20] Cf. Irenaeus, *Adv. Haer.* 1.23.1 (*bis*); 3.12.1, 2 (*bis*), 3, 4, 5 (*saepe*), 7 (*saepe*), 8 (*bis*), 9 (*saepe*), 10, 13, 14 (*bis*), 15 (*bis*); 3.14.1 (*saepe*), 2; 3.15.1 (*bis*); 4.15.1.

[21] e.g. Tertullian, as 'Acts' in *De Bapt.* 7; *De Resur. Carnis* 23; *Scorp.* 15; *Adv. Praxean* 17; and as 'Acts of the Apostles' in *De Bapt.* 10; *Scorp.* 15; *De Carne Christi* 15; *De Resur. Carnis* 39; *Adv. Praxean* 28; *Praescript.* 1 (*bis*).

[22] Knox, *Marcion*, 160; Campenhausen, 248 n. 214.

[23] M. R. James, *The Apocryphal New Testament* (Oxford, 1924), 228.

Psalter (*c.* 340), preserved in a Coptic translation, reveals knowledge of the Acts of these five apostles.[24] There is also an allusion to these same five apostles by the Manichaean Faustus of Mileve (Augustine, *C. Faust.* 30.4). Filaster of Brescia mentioned Acts of Andrew, John, Peter, and Paul in the hands of the Manichees (*De Haer.* 88.6).[25] And Innocent I rejected writings 'under the names of Peter and John, which were composed by a certain Leucius; and under the name of Andrew, by the philosophers Xenocharides and Leonidas; and under the name of Thomas' (*Ad Exup. Tol.*). The mention of Leucius suggests that apocryphal Acts are in question. The statements of Filaster and Innocent further suggest the use of a collection of apocryphal Acts by the Manichees. There is not much significance in the fact that Filaster and Innocent represented the contents of the collection as different from that presupposed by the Manichaean Psalter and Faustus of Mileve. Filaster's omission of the Acts of Thomas and Innocent's of the Acts of Paul need mean only that they were insufficiently informed.

It seems that the collection described by Photius appeared in the fourth century as a clearly defined corpus of apocryphal Acts in use among the Manichees and substituted by them for the Lucan Acts. K. Schaferdiek concluded with 'the assumption that it was the initiative taken by Manichaean circles that was responsible for uniting within this corpus the Acts which they found and took over, which had been circulating separately or in loose association among Christian sects, and in the case of the Acts of Paul within the Church itself.'[26] This situation may account for the amplifications in describing Acts in Cyril, *Doctrina Addai*, Gregory of Nazianzus, and Amphilochius. Likewise, this situation may account for the description of Acts in the Fragment, if the Fragment is a fourth-century Eastern document. No adequate explanation of the title is given if the Fragment is traditionally dated.

Like Irenaeus, the Fragmentist (ll. 34–5) knew the tradition of Luke's authorship of Acts. Clement of Alexandria (*Strom.* 5.82.4), Tertullian (*Adv. Marc.* 5.2; *Praescript.* 23), and Origen

[24] K. Schaferdiek, 'Second and Third Century Acts of Apostles', in W. Schneemelcher (ed.), *New Testament Apocrypha*, ii. 179–81.

[25] Ibid. 180.

[26] Ibid. 181.

(Eusebius, *HE* 6.25) also knew Luke as its author. Earlier in the Fragment (l. 3) he was identified as a physician (cf. Col. 4.14), a tradition repeated in Irenaeus (*Adv. Haer.* 3.14.1), Eusebius (*HE* 3.4.6), and the so-called Monarchian Prologue to Luke.[27] The Fragment (ll. 4, 35–6) also identified him as a companion of Paul (cf. Philem. 24, 2 Tim. 4.11). Irenaeus portrayed him as an 'inseparable' companion of Paul (*Adv. Haer.* 3.14.1), although elsewhere he (*Adv. Haer.* 3.10.1, 14.2) and the 'Monarchian prologue' portrayed him as a pupil of a number of apostles. The 'we' sections of Acts were probably the source for the tradition in the Fragment (l. 36) that Luke was an eyewitness to the accounts in Acts, a tradition repeated by Eusebius (*HE* 3.4.8).

Parts of the description of Acts in the Fragment, however, relied upon some tradition or traditions in addition to the work itself, since it states that Luke was not present at the passion of Peter and that Paul, without Luke, journeyed to Spain, facts not deducible from Acts alone. There are few early traditions about Luke and no trace of any from independent sources until the third century.[28] The notion in the Fragment, for instance, that Luke (and Mark) were not disciples (*dñm tamen nec Ipse (d)uidit in carne*, ll. 6–7) was repeated by Megethios in the Dialogue of Adamantius called *De Recta in Deum Fide* (*c.* 300). But Adamantius replied that they were in fact two of the seventy disciples (Luke 10:1). The tradition that Paul travelled to Spain, as he himself proposed (Rom. 15:24, 28), which may be hinted at by Clement of Rome (1 Clem. 5:7), was widely accepted in the East from the second half of the fourth century, for instance by Cyril of Jerusalem, Epiphanius, Jerome, and Chrysostom. The Fragmentist's insistence that Luke was absent from the trip to Spain and from Peter's crucifixion suggests that he was familiar with accounts of both. The Acts of Peter, which seems to have come from Syria or Palestine, gave a

[27] This prologue, which used to be assigned to the first half of the 3rd c. (Corssen), is now thought to have been composed at the end of the 4th (Chapman). The so-called anti-Marcionite prologue to Luke, previously dated between 160 and 180 (De Bruyne and Harnack), is now also thought to be much later, either 3rd c. (Heard) or late 4th (Gutwenger); and there are several indications that the 'Monarchian' prologue previously thought dependent upon it (De Bruyne, Harnack, Heard), is really its basis (Gutwenger). It is therefore not considered in this chapter.

[28] Haenchen, 3–14.

detailed account of Paul's departure for Spain, omitting any mention of Luke; it also contains an account of Peter's Passion. C. Schmidt concluded therefore that the Fragmentist knew this work.[29] Origen (Eusebius, *HE* 3.1.2) and Commodian (*Carmen Apol.* 626, 629–30) also related traditions found in it; the Didascalia and the Acts of Paul seem to have actually used it.[30] The sources mentioning it become rather more plentiful in the fourth century,[31] but its use in the Manichaean Psalter probably led to its almost total disappearance thereafter. Thus traditions that relied upon the Acts of Peter are more likely to be fourth-century.

## THE EPISTLE TO THE LAODICEANS

Following the listing of Paul's canonical epistles, the Fragment mentions two letters, one to the Laodiceans and another to the Alexandrians, which the Fragment declared were forged in Paul's name by the Marcionites (ll. 63–8).

> sunt Fertur etiam ad
> Laudecenses alia ad alexandrinos Pauli no
> mine fincte ad he*re*sem marcionis et alia plu
> ra quae In c(h)atholicam eclesiam recepi non
> potest Fel enim cum melle misceri non con
> cruit

This remark in the Fragment about the epistle to the Alexandrians is all that is known about the work. Attempts to identify the reference with Hebrews have been unconvincing.[32] Zahn believed he had found a fragment of Alexandrians in a lesson from an eighth-century sacramentary and lectionary at Bobbio. The lection was headed 'Epistle of Paul the Apostle to the Colossians', but it was not from Colossians or any other known Pauline letter.[33] M. R. James doubted Zahn's con-

[29] C. Schmidt, *Die alten Petrusakten* (TU 24/1; Leipzig, 1903), 105; id., 'Studien zu den alten Petrusakten, II. Die Komposition' (hereafter 'Studien'), *ZKG* 45 (1926), 481–513, at 495. Cf. L. Vouaux, *Les Actes de Pierre: Introduction, textes, traduction et commentaire* (Paris, 1922), 110–11.

[30] Schmidt, *Die alten Petrusakten*, 147; id., 'Studien', 507; Vouaux, 119–20.

[31] Schneemelcher, *New Testament Apocrypha*, ii. 261–2, 265–6.

[32] Hesse, 201–22.

[33] Zahn, *Geschichte*, ii. 586–92.

clusions and suggested further that the word 'fincte' in the Fragment (l. 65) might have applied only to the second letter, that to the Alexandrians, and should be in the singular, leaving the letter to the Laodiceans possibly unrelated to the Marcionites.[34] The evidence of numerous scribal errors may lend credence to such a hypothesis, for there is obviously some corruption in the text. Lightfoot suggested that there is a hiatus after 'Pauli nomine' (ll. 64–5), and that 'fincte' refers to the mutilated epistles of Marcion, and not to the epistles to the Laodiceans or Alexandrians, so that neither of these letters should be considered Marcionite forgeries.[35]

Tertullian reported (*Adv. Marc.* 5.11, 17) that the Marcionites regarded the canonical 'Ephesians' as an epistle to the 'Laodiceans', and that Marcion himself had made the change in the title. The address to the Ephesians in the text (l. 1) is absent in the earliest manuscripts.[36] None the less, the Fragmentist listed the canonical epistle to the Ephesians among the letters of Paul to the seven churches (l. 51). Since both Ephesians and Laodiceans are listed in the Fragment, the Fragmentist must have been either (*a*) confused about Laodiceans, not realizing that the Marcionite Laodiceans was the same as the canonical Ephesians, or else (*b*) aware of a letter to the Laodiceans that was distinct from the canonical Ephesians. Since the Fragmentist listed two separate works, the presumption should be that he knew two different epistles.

The Fragmentist therefore may have been referring to the so-called Latin Epistle to the Laodiceans, if no other pseudo-Pauline epistles to Laodicea are assumed.[37] The Latin Laodiceans, which is found in many biblical manuscripts of the sixth to fifteenth centuries and in early printed editions of the New Testament, consists of only twenty verses, with words and sentences taken from canonical Pauline letters, especially Philippians. A reference to an epistle to the Laodiceans in Colossians (4:16) probably provided the motivation for the obvious forgery. Indeed, in the same way, Marcion or some

[34] James, *The Apocryphal New Testament*, 480, 478.

[35] Lightfoot, *Colossians and Philemon*, 290 n. 1.

[36] Kummel, 248–9.

[37] Harnack, *The Apocryphal Epistles of S. Paul to the Laodiceans and the Corinthians* (hereafter *Apocryphal Epistles*) (Materials for the Use of Theological Lecturers and Students, 12; Cambridge, 1905), 2–6.

contemporary may have been led by this reference to give the title 'Laodiceans' to the probably untitled work which he possessed and which only later became known as 'Ephesians'.

Harnack promoted the hypothesis that the Latin Laodiceans was indeed a Marcionite forgery.[38] He saw the opening verse adapted from Gal. 1:1 as evidence, along with several departures from corresponding verses in Philippians. More recently G. Quispel has propounded the Marcionite character of the Latin Laodiceans.[39] Yet their thesis has not been generally accepted.[40] The Latin Laodiceans is devoid of any apparent purpose, doctrinal or otherwise, to suggest that it is of the Marcionite character that would be expected on the basis of its description in the Fragment. The text is so brief that Schneemelcher concluded 'the Marcionite origin of the Latin Epistle to the Laodiceans is an hypothesis that can neither be proved nor sustained'.[41]

The Marcionites would be unlikely to forge an epistle to the Laodiceans so long as they considered the canonical Ephesians to be a letter to the Laodiceans. The vital question here is when the Marcionites began to accept the title 'Ephesians' for their 'Laodiceans'? Harnack suggested that the Latin Laodiceans was forged by one of Marcion's disciples between 160 and 190, using the Fragment as traditionally dated as the *terminus ad quem*. Yet Tertullian (*c.* 212) declared that the Marcionites still called Ephesians 'Laodiceans' (*Adv. Marc.* 5.11), and he would have certainly mentioned it had the Marcionites known to him referred to any other epistle as 'Laodiceans'. Epiphanius (374–7), however, did list an epistle to the Laodiceans along with one to the Ephesians among the collection of the Marcionites (*Pan.* 42.9.4, 42.12.3). Since both Ephesians and Laodiceans are listed in Epiphanius, he too must have either (*a*) been confused about Laodiceans, not realizing that the Marcionite Laodiceans was the same as the canonical Ephesians, or else (*b*) been

[38] Harnack, *Marcion*, 134–49.

[39] Quispel, 'De Brief aan de Laodicensen een Marcionitische vervalsing', *Nederlands Theologisch Tijdschrift*, 5 (1950), 43–6.

[40] B. Capelle, *Bulletin d'ancienne littérature chrétienne latine, supplément à la Revue Bénédictine*, 1 (1929), no. 283, 103–1; W. J. MacKnight, 'The Letter to the Laodiceans', *The Biblical Review*, 16 (1932), 519–39.

[41] Schneemelcher, *New Testament Apocrypha*, ii. 131.

aware of a letter to the Laodiceans that was distinct from the canonical Ephesians.

The first certain mention of the Latin Laodiceans occurs in the fifth century with a quotation of v. 4 in the pseudo-Augustinian *Speculum* (CSEL 12.516). The earliest manuscript which contains the Latin Laodiceans is the Fuldensis (546–7).[42] However, an epistle to the Laodiceans is referred to earlier both in the East and in the West. Filaster of Brescia (385–91) briefly mentioned an epistle to the Laodiceans in a discussion about Hebrews (*Haer.* 84). Later Gregory the Great (*c.* 595) acknowledged that Paul wrote one more letter than the recognized fourteen (*Moralia* 35.20.48), probably implying the Latin Laodiceans. Haymo of Halberstadt (d. 853), Aelfric abbot of Eynsham (d. 1020), Hervey of Dôle (*c.* 1130), and John of Salisbury (d. 1180) reveal similar support for it.[43] The letter appears to have been generally accepted in the West; it was widely disseminated in Western manuscripts and translated into Western vernaculars.[44]

By contrast, although an epistle to the Laodiceans was known to the Eastern Fathers of the late fourth and fifth centuries, they generally rejected it. It is placed among the collection of the Marcionites by Epiphanius. Jerome, writing from Bethlehem, reported that Laodiceans was read by some people, but rejected by all (*De Vir. Ill.* 5). Theodore of Mopsuestia condemned Laodiceans as spurious (Rab. Maur. *Op.* 6), as did Theodoret. Timotheus, who became Patriarch of Constantinople in 511, included an epistle to the Laodiceans in a list of works forged by the Manichees, whom he may have been confusing with the Marcionites. Several centuries later the Second Council of Nicaea (787) found it necessary to warn people against 'a forged epistle to the Laodiceans' (Act. 6, Tom. 5). Thus, while the epistle is not found in any extant Greek manuscript, an epistle to the Laodiceans was certainly known in the East.

Latin origin is often postulated for Laodiceans because of the absence of a Greek text. Since the epistle is a cento of Pauline passages, one would expect the Latin in that case to have been

[42] The principal MSS containing this epistle are listed in Lightfoot, *Colossians and Philemon*, 280–2.

[43] Lightfoot, ibid. 293–4.

[44] Ibid. 295–7.

taken directly from the Latin versions of Paul's letters. Yet the Latin of Laodiceans differs widely from both the Old Latin and the Vulgate versions.[45] Moreover, there is ample evidence that the work was known to Eastern writers. Lightfoot argued for a Greek original because of its close adherence to Greek idiom. He suggested that the habitual divergences from the Latin versions indicate that the author wrote in Greek and was more familiar with Paul's letters in that language.[46]

A date for the epistle is uncertain. Regardless of whether the original was Latin or Greek, the Latin Laodiceans appears in Western manuscripts from the sixth century. In the fifth century it was quoted by Pseudo-Augustine. From the end of the fourth century it is presumably referred to by a number of writers: Epiphanius, Filaster, Jerome, Theodore of Mopsuestia, Theodoret, and Timotheus. Even if Laodiceans was a Marcionite forgery, there is no evidence of its existence earlier than the late fourth century. The Muratorian Fragment, if it is a late fourth-century Eastern list, would fit in with the other existing evidence, taking its place among other Eastern witnesses, of that time, which rejected the epistle to the Laodiceans. It would particularly parallel the testimony of Epiphanius, who also listed letters to both the Ephesians and Laodiceans. Such a provenance for the Fragment would also remove the question of confusion by the Fragmentist. However, if traditionally dated, the Fragmentist must be seen either as confused, or as providing a unique Western witness for the rejection of the Latin Laodiceans over 150 years before any other extant mention of the work.

## THE WISDOM OF SOLOMON

After mentioning Jude and the epistles of John, the Fragmentist continued his catalogue with the inclusion of the Wisdom of Solomon (ll. 69–71).

> In catholica habentur Et sapi entia ab amicis salomonis in honorē ipsius scripta

[45] Harnack, *Apocryphal Epistles* 4–6.

[46] Lightfoot, *Colossians and Philemon*, 289–90.

The Fragment's mention of the Wisdom of Solomon is remarkable on two accounts: that the Fragmentist apparently denied the Solomonic authorship of Wisdom, and that he included it in a list of New Testament Scriptures.

The Wisdom of Solomon professes King Solomon as its author (7:1–4, 8:17–19:18 recall Solomon's prayer for wisdom in1 Kgs. 3:6–9 and 2 Chron. 1:8–10).[47] The Fragment states that the work was written 'in honour of Solomon', and by his 'friends', or perhaps 'Philo'.[48] Yet the earliest Church Fathers unanimously attributed this oft-quoted work to Solomon, specifically Clement of Alexandria (e.g. *Strom.* 6.93.2), Tertullian (e.g. *Adv. Val.* 2.2), Cyprian (e.g. *Adv. Fort.* 12), Pseudo-Cyprian(s) (e.g. *De Sing. Cler.* 14, 16, 17; *De Mont. Sina et Sion* 7, 13), Pseudo-Hippolytus (e.g. *Adv. Iudaeos* 16, 17–18, 20), Lactantius (e.g. *Epitome* 42), and Cyril (e.g. *Catech.* 9.2).[49] Origen acknowledged that the Wisdom of Solomon was not deemed authoritative by all (*De Princ.* 4.1.33), but the dispute which Origen noted was probably not about the authorship of the work, for Origen himself quoted it frequently as a work of Solomon (e.g. *Contra Celsum* 5.29). The dispute he mentioned was possibly about its absence from the Jewish canon (cf. Eusebius, *HE* 6.25.2).

Augustine, who quoted from Wisdom almost 800 times, is the earliest extant witness to deny that Solomon was the author (*City of God* 17.20). Nevertheless, Augustine acknowledged that the work was Scripture and a part of the Christian canon (*De Praed. Sanct.* 14.26–9; *De Doct. Christ.* 2.13). In *De Doctrina Christiana* Augustine suggested that Ben Sira might have been the author (2.8), a suggestion which he later retracted (*Retract.* 2.4). Jerome in Bethlehem (392) noted in his *Preface to the Books of Solomon* that the style of the work was Greek, not Hebrew, and that some thought Philo was its author. If Tregelles's suggestion for the original Greek at this point in the Fragment's text is correct, then Jerome may have seen the Fragment or derived his information from it. None the less, there is no expressed doubt about the Solomonic authorship of Wisdom

[47] J. Reider, *The Book of Wisdom* (New York, 1957); A. T. S. Goodrick, *The Book of Wisdom* (London, 1913).

[48] Tregelles, 53–5.

[49] C. Larcher, *Études sur le Livre de la Sagesse* (Paris, 1969), 36–46.

until the very end of the fourth century. The Fragment, if traditionally dated, would then be unusual for its claims regarding the authorship of Wisdom. However, redating the Fragment would support and confirm the dispute about authorship in the late fourth century, and could well be the very source of Jerome's information.

The presence of Wisdom in a New Testament catalogue is also particularly remarkable. It is precisely this listing which first attracted Sundberg's attention to the question of the place and date of the Fragment.[50] Sundberg saw in this inclusion evidence that the Old Testament canon was closed at the time of the Fragment. Moreover, he thought this implication was further supported by a later statement in the Fragment: 'And therefore it [the *Shepherd*] ought indeed to be read, but it cannot be read publicly in the Church to the people either among the prophets, *whose number is settled*, or among the apostles to the end of time' (ll. 77–80).

Sundberg understood the phrase 'among the prophets' (*inter profetas*, ll. 78–9) to refer to the Old Testament, and 'among the apostles' (*inter apostolos*, ll. 79–80) to refer to the New Testament. 'Prophets' would hardly refer to apocalypses—the Revelations to John and Peter (ll. 71–2)—since the Fragmentist nowhere named their authors as 'prophets' and no closed collection of apocalypses as such was known in the churches. The suggestion that 'prophets' referred to Montanist prophets also seems unlikely. The context suggests public readings in church (*puplicare uero in eclesia populo*, ll. 77–8), not ecstatic revelations, and such an interpretation would strangely require the qualifier 'whose number is settled' (*conpletum numero*, l. 79) to be applied to Montanist prophets, but not to the apostles. A reference to 'prophets and apostles' was, however, a common designation for the Old Testament and Christian writings in the churches, and the phrase should be interpreted in that way in the Fragment (cf. 2 Clem. 14: 2; Polycarp, *Phil.* 6.3; Justin, *1 Apol.* 76.3; Irenaeus, *Adv. Haer.* 3.19.2, 24.1; Hippolytus, *Comm. Dan.* 4.12.1; Tertullian, *De Pud.* 12.2; Origen, *De Princ.* 4.2.7). The use of the qualifier 'whose number is settled' suggests that the Old Testament canon was closed, but that a

[50] Sundberg, 'Canon Muratori', 15–18.

New Testament canon was not yet established. Such a circumstance may explain the motivation for the Fragmentist's drawing up this list of New Testament works.

Until recently the inclusion of Wisdom in a New Testament catalogue was something of an enigma. This was because it had long been assumed that early Christianity received a closed canon from Judaism, not the Jewish canon *per se*, but a larger collection including the books of the Apocrypha, thought to be the Alexandrian canon of diaspora Judaism. This larger collection included Wisdom, so there was no need to include it in a New Testament list, except perhaps by mistake. However, as Sundberg has demonstrated in his monograph *The Old Testament of the Early Church*, the supposed Alexandrian canon never existed.[51] Consequently it is now understood that the closing of the Old Testament canon within the Church was a longer and more complex process than previously assumed, and so far as our existing information reveals, it would appear that the church in the West was particularly slow in concerning itself with the closing of the Old Testament. When the churches did take up the matter, the Old Testament canon of the Western church usually included Wisdom (e.g. Augustine, *De Doct. Christ.* 2 13; Council of Carthage, canon 26).

In the Eastern church, however, the impact of the closing of the Jewish canon in the late first or early second century was more immediate. This is evidenced in the lists of the Jewish canon drawn up first by Melito and Origen (Eusebius, *HE* 4.26.14, 6.25.2, respectively). In the East, the tendency in the churches was to exclude the books which are now called the Apocrypha from the Old Testament, including Wisdom. Some of these 'deuterocanonical' works were included under titles from the Jewish canon (e.g. Athanasius, *Ep. Fest.* 39.4; Cyril, *Catech.* 4.35; Epiphanius, *Pan.* 1.1.8): the heading of 'Daniel' in many Eastern lists included the Song of the Three Holy Children, the History of Susanna, and the story of Bel and the Dragon, all of which were excluded from the Hebrew Bible. Similarly for the Christians 'Esdras' implied 1 Esdras, Ezra, and Nehemiah; and 'Jeremiah' included Lamentations, Baruch, and the Epistle of Jeremy. Other deuterocanonical

[51] For references, see Introd. n. 1.

works were recommended for secondary reading, or considered with the New Testament writings.

Athanasius (367), for example, excluded Wisdom from his Old Testament catalogue, but included it among a list suitable for the catechumens, along with Sirach, Esther, Judith, Tobit, the Didache, and the Shepherd (*Ep. Fest.* 39). Another Eastern Father, Epiphanius of Salamis, also omitted Wisdom from his Old Testament catalogues but, like the Fragmentist, included it in his New Testament catalogue, along with Sirach (*Pan.* 76). Eusebius, when illustrating Irenaeus' use of scriptures, included a quotation of his from Wisdom along with other passages mentioning Matthew, Mark, Luke, John, Revelation, 1 John, 1 Peter, and the Shepherd (*HE* 5.8.1–8). The association of Wisdom with these New Testament Scriptures appears to have been made by Eusebius, not Irenaeus. Eusebius derived his reference from *Adversus Haereses* (4.38.3), where Irenaeus quoted Wisd. 6: 19 without mentioning the source of the quotation and even without acknowledging that he was quoting written material; nor was Wisdom quoted there by Irenaeus among New Testament Scriptures. Elsewhere (*Adv. Haer.* 2.28.9), Irenaeus may have again alluded to passages from Wisdom (9.13–17) without mentioning his source. Rufinus, perhaps influenced by his time in the East, listed it among his 'ecclesiastical' works (*Comm. in Symb. Apost.* 38). Thus in the fourth century Wisdom, among other works, was excluded from the Old Testament of the churches and was sometimes placed among New Testament Scriptures or accepted as secondary readings, as in Eusebius, Athanasius, Epiphanius, and Rufinus.

According to Sundberg, it is probable that Sirach, Wisdom, Judith, and Tobit were excluded from the Old Testament canon of the Eastern church because they were not a part of the Jewish canon (cf. Eusebius, *HE* 4.26.14; 6.25.2) and could not be included by the process of agglomeration under the titles in the Jewish list.[52] The full impact of the closed Jewish canon upon the formation of a Christian Old Testament does not appear to have become an issue until the fourth century.[53] The inclusion by Epiphanius and Eusebius of

[52] Sundberg, *The Old Testament of the Early Church*, 129–69.

[53] Ibid. 134–60.

Wisdom among New Testament scriptures, like its presence as catechumenate reading in Athanasius, was probably due to a continued interest in the usefulness of this work in the church even though it could not be seen as part of the Jewish canon. Since there are no parallels in the West to the placing of the Wisdom of Solomon among New Testament Scriptures, its presence in the Fragment would seem to suggest an Eastern provenance. Since the Old Testament canon was not an issue for the churches until the fourth century, the book's inclusion in the Fragment would appear to suggest a later date than traditionally given.

## THE REVELATION OF PETER

The Fragment included the Revelations of John and of Peter at the end of its list of canonical books (ll. 71–3). The Fragmentist noted, however, that some people did not want the Revelation of Peter read in Church.

> apocalapse etiam Iohanis et Pe
> tri tantum recip(e)*i*mus quam quidam ex nos
> tris legi In eclesia nolunt

The presence of this work (written *c.* 125–*c.* 150) in the Fragment may be significant in determining the latter's provenance, since there is only the scantiest evidence for its use in the West. The first explicit references to the work there are found in the fourth-century *Homily on the Ten Virgins* (ll. 58–9).[54]

Egypt, whence all the known manuscripts of the Revelation of Peter derive, is its probable place of origin. The text is known primarily from an eighth- or ninth-century Greek fragment discovered in Upper Egypt in 1887 and an Ethiopic translation of the seventh or eighth century found in 1910.[55] Besides these, there are two small Greek fragments: one from the fifth century, which was bought in Egypt in 1894/5, and one from

[54] E. Klostermann, *Apocrypha I: Reste des Petrusevangeliums, der Petrusapokalypse und des Kerygma Petri* (KT 3; Bonn, 1908), 8–16.

[55] For the Greek, cf. J. Armitage Robinson and M. R. James, *The Gospel according to Peter and the Revelation of Peter* (London, 1892), 89–96; for the Ethiopic, cf. S. Grébaut, 'Littérature éthiopienne pseudo-clémentine', *Revue de l'Orient chrétien*, 15 (1910), 198–214, 307–23, 425–39.

a third- or fourth-century manuscript.[56] The oldest surviving quotations of the work come from Clement of Alexandria.

According to Ch. Maurer, all the significant citations of the Revelation of Peter are from Eastern Fathers.[57] Theophilus of Antioch alluded to it (*Ad Autolyc.* 2.19) around 180. Clement of Alexandria appears to have quoted from it in *Eclogae ex Propheticis Scripturis* (41.1), and later, on several other occasions, cited it by name (41.2, 48.1, 49). Methodius of Olympus (d. 311) quoted from ch. 8 (*Symposium* 2.6); Macarius of Magnesia (*c.* 400) quoted once each from chs. 4 and 5 (*Apocriticus* 6, 7). A number of Eastern apocrypha used it, for instance the Epistle of the Apostles (*c.* 150), book 2 of the *Sibylline Oracles* (*c.* 150), the Acts of Paul (*c.* 185), the Acts of Thomas (*c.* 250), and the Revelation of Paul (latter half of the fourth century).[58]

A dispute about the Revelation of Peter is first reflected in the fourth century and solely among Eastern writers. Eusebius noted that Clement of Alexandria in his *Hypotyposes* gave 'abridged accounts of all canonical Scripture [ἐνδιαθήκου γραφῆς], not omitting the disputed (ἀντιλεγομένας) books—I refer to Jude and the other catholic epistles, and Barnabas and to the so-called Revelation of Peter' (*HE* 6.14.1). The description of the Revelation of Peter as a 'disputed' work reflected Eusebius' judgement, not Clement's. Clement clearly considered the book to be Scripture (*Eclog. Proph.* 41.1) and the author to be Peter (41.2, 48.1, 49). Methodius too reckoned it among the inspired (θεόπνευστοι) writings (*Symposium* 2.6). The catalogue in the Codex Claramontanus accepted it among the books of the New Testament.[59] The list is believed to be Eastern, possibly Alexandrian, and dated perhaps in the second quarter of the fourth century. It will be recalled, however, that the scribe placed a horizontal line before Barnabas, the Shepherd, the Acts of Paul, and the Revelation of Peter, perhaps indicating some reservation about these works. Nevertheless, the fact that the Revelation of Peter was listed in the

[56] James, 'The Rainer Fragment of the Apocalypse of Peter', *JTS* 32 (1931), 270–9, at 278.

[57] Ch. Maurer, 'Apocalypse of Peter', trans. D. Hill, in W. Schneemelcher (ed.), *New Testament Apocrypha* ii. 663–83, at 684.

[58] M. S. Enslin, 'Apocalypse of Peter', *IDB* iii (New York, 1962), 758.

[59] Zahn, *Geschichte*, ii. 159.

Codex Claromontanus even with a scribal mark and that Clement and Methodius considered the work inspired Scripture suggests that any dispute about the work was only just beginning.

In one place Eusebius completely rejected the Revelation of Peter along with the Acts of Peter, the Gospel of Peter, and the Preaching of Peter, noting that 'no ecclesiastical writer of the ancient time or of our own has used their testimonies' (*HE* 3.3.2). Yet this was certainly an overstatement on the part of Eusebius, for elsewhere he reported that Clement of Alexandria commented on the Revelation of Peter (*HE* 6.14.1). Moreover, in Eusebius' own listing of canonical Scriptures, the Revelation of Peter appeared among the 'spurious' (νόθοι) works along with the Acts of Paul, the Shepherd, Barnabas, the Didache, and perhaps Revelation and the Gospel according to the Hebrews (*HE* 3.25.4–5), not among the heretical works which followed (namely the gospels of Peter, Thomas, and Matthias, or the Acts of Andrew, John, and the other apostles), 'which no one belonging to the succession of ecclesiastical writers has deemed worthy of mention in his writings' (*HE* 3.25.7).

Jerome, after he moved East, in 392 wrote his *De Viris Illustribus sive de Scriptoribus Ecclesiasticis*. In the very first chapter, having noted the acknowledged writings of Peter, he went on to list books attributed to Peter but rejected; and among them is included the Revelation of Peter. Jerome's list is similar to Eusebius', and it is perhaps likely that Jerome became acquainted with the Revelation of Peter in Palestine. Despite the rejections by Eusebius and Jerome, Sozomen (439–50) reported that it was being read in his day in some of the churches in Palestine on the Day of Preparation (*Hist.* 7.19). The references to the work in Macarius of Magnesia's *Apocriticus* (6, 7) might also suggest continued use of the work by Christians in Palestine (*c.*400).[60] The Stichometry of Nicephorus (*c.*850) listed the Revelation of Peter among the 'antilegomena' along with Revelation, Barnabas, and Gospel according to the Hebrews (ll. 44–8). These works were distinguished from the 'apocrypha' of the New Testament (ll. 62–70), which included the travels of Peter, John, and Thomas, the

[60] T. W. Crafer, *The Apocriticus of Macarius Magnes* (London, 1919), 129–30, cf. p. xxv.

Gospel of Thomas, Didache, 1 and 2 Clement, Ignatius, Polycarp, and the Shepherd.

The surviving evidence clearly shows that the Revelation of Peter circulated primarily in the Eastern church, witnesses to it being especially concentrated in Syria and Palestine: for example, Theophilus of Antioch, Methodius of Tyre,[61] Eusebius in Caesarea, the Stichometry of Nicephorus in Jerusalem, Macarius in Syria,[62] Jerome in Bethlehem, and Sozomen, a native of Bethelia in Palestine (exceptions are Clement of Alexandria and the probably Alexandrian catalogue in the Codex Claromontanus). A dispute about the work does not appear until the fourth century; the earlier Eastern Fathers who quoted it, such as Theophilus, Clement of Alexandria, and Methodius, indicate no doubts concerning its authority. Reservations about the work are reflected in the scribal mark in the catalogue of the Codex Claromontanus and in the writings of Eusebius, Jerome, and perhaps Macarius. Though rejected by some in the fourth century, the book was favoured by others, as is shown by Methodius and Sozomen. It is in the fourth century, then, that the reservations mentioned in the Fragment would find the strongest parallel. On the other hand, there is almost no evidence to support Western second-century doubts about (or approval of) the work, as would be suggested by the Fragment as traditionally dated.

## THE CATALOGUE OF HERESIES

The concluding lines of the Fragment (ll. 81–5) break off abruptly, after which a little more than half a line is left vacant. The next line in the Codex Muratorianus begins with a passage from Ambrose, so that any possible defect at the end of the Fragment does not arise from mutilation of the manuscript. Excerpts from the Fragment in the Benedictine texts (ll. 33–7) include the last lines of the Fragment, but add nothing.

The concluding lines appear to refer to works which were

[61] Jerome asserted that Methodius was bishop of Tyre (*De Vir. Illus.* 83), as did Sozomen (*HE* 6.13).

[62] Crafer, op. cit., pp. xix–xxiii, demonstrated that Macarius was from Syria; cf. id., 'Macarius Magnes. A Neglected Apologist', *JTS* 8 (1907), 401–23, at 401–6.

entirely rejected, as contrasted with the Revelation of Peter, whose public reading some objected to (ll. 72–3), and the Shepherd of Hermas, which ought only to be read privately (ll. 77–8). Westcott wrote of these lines: 'The conclusion is hopelessly corrupt, and evidently was so in the copy from which the Fragment was derived.'[63]

> Arsinoi autem seu ualentini uel mitiad(ei)*i*s
> nihil In totum recipemus. Qui etiam nouũ
> psalmorum librum marcioni conscripse
> runt una cum basilide assianum catafry
> cum conſtitutorem

Miltiades is the presumed referent of 'mitiad(ei)*i*s' (l. 81) in the Fragment (cf. *Mitiadis* CC[1], *Mi(ti)adis* C[2], *Mitididis* C[3]). An anonymous writer quoted in Eusebius mentioned a certain 'Miltiades' in the company of Justin, Tatian, and Clement as among the writers who, before Victor's episcopate, had written 'in behalf of truth against the heathen, and against the heresies which existed in their day' (*HE* 5.28.4). Tertullian also named a Miltiades in the company of Justin, Irenaeus, and one Proculus, as a writer against heresy (*Adv. Val.* 5). Eusebius himself mentioned Miltiades as the author of a work against the Montanists, another against the Greeks, another against the Jews and an 'Apology' addressed to 'the earthly rulers' (*HE* 5.17.1–5). Jerome twice mentions Miltiades (*De Vir. Ill.* 39; *Ep. ad Magnum*), but provides no further information.

In ch. 17 of Eusebius' *Church History* there is some confusion about Miltiades (*HE* 5.17.1). Eusebius here continues to quote a series of extracts from an anonymous anti-Montanist writer which he had begun in ch. 16. Eusebius notes, 'In this [unnamed] work he [the anonymous anti-Montanist author] mentions a writer, Miltiades, stating that he also wrote a certain book against the above-mentioned heresy [Montanism]' (*HE* 5.17.1), and then proceeds to quote the reference. The reference, however, names 'Alcibiades' as the author of the anti-Montanist work, not 'Miltiades' (*HE* 5.17.1). All the manuscripts and versions unanimously testify to 'Alcibiades', and not 'Miltiades', although most editors have thought it necessary to change the reference to Miltiades to make

[63] Westcott, *Canon of the New Testament*, 530 n. 8.

Eusebius consistent with himself.[64] Immediately after the extracts from the anonymous anti-Montanist writer, Eusebius notes, 'But the Miltiades to whom he [the anonymous anti-Montanist writer] refers has left other monuments of his own zeal for the Divine Scriptures' (*HE* 5.17.5), which Eusebius then lists. Eusebius seems to have mistakenly named Alcibiades in his text where the anti-Montanist author had apparently written, and Eusebius had read, Miltiades.

Earlier in the *Church History* (*HE* 5.3.2–4), Eusebius did mention an Alcibiades, a prominent *follower* of Montanus, who along with one Theodotus was widely received because of the many miracles associated with them. A Montanist Theodotus is also mentioned near the end of ch. 16 (*HE* 5.16.14–5), and this association may account for Eusebius' confusion at the beginning of ch. 17. This confusion is perhaps confirmed at the beginning of ch. 16 (*HE* 5.16.3), where Eusebius records within the context of opponents of the Phrygian heresy an anonymous author who mentions writing 'a treatise against the heresy of those who are called after *Miltiades*'. It seems likely that there has been a confusion of persons, unless one assumes two Miltiadae are mentioned in consecutive chapters, one an anti-Montanist (*HE* 5.17.1) and one a Montanist (*HE* 5.16.3). To leave the texts uncorrected would also suggest two Alcibiadae, one a Montanist (*HE* 5.3.2–4) and the other an anti-Montanist writer (*HE* 5.17.1).

There is no explicit evidence for a Montanist named Miltiades to support Eusebius' reference in ch. 16 (*HE* 5.16.3). Tertullian, as noted, mentioned a Miltiades (*Adv. Val.* 5), even giving him the appellation *Sophista Ecclesiarum*, evidently intended in a commendatory sense. But Tertullian's favourable mention is not enough to suggest that he was a Montanist, for Tertullian was equally commendatory in this passage of Justin and Irenaeus. In the confusing last lines of the Muratorian Fragment a Miltiades is apparently named in connection with Marcion, Arsinous, Valentinus, Basilides, and the 'Cataphrygians'. Yet this passage is so corrupt that it cannot count for direct support of a Montanist Miltiades. Rather it would seem more likely that Eusebius, or his copyists, simply con-

[64] H. J. Lawlor and J. E. L. Oulton, *Eusebius*, ii: *Introduction, Notes, and Index* (London, 1928), 175–6.

# 6

# REDATING THE FRAGMENT

THERE is clearly a strong case for proposing that the Fragment is an Eastern list of New Testament works originating from the fourth century. This provenance is supported by many details.

Eusebius appears to be the individual within the history of the Canon who developed and prompted New Testament catalogues, and thus the Fragment most probably derives from some time after Eusebius. And if the Fragment's mention of Miltiades is dependent, as suggested, upon a copyist's error in Eusebius' *Church History*, that points to the same conclusion. Thus Eusebius' *Church History* (*c.* 303–24) can reasonably be suggested as the *terminus a quo* for the Fragment. If Jerome's ascription of the authorship of the Wisdom of Solomon is dependent, as suggested, upon the Fragment's supposed original Greek, then Jerome's *Lives of Illustrious Men* (392) would be the *terminus ad quem*. Thus the Fragment would need to be dated between 303 and 392.

The supposed Greek original would require the Fragment, if dated during this period, to be Eastern in origin. The Fragment is found in a Codex in which over two-thirds of the attributable contents are known to be of Eastern derivation (85 pages out of 121), and all the attributable contents are known to be fourth- or fifth-century. An Eastern origin for the Fragment is also supported by its ordering of the gospels and its interpolation of a legend about Andrew. Yet further support for a fourth-century date is provided by the introduction of *episcopi* into the legend about the origin of John's gospel. An Eastern fourth-century provenance is still further supported by the Fragment's description of Acts and its consideration of the Shepherd as a secondary work suitable for private reading, but not for public use. The inclusion of the Wisdom of Solomon among New Testament works, as in Eusebius and Epiphanius, also suggests an Eastern fourth-century provenance, reflecting the

Eastern churches' inhibitions at that time about using works excluded from the Jewish canon. The inclusion of the Revelation of Peter clearly suggests an Eastern origin for the Fragment, and the mention of dispute about its use would suggest a fourth-century date.

While Sundberg argued that the Fragment was early fourth-century, a later date may be preferable for a number of reasons. The Fragment's denial of Solomonic authorship for Wisdom, as in Jerome and Augustine, and the apparent mention (and rejection) of the Latin Laodiceans, as in Epiphanius, Filaster, Jerome and Theodore of Mopsuestia, are both unparalleled until late in the fourth century. Similarly, the introduction of the term 'Cataphrygians' might suggest an Eastern source and a date in the second half of the fourth century; so Cyril, Athanasius, and Epiphanius, as might the mention of a Marcionite Psalter as in Maruta. The Fragment's inclusion of the scheme of Pauline letters to seven churches is also not found in writers in the East until this time, such as Jerome and Amphilochius, and may explain the omission of Hebrews.

If the Fragment's association of Pius I and Hermas is dependent, as suggested, upon the Liberian Catalogue, then the Fragment would have to be dated in the second half of the fourth century. There were frequent travellers between the West and the East by which the tradition might have passed. Liberius himself was exiled to Beroea (Thracia) for several years (355–8). The presence of Revelation in the Fragment might discourage a date in the last two decades of the fourth century, for Eastern catalogues of that time generally omit mention of it (the Apostolic Canons, Gregory of Nazianzus, the Syrian Catalogue, and the Peshitta), or else declare it spurious (so Amphilochius). Revelation is, however, present without comment in the Codex Alexandrinus (*c.*425). While reservations about Revelation are apparent earlier (as in Eusebius), and the work is omitted by Cyril, it is listed without distinction in the Alexandrian catalogue of the Codex Claromontanus, Athanasius, Epiphanius, and Jerome. Thus a date for the Fragment of *c.*375 is early enough to include Revelation without explanation, but late enough to employ the term 'Cataphrygians', to deny Solomonic authorship for Wisdom, to mention the Latin Laodiceans and the Marcionite Psalter, to note in the East the seven-church scheme for Pauline letters, and to be informed by the Liberian Catalogue. A slightly later date would also be possible.

Sundberg argued for a Syrian/Palestinian provenance for the Fragment primarily on the grounds of its inclusion of the Revelation of Peter and parallels with Eusebius. Alexandria/Egypt would seem an unlikely source, since the Fragment omits Hebrews and employs the seven-churches scheme, also found in Jerome and Amphilochius. The Fragment's inclusion of the Shepherd and the Revelation of Peter, without mention of Barnabas, the Didache, or the Acts of Paul, also discourage locating the Fragment in Alexandria/Egypt, for even in the second half of the fourth century the Didache, Barnabas, or the Acts of Paul were sometimes included in Alexandria among New Testament Scriptures. Their absence in the Fragment suggests a different provenance.

An interest in New Testament catalogues is not apparent in Asia Minor until very late in the fourth century. Moreover, the catalogues, when they do appear in Gregory of Nazianzus and Amphilochius, are noted primarily for their rejection of Revelation, which the Fragment includes. Amphilochius noted that some maintain Hebrews to be spurious, which may explain why it is absent in the Fragment; but again Jerome in Bethlehem also noted that Hebrews is not generally counted in with the others. Thus there is no strong case for an origin of the Fragment in Asia Minor either.

Several remarkable parallels with Epiphanius would seem to confirm a Syrian/Palestinian provenance around 375 for the Fragment, specifically the inclusion of the Wisdom of Solomon in a New Testament catalogue, the mention of a Marcionite Laodiceans (in addition to the canonical Ephesians), and the presence of Revelation without comment. These, combined with the public reading of the Revelation of Peter noted in the Fragment and Sozomen, and various similarities with Jerome (392), namely the seven-letter Pauline scheme, Philo as the author of Wisdom, a rejection of Laodiceans, the inclusion of Revelation, and doubts about Hebrews, would seem to confirm that the Muratorian Fragment is not a Western late second-century document, but is instead a late fourth-century Eastern catalogue, probably deriving from Western Syria or Palestine.

Redating the Fragment removes it as an anomaly in the formation of the New Testament. The early development of the Christian canon can be seen to be a gradual accumulation of valued writings to complement the inherited collection of Jewish scriptures. The Fourfold Gospel is the only subcanon that appears closed before the fourth century. The other New Testament collections, namely of Pauline letters and catholic epistles, seem to have gone through a process of expansion and adjustment lasting into the fourth century. It was only at that time that they, along with the Old Testament canon, were finally established for the churches. Thus the decisive period in the formation of the Christian Canon is to be located in the fourth century. It is at that time that the Church appropriated the word 'canon' to describe its collection of sacred writings, and that the earliest extant manuscripts of the whole Christian Bible are dated. And it is also at that time that fifteen catalogues of the Christian Canon appear in various churches. The redated Muratorian Fragment should find its place among these.

# BIBLIOGRAPHY


ALLBERRY, C. R. C. (ed.) *Manichaean Manuscripts in the Chester Beatty Collection*, II: *A Manichaean Psalm-Book, Part II* (Stuttgart, 1938).

ALTANER, B., *Patrology*, trans. H. C. Graef (London, 1960).

ANDERSON, C. P., 'The Epistle to the Hebrews and the Pauline Letter Collection', *HTR* 59 (1966), 429–38.

ANDRY, C. F., 'Barnabae Epist. ver. DCCCL', *JBL* 70 (1951), 233–8.

AUDOLLENT, A., *Defixionum Tabellae* (Paris, 1904).

BABUT, E. Ch., *Priscillien et le priscillianisme* (Bibliothèque de l'École des hautes études, 169; Paris, 1909).

BARDENHEWER, O., *Patrology: The Lives and Works of the Fathers of the Church*, trans. T. S. Shahan (Freiburg i. B., 1908).

BARMBY, J., 'Pius I', *DCB* iv (London, 1887), 416–17.

BARNARD, L. W., 'The Shepherd of Hermas in Recent Study', *HeyJ* 9 (1968), 29–36.

BARNES, T. D., *Constantine and Eusebius* (London, 1981).

BARNETT, A. E., *Paul Becomes a Literary Influence* (Chicago, 1941).

BARTLET, V., 'Melito the Author of the Muratorian Canon', *The Expositor*, 7th ser., 2 (1906), 210–24.

BAUCKHAM, R. J., 'The Great Tribulation in The Shepherd of Hermas', *JTS*, NS 25 (1974), 27–40.

BAUER, A., *Die Chronik des Hippolytos im Matritensis graecus 121* (TU 29. 1; Leipzig, 1905).

BAUER, F. Ch., 'Bemerkungen über die Bedeutung des Wortes *Κανών*', *ZWT* 1 (1858), 141–50.

BAUR, C., *John Chrysostom and His Time*, trans. M. Gonzaga, 2 vols. (1959–60).

BECKWITH, R., *The Old Testament Canon of the New Testament Church and its Background in Early Judaism* (London, 1985).

BEUMER, JOHANNES VON, 'Das Fragmentum Muratori und seine Rätsel', *Theologie und Philosophie*, 48 (1973), 534–50.

BEYER, H. W., *Κανών*, *TDNT*, ed. G. Kittel, trans. G. W. Bromiley, iii (1965), 596–602.

BIGG, C., *The Origins of Christianity*, ed. T. B. Strong (Oxford, 1909).

BLACK, M., 'Rabbula of Edessa and the Peshitta', *BJRL* 33 (1950–1), 203–10.

—— *An Aramaic Approach to the Gospels and Acts* (Oxford, 1946).

BLACKMAN, E. C., *Marcion and His Influence* (London, 1948).

BLAISE, A., *Dictionnaire latin-français des auteurs chrétiens* (Turnhout, 1954).

BLEEK, F., 'Ueber die Stellung der Aprokryphen des Alten Testamentes im christlichen Kanon', *Theologische Studien und Kritiken*, 26 (1853), 268–354.

—— An Introduction to the New Testament, trans. W. Urwick, 2 vols. (London, 1869).

BONE, K. G., *Περὶ τῆς μητρὸς τῆς ἁγίας Ὀλυμπιάδος*, *Studi bizantini e neoellenici*, 8. 2 (1953), 3–10.

BONNER, C., *A Papyrus Codex of the Shepherd of Hermas* (Ann Arbor, Mich., 1934).

BONNET, M., *Le latin de Grégoire de Tours* (Paris, 1890).

BONWETSCH, N., 'Hippolytisches', *Nachrichten von der Königlichen Gesellschaft der Wissenschaften zu Göttingen* (Berlin, 1924), pt. 1, 27–32.

—— 'Nachtrag zu dem Aufsatz "Hippolytisches"', *Nachrichten von der Königlichen Gesellschaft der Wissenschaften zu Göttingen*, pt. 2 (Berlin, 1924), 63–4.

BOX, G. H., *The Ezra-Apocalypse, Being Chapters 3–14 of the Book Commonly Known as 4 Ezras (or II Esdras)* (London, 1912).

BRANDES, W., 'Zwei Victoringedichte des Vatic. Regin. 582 und das Carmen adversus Marcionitas', *Wiener Studien*, 12 (1890), 310–16.

BROOKE, A. E., *A Critical and Exegetical Commentary on the Johannine Epistles* (Edinburgh, 1912).

BROWN, R. E., *The Epistles of John* (New York, 1982).

BUCHANAN, E. S., 'The Codex Muratorianus', *JTS* 9 (1907), 537–45.

BUCK, C., 'The Early Order of the Pauline Corpus', *JBL* 68 (1949), 351–7.

BUCKLEY, E. R., 'Justin Martyr's Quotations from the Synoptic Tradition', *JTS* 36 (1935), 173–6.

BUNSEN, C., *Analecta Ante-Nicaena*, 3 vols. (London, 1854).

BURKITT, F. C., *S. Ephraim's Quotations from the Gospel* (TxSt 7. 2, Cambridge, 1901).

—— *Evangelion da-Mepharreshe*, 2 vols. (Cambridge, 1904).

—— 'Tatian's Harmony and the Dutch Harmonies', *JTS* 25 (1923–4), 113–30.

—— *Religion of the Manichees* (Cambridge, 1925).

—— 'The Dura Fragment of Tatian', *JTS* 36 (1935), 255–9.

CAMPENHAUSEN, H. VON, *The Formation of the Christian Bible*, trans. J. A. Baker (Philadelphia, 1972).

CAMPOS, J., 'Época del Fragmento Muratoriano', *Helmantica: Revista de Humanidades Clásicas*, 11 (1960), 485–96.

CAPELLE, B., *Bulletin d'ancienne littérature chrétienne latine, supplément à la Revue Bénédictine*, 1 (1924), 130–1, no. 283.

CARNOY, A., *Le Latin d'Espagne d'après les inscriptions* (Louvain, 1902).
CARROLL, K. L., 'The Expansion of the Pauline Corpus', *JBL* 72 (1953), 230–7.
—— 'The Creation of the Fourfold Gospel', *BJRL* 37 (1954–5), 68–77.
CASEY, R., 'The Armenian Marcionites and the Diatessaron', *JBL* 57 (1938), 185–94.
CASPAR, E., *Die älteste römische Bischofsliste* (Berlin, 1926).
CHADWICK, H., 'The New Edition of Hermas', *JTS*, NS 8 (1957), 274–80.
CHAPMAN, J., 'Clément d'Alexandrie sur les Évangiles, et encore le Fragment de Muratori', *RBén* 21 (1904), 369–74.
—— *Notes on the Early History of the Vulgate Gospels* (Oxford, 1908).
—— 'On the Decretum Gelasianum de libris recipiendis et non recipiendis', *RBén* 30 (1913), 187–207, 315–33.
CHARLESWORTH, J., 'Tatian's Dependence upon Apocryphal Traditions', *HeyJ* 15 (1974), 5–17.
CHARTERIS, A. H., *Canonicity: A Collection of Early Testimonies to the Canonical Books of the New Testament* (Edinburgh, 1880).
CHILDS, B., *Introduction to the Old Testament as Scripture* (London, 1979).
COLEBURNE, W., 'A Linguistic Approach to the Problem of Structure and Composition of *The Shepherd of Hermas*', *ANZTR* 3 (1969), 133–42.
—— '*The Shepherd of Hermas*: Case for Multiple Authorship and Some Implications', *StudPat* 10/1 (1970), 65–70.
COLLINS, R., *Introduction to the New Testament* (London, 1983).
CORSSEN, P., *Monarchianische Prologe zu den vier Evangelien* (TU 15/1; Leipzig, 1896).
—— 'Zur Überlieferungsgeschichte des Römerbriefes', *ZNW* 10 (1909), 1–45, 97–102.
COZZA-LUZI, J., *Novum Testamentum e Codice Vaticano 1209 Nativi Textus Graeci primo omnium phototypice Repraesentatum* (Rome, 1889).
CRAFER, T. W., 'Marcarius Magnes, A Neglected Apologist', *JTS* 8 (1907), 401–23.
—— *The Aprocriticus of Macarius Magnes* (London, 1919).
CREDNER, K. A., *Zur Geschichte des Kanons* (Halle, 1847).
—— *Geschichte des neutestamentlichen Kanons*, ed. G. Volkmar (Berlin, 1860).
CROSS, F. L., 'The Priscillianist Prologues', *Expository Times*, 48 (1936–7), 188–9.
CURETON, W., *Remains of a Very Ancient Recension of the Four Gospels in Syriac* (London, 1858).

DAHL, N. A., 'Welche Ordnung der Paulusbriefe wird vom Muratorischen Kanon vorausgesetzt?', *ZNW* 52 (1961), 39–53.

—— 'The Particularity of the Pauline Epistles as a Problem in the Ancient Church', in *Neotestamentica et Patristica* (*Novum Testamentum*, suppl. 7; Leiden, 1962), 261–71.

—— 'The Origin of the Earliest Prologues to the Pauline Letters', *Semeia*, 12 (1978), 233–77.

DANIÉLOU, J., *Origen*, trans. W. Mitchell (London, 1955).

DE BRUYNE, D., 'Prologues bibliques d'origine marcionite', *RBén* 24 (1907), 1–16.

—— 'Les plus anciens prologues latins des Evangiles', *RBén* 40 (1928), 193–214.

DIBELIUS, M., *Der Hirt des Hermas* (Tübingen, 1923).

DI BERARDINO, A. (ed.) *Patrology*, Vol. 4, trans. P. Solari (Westminster, Md., 1986).

DOBSCHÜTZ, E. von, *Das Decretum Gelasianum* (Leipzig, 1912).

DONALDSON, J., *A Critical History of Christian Literature and Doctrine from the Death of the Apostles to the Nicene Council*, 3 vols. (London, 1866).

DUCHESNE, L., *Le Liber Pontificalis*, 2 vols. (Paris, 1886–92).

DVORNIK, F., *The Idea of Apostolicity and the Legend of the Apostle Andrew* (Cambridge, Mass., 1958).

EHRHARDT, A. A. T., 'The Gospels in the Muratorian Fragment', *Ostkirchliche Studien*, 2 (1953), 121–38.

EHRMAN, B. D., 'The New Testament Canon of Didymus the Blind', *VC* 37 (1983), 1–21.

ENSLIN, M. S., 'Apocalypse of Peter', *IDB* iii (New York, 1962), 758.

ERBES, C., 'Die Zeit des Muratorischen Fragments', *ZKG* 35 (1914), 331–62.

FABRICIUS, G., *Poetarum Veterum Ecclesiasticorum Opera Christiana* (Basle, 1564).

FARKASFALVY, D. M., 'The Ecclesial Setting of Pseudepigraphy in Second Peter and Its Role in the Formation of the Canon', *The Second Century*, 5 (1985–6), 3–29.

FARMER, W. R., and FARKASFALVY, D. M., *The Formation of the New Testament Canon* (New York, 1983).

FERGUSON, E., 'Canon Muratori: Date and Provenance', *StudPat* 17/2 (Oxford, 1982), 677–83.

FIGGIM, C., 'Agrippino o Callisto?', *Scuola cattolica*, 6/3 (1924), 204–11.

FINEGAN, J., 'The Original Form of the Pauline Corpus', *HTR* 49 (1956), 85–103.

FRANK, I., *Der Sinn der Kanonbildung. Eine historisch-theologische Unter-*

*suchung der Zeit vom I. Clemensbrief bis Irenaeus von Lyon* (Freiburger Theologische Studien, 90; Freiburg i. B., 1971).

FREDE, H. J., *Altlateinische Paulus-Handschriften* (Vetus Latina; Freiburg i. B., 1964).

—— *Epistula ad Colossenses* (Vetus Latina; Freiburg i. B., 1969).

FREND, W. H. C., *Martyrdom and Persecution in the Early Church: A Study of a Conflict from the Maccabees to Donatus* (Oxford, 1965).

FULLER, R. H., *A Critical Introduction to the New Testament* (Letchworth, 1971).

FUNK, F. X., *Didascalia et Constitutiones Apostolorum*, i (Paderborn, 1906).

GAAB, G., *Der Hirt des Hermas* (Basle, 1866).

GAMBLE, H. Y., 'The Redaction of the Pauline Letters and the Formation of the Pauline Corpus', *JBL* 94 (1975), 403–18.

—— *The Textual History of the Letters to the Romans* (Studies and Documents, 42; Grand Rapids, Mich., 1977).

—— *The New Testament Canon: Its Making and Meaning* (Philadelphia, 1985).

GIET, S., *Hermas et les Pasteurs: Les trois auteurs du Pasteur d'Hermas* (Paris, 1963).

GOODRICK, A. T. S., *The Book of Wisdom* (London, 1913).

GOODSPEED, E. J., *The Formation of the New Testament* (Chicago, 1926).

—— *New Solutions of New Testament Problems* (Chicago, 1927).

—— *The Meaning of Ephesians* (Chicago, 1933).

—— *An Introduction to the New Testament* (Chicago, 1937).

—— 'Ephesians and the First Edition of Paul', *JBL* 70 (1951), 285–91.

—— 'Phoebe's Letter of Introduction', *HTR* 44 (1951), 55–7.

GRANT, R. M., 'The Fourth Gospel and the Church', *HTR* 35 (1942), 95–116.

—— *The Earliest Lives of Jesus* (New York, 1961).

—— *The Formation of the New Testament* (London, 1965).

—— *Eusebius as Church Historian* (Oxford, 1980).

GRÉBAUT, S., 'Littérature éthiopienne pseudo-clémentine', *Revue de l'Orient chrétien*, 15 (1910), 198–214, 307–23, 425–39.

GROSHEIDE, F. W., *Some Early Lists of the Books of the New Testament* (Textus Minores, 1; Leiden, 1948).

GUTWENGER, E., 'The Anti-Marcionite Prologues', *TSt* 7 (1946), 393–409.

GWATKIN, H. M., *Early Church History to AD 313*, 2 vols. (London, 1909).

GWILLIAM, G. H., 'The Materials for the Criticism of the Peshitto

New Testament, with Specimens of the Syriac Massorah', *StudBib* 3 (1891), 47–104.

GWYNN, J., 'Hippolytus and his "Heads against Caius"', *Hermathena*, 6 (1886–8), 397–418.

HAENCHEN, E., *The Acts of the Apostles: A Commentary* (Oxford, 1971).

HAHN, A. (ed.) *Bibliothek der Symbole und Glaubensregeln der alten Kirche* (Breslau, 1897).

HANSON, A. T., *The Pastoral Epistles* (London, 1982).

HANSON, R. P. C., *Origen's Doctrine of Tradition* (London, 1954).

HARNACK, A., 'Geschichte der marcionitischen Kirchen', *ZWT* 19 (1875), 115–20.

—— *Hermae Pastor Graece, Addita Versione Latina Recentiore e Codice Palatino* (Leipzig, 1877).

—— *Der pseudocyprianische Tractat de Aleatoribus* (TU 5/1; Leipzig, 1889).

—— 'Excerpte aus dem Muratorischen Fragment (saec. xi et xii)', *Theologische Literaturzeitung*, 23 (1898), 131–4.

—— *The Apocryphal Epistles of St Paul to the Laodiceans and the Corinthians* (Materials for the Use of the Theological Lecturers and Students, 12; Cambridge, 1905).

—— 'Miltiades', *The New Schaff–Herzog Encyclopedia of Religious Knowledge*, ed. S. M. Jackson, xii (London, 1910), 381–2.

—— *Marcion: Das Evangelium vom fremden Gott* (TU 45; Leipzig, 1921).

—— 'Über den Verfasser und den literarischen Charakter des Muratorischen Fragments', *ZNW* 24 (1925), 1–16.

—— *The Origin of the New Testament and the most Important Consequences of the New Creation*, trans. J. R. Wilkinson (London, 1925).

—— 'Der marcionistische Ursprung der ältesten Vulgata-Prologe zu den Paulusbriefen', *ZNW* 24 (1925), 204–17.

—— 'Die Marcionitischen Prologe zu den Paulusbriefen, eine Quelle des Muratorischen Fragments', *ZNW* 25 (1926), 160–2.

—— 'Die ältesten Evangelien-Prologe und die Bildung des Neuen Testamentes', *Sitzungsberichte der Preußichen Akademie der Wissenschaft, phil.-hist. Klasse*, 24 (1928), 322–41.

—— *Studien zur Geschichte des Neuen Testaments und der alten Kirche*, i: *Zur neutestamentlichen Textkritik* (no more published) xix (Arbeiten zur Kirchengeschichte, 19; Berlin, 1931).

—— *Lehrbuch der Dogmengeschichte*, 5th edn., 3 vols. (Tübingen, 1931).

—— *Geschichte der altchristlichen Literatur bis Eusebius*, 4 pts. in 2 vols. (Leipzig, 1958).

HARRIS, J. RENDEL, 'Hermas in Arcadia', *JBL* 21 (1887), 69–83.

—— 'Appendix: On the Common Origin of Codices א and B', *Stichometry* (London, 1893), 69–89.

—— *Hermas in Arcadia and Other Essays* (Cambridge, 1896).

—— 'Marcion and the Canon', *Expository Times*, 18 (1906–7), 392–4.

HARRISON, P. N., *The Problem of the Pastoral Epistles* (Oxford, 1921).

—— *Polycarp's Two Epistles to the Philippians* (Cambridge, 1936).

HATCH, W. H. P., 'The Position of Hebrews in the Canon of the New Testament', *HTR* 29 (1936), 133–51.

HEARD, R. G., 'The Old Gospel Prologues', *JTS*, NS 6 (1955), 1–16.

HEFELE, C. J., *A History of the Councils of the Church from the Original Documents*, trans. H. N. Oxenham, ii (Edinburgh, 1876).

HESSE, F. H., *Das Muratorische Fragment* (Giessen, 1873).

HILGENFELD, A., *Der Kanon und die Kritik des Neuen Testaments in ihrer geschichtlichen Ausbildung und Gestaltung, nebst Herstellung und Beleuchtung des Muratorischen Bruchstucks* (Halle, 1863).

—— *Hermae Pastor* (Leipzig, 1873).

—— *Historisch-kritische Einleitung in das Neue Testament* (Leipzig, 1875).

—— review of Huckstadt, *Über das pseudotertullianische Gedicht Adversus Marcionem*, *ZWT* 19 (1876), 154–9.

HOFFMAN, R. J., *Marcion: On the Restitution of Christianity: An Essay on the Development of Radical Paulinist Theology in the Second Century* (Chicago, 1984).

HOLL, K., 'Über Zeit und Heimat des pseudotertullianischen Gedichts adv. Marcionem', *Gesammelte Aufsätze*, iii (Tübingen, 1928), 13–53.

HORNSCHUH, M., 'Acts of Andrew', trans. E. Best, in Wilhelm Schneemelcher (ed.), *New Testament Apocrypha* (Philadelphia, 1964), 390–425.

HORT, F. J. A., 'Arsinous', *DCB* i (London, 1877), 174.

—— 'Bardaisan', ibid. 250–60.

HOWARD, W. F., 'The Anti-Marcionite Prologues to the Gospels', *Expository Times*, 47 (1935–6), 534–8.

HOWORTH, H. H., 'The Influence of St. Jerome on the Canon of the Western Church. 1', *JTS* 10 (1908–9), 481–96.

—— 'The Influence of St. Jerome on the Canon of the Western Church. 2', *JTS* 11 (1909–10), 321–47.

—— 'The Influence of St. Jerome on the Canon of the Western Church. 3', *JTS* 13 (1911–12), 1–19.

—— 'The Decretal of Damasus', *JTS* 14 (1913), 321–37.

HUCKSTADT, E., *Über das pseudotertullianische Gedicht Adversus Marcionem* (Leipzig, 1875).

JAMES, M. R., *The Apocryphal New Testament: Being the Apocryphal Gospels, Acts, Epistles, and Apocalypses with Other Narratives and Fragments* (Oxford, 1924).

JAMES, M. R., 'The Rainer Fragment of the Apocalypse of Peter', *JTS* 32 (1931), 270–9.

JEFFREY, A., 'The Canon of the Old Testament', *The Interpreter's Bible*, i (New York, 1952), 32–45.

JEPSEN, A., 'Kanon und Text des Alten Testaments', *Theologische Literaturzeitung*, 74 (1949), 65–74.

JOHNSON, A. C., GEHMAN, H. S., and KASE, E. H., *The John H. Scheide Biblical Papyri: Ezekiel* (Princeton, 1938).

JOLY, R., *Hermas: Le Pasteur* (Paris, 1958).

—— 'Hermas et le Pasteur', *VC* 21 (1967), 201–18.

JÜLICHER, A., *An Introduction to the New Testament*, trans. J. Ward (London, 1904).

KATZ, P., 'The Johannine Epistles in the Muratorian Canon', *JTS*, NS 8 (1957), 273–4.

KELLY, J. N. D., *Rufinus: A Commentary on the Apostles' Creed* (Ancient Christian Writers, 20; London, 1955).

—— *The Athanasian Creed* (London, 1964).

—— *The Oxford Dictionary of Popes* (Oxford, 1986).

KENYON, F., *The Chester Beatty Biblical Papyri: Description and Texts of the Twelve Manuscripts on Papyrus of the Greek Bible*, 8 fasciculi (London, 1933–58).

—— *Our Bible and the Ancient Manuscripts*, rev. A. W. Adams (London, 1958).

KIRSCH, J. P., 'Muratorian Canon', *The Catholic Encyclopaedia*, x (London, 1911), 642.

KLOSTERMANN, E., *Apocrypha I: Reste des Petrusevangeliums, der Petrusapokalypse und des Kerygma Petri* (KT 3; Bonn, 1908).

KNOX, J., *Philemon among the Letters of Paul* (Chicago, 1935).

—— *Marcion and the New Testament* (Chicago, 1942).

—— 'A Note on the Text of Romans: An Essay in the Early History of the Canon', *NTSt* 2 (1955–6), 191–3.

KOCH, H., 'Zur Schrift Adversus aleatores', *Festgabe K. Müller* (Tübingen, 1922), 58–67.

—— 'Zu A. v. Harnacks Beweis für den amtlichen römischen Ursprung des Muratorischen Fragments', *ZNW* 25 (1926), 154–60.

KOEHLER, W., 'Zum Toleranzedikt der römischen Bischofs Calixt', *ZKG* 61 (1942), 124–35.

KÖSTER (KOESTER), H., *Synoptische Überlieferung bei den apostolischen Vätern* (TU 65; Berlin, 1957).

—— '*Γνῶμαι διάφοροι*: The Origin and Nature of Diversification in the History of Early Christianity', *HTR* 58 (1965), 279–318.

—— 'Apocryphal and Canonical Gospels', *HTR* 73 (1980), 105–30.

KUENEN, A., 'Über die Männer der großen Synagoge', *Gesammelte*

*Abhandlungen zur biblischen Wissenschaft von Dr. Abraham Kuenen* (Freiburg i. B., 1894).

KÜHN, G., *Das Muratorische Fragment* (Zurich, 1892).

KÜMMEL, W. G., *Introduction to the New Testament*, trans. H. C. Kee (London, 1975).

KURFESS, A., 'The Apocryphal Correspondence between Seneca and Paul', trans. G. Ogg, in *New Testament Apocrypha*, Wilhelm Schneemelcher (ed.), ii (Philadelphia, 1964), 133–41.

LAGRANGE, M. J., 'L'auteur du canon de Muratori', *RBib* 35 (1926), 83–8.

—— 'Le Manuscrit Sinaïtique: II. L'Origine médiate et immédiate du ms. sinaïtique', ibid. 91–3.

—— 'Le canon d'Hippolyte et le fragment de Muratori', *RBib* 42 (1933), 161–86.

—— *Introduction à l'étude du Nouveau Testament*, i. *Histoire ancienne du Canon du Noveau Testament* (Paris, 1933).

LAKE, H., and LAKE, K., *Codex Sinaiticus Petropolitanus: The New Testament, The Epistle of Barnabas, and The Shepherd of Hermas*, 2 vols. (Oxford, 1911–23).

LAKE, K., *Facsimiles of the Athos Fragments of The Shepherd of Hermas* (Oxford, 1907).

—— 'The Sinaitic and Vatican Manuscripts and the Copies Sent by Eusebius to Constantine', *HTR* 11 (1918), 32–5.

—— 'The Shepherd of Hermas', *HTR* 18 (1925), 279–80.

—— *The Text of the New Testament* (London, 1928).

LAMPE, G. W. H., *A Patristic Greek Lexicon* (Oxford, 1961).

LA PIANA, G., 'The Roman Church at the End of the Second Century', *HTR* 18 (1925), 201–77.

LARCHER, C., *Études sur le Livre de la Sagesse* (Paris, 1969).

LAWLOR, H. J., and OULTON, J. E. L., *Eusebius, Bishop of Caesarea: The Ecclesiastical History and The Martyrs of Palestine*, 2 vols. (London, 1928).

LEFORT, L. Th., 'Le Pasteur d'Hermas: En Copte-Sahidique', *Le Muséon* 51 (1938), 239–76.

LEIMAN, S., *The Canonization of the Hebrew Scripture* (Hamden, Conn., 1976).

LEWIS, A. S., *Catalogue of the Syriac MSS in the Convent of S. Catherine on Mount Sinai* (Studia Sinaitica, 1; London, 1894).

—— *The Old Syriac Gospels* (London, 1910).

LIETZMANN, H., *Das Muratorische Fragment und die monarchianischen Prologe zu den Evangelien* (KT 1; Bonn, 1908).

LIGHTFOOT, J. B., *The Apostolic Fathers*, rev. edn, 2 pts. in 5 vols. (London, 1889, 1890).

LIGHTFOOT, J. B., *Saint Paul's Epistles to the Colossians and to Philemon* (New York, 1875).

—— *Saint Paul's Epistle to the Philippians* (London, 1891).

LINDSAY, W. M., *The Latin Language* (Oxford, 1894).

LIPSIUS, R. A., *Chronologie der römischen Bischöfe bis zur Mitte des vierten Jahrhunderts* (Kiel, 1869).

MCFAYDEN, D., 'The Occasion of the Domitianic Persecution', *AJT* 24 (1920), 46–66.

MACKNIGHT, W. J., 'The Letter to the Laodiceans', *The Biblical Review*, 16 (1932), 519–39.

MAGISTRIS, S. DE, *Daniel secundum LXX ex Tetraplis Originis* (Rome, 1772).

MANSON, T. W., 'Entry into Membership of the Early Church, Additional Note: The Johannine Epistles and the Canon of the New Testament', *JTS* 48 (1947), 32–3.

—— 'St. Paul's Letter to the Romans—and Others', *BJRL* 31 (1948), 224–40.

MARSHALL, J. T., 'Eldad and Modad, Book of', *A Dictionary of the Bible*, ed. J. Hastings, i (Edinburgh, 1898), 676.

MARTIN, V., and KASSER, R., *Papyrus Bodmer XIV* (Cologny-Geneva, 1961).

MARTINI, C., *Ambrosiaster. De Auctore, Operibus, Theologia* (Rome, 1944).

MAURER, Ch., 'Apocalypse of Peter', trans. D. Hill, in Wilhelm Schneemelcher (ed.), *New Testament Apocrypha*, ii (Philadelphia, 1964), 663–83.

MERCATI, G., 'Anonymi Chiliastae in Matthaeum Fragmenta', in *Varia Sacra* (Studi e Testi, 11; Rome, 1903), 1–49.

MERKEL, H., 'Widersprüche zwischen den Evangelien', *WUNT* 13 (1971), 56–62.

METZGER, B. M., *The Text of the New Testament: Its Transmission, Corruption, and Restoration* (Oxford, 1964).

—— *The Early Versions of the New Testament* (Oxford, 1977).

—— *The Canon of the New Testament* (Oxford, 1987).

METZGER, M., *Les Constitutions apostoliques* (SCh 320; Paris, 1985).

MEYER, R., 'The Canon and the Apocrypha in Judaism', *TDNT* iii (1965), 978–87.

MILBURN, R. L. P., 'The Persecution of Domitian', *CQR* 139–40 (1944–5), 154–64.

MILNE, H. J. M., and SKEAT, T. C., *Scribes and Correctors of the Codex Sinaiticus* (London, 1938).

MITTON, C. L., *The Epistle to the Ephesians: Its Authorship, Origin, and Purpose* (Oxford, 1951).

—— *The Formation of the Pauline Corpus of Letters* (London, 1955).

MOHRMANN, C., 'Les origines de la latinité chrétienne à Rome', *VC* 3 (1949), 67–106, 163–83.

—— 'Le latin langue de la chrétienté occidentale', *Aevum*, 24 (1950), 133–61.

—— 'Quelques observations sur l'originalité de la littérature latine chrétienne', *Rivista di storia della chiesa in Italia*, 4 (1950), 153–63.

—— 'L'étude de la latinité chrétienne: État de la question méthodes, résultats', *Conférences de l'Institut de linguistique de l'Université de Paris*, 10 (1950–1), 125–41.

MOMMSEN, Th., *Über den Chronographen vom Jahre 354 mit einem Anhange über die Quellen der Chronik des Hieronymus* (Leipzig, 1850).

—— 'Zur lateinischen Stichometrie', *Hermes*, 21 (1886), 142–56.

MOORE, G. F., *Judaism in the First Centuries of the Christian Era: The Age of Tannaim*, 3 vols. (Cambridge, 1927).

MOULE, C. F. D., *The Birth of the New Testament* (London, 1962).

MÜLLER, M., *Untersuchungen zum Carmen adversus Marcionitas* (Ochsenfurt, 1936).

MUNCK, J., *Paul and the Salvation of Mankind*, trans. F. Clarke (London, 1959).

MUNDLE, W., 'Die Herkunft der "Marcionitische" Prologe zu den Paulischen Briefen', *ZNW* 24 (1925), 56–77.

MURATORI, L. A., *Antiquitates Italicae Medii Aevi*, 6 vols. (Milan, 1738–48).

NESTLE, E., *Introduction to the Textual Criticism of the Greek New Testament*, trans. W. Edie (London, 1901).

OEHLER, F., *Quinti Septimi Florentis Tertulliani quae supersunt omnia*, 3 vols. (Leipzig, 1853).

OEPKE, A., '*Βίβλοι ἀπόκρυφοι* in Christianity', *TDNT* iii (1965), 987–1000.

OPITZ, L. H., *Athanasius Werke*, 9 vols. (Berlin, 1935–41).

OULTON, J. E. L., 'Rufinus's Translation of the Church History of Eusebius', *JTS* 30 (1928–9), 150–74.

OXE, A., *Prolegomena de Carmine adversus Marcionitas* (Leipzig, 1888).

PERNVEDEN, L., *The Concept of the Church in the Shepherd of Hermas*, trans. I. and N. Reeves (Lund, 1966).

PERRIN, N., and DULING, D. C., *The New Testament: An Introduction* (London, 1982).

PETERSON, P. M., *Andrew, Brother of Simon Peter: His History and His Legends* (Novum Testamentum, suppl. 1; Leiden, 1958).

PFEIFFER, R., *History of Classical Scholarship from the Beginnings to the End of the Hellenistic Age* (Oxford, 1968).

PHILLIPS, G., *The Doctrine of Addai, the Apostle* (London, 1876).

PIEDAGNEL, A., *Catéchèses mystagogiques* (SCh 126; Paris, 1966).

QUASTEN, J., *Patrology*, 3 vols. (Westminster, Md., 1953).

QUINN, J. D., 'P$^{46}$—The Pauline Canon?', *CBQ* 36 (1974), 379–85.

QUISPEL, G., 'De Brief aan de Laodicensen een Marcionitische vervalsing', *Nederlands Theologisch Tijdschrift*, 5 (1950), 43–6.

—— 'The Gospel of Thomas and the New Testament', *VC* 11 (1957), 189–207.

—— and GRANT, R. M., 'Note on the Petrine Apocrypha', *VC* 6 (1952), 31–2.

RAMSAY, W. M., *The Church in the Roman Empire before A.D. 170* (London, 1893).

RAUSCHEN, G., 'Monumenta Minora Saeculi Secundi', *FP* 3 (1914), 24–34.

REIDER, J., *The Book of Wisdom* (New York, 1957).

REILING, J., *Hermas and Christian Prophecy: A Study of the Eleventh Mandate* (Leiden, 1973).

REUSS, E., *Die Geschichte der heiligen Schriften Neuen Testaments* (Brunswick, 1853).

RITTER, S., 'Il Fragmento Muratoriano', *Rivista di archeologia cristiana*, 3 (1926), 226–31.

ROBERTS, B. J., 'The Dead Sea Scrolls and the Old Testament Scriptures', *BJRL* 36 (1953–4), 75–96.

ROBERTS, C. H., 'The Christian Book and the Greek Papyri', *JTS* 50 (1949), 155–68.

ROBINSON, JOHN A. T., *Redating the New Testament* (London, 1976).

ROBINSON, J. ARMITAGE, *A Collation of the Athos Codex of the Shepherd of Hermas* (Cambridge, 1888).

—— *The Passion of S. Perpetua together with an Appendix of the Scillitan Martyrdom* (TxSt 1/2; Cambridge, 1891).

—— *Barnabas, Hermas, and the Didache* (London, 1920).

—— and JAMES, M. R., *The Gospel according to Peter and the Revelation of Peter* (London, 1892).

ROBINSON, T. H., 'The Authorship of the Muratorian Canon', *The Expositor*, 7th ser., 1 (1906), 481–95.

ROTTENMANNER, O., 'S. Augustin sur l'auteur de l'épître aux Hébreux', *RBén* 18 (1901), 257–61.

ROUTH, M. J., *Reliquiae Sacrae*, 2nd edn., 5 vols. (Oxford, 1846–8).

RUWET, J., 'Les "Antilegomena" dans les œuvres d'Origène', *Biblica*, 23 (1942), 18–42.

—— 'Clément d'Alexandrie: Canon des Écritures et apocryphes', *Biblica*, 29 (1948), 391–408.

RYDER, H. I. D., 'Harnack on the "De Aleatoribus"', *The Dublin Review*, 3rd ser., 22/43 (1889), 82–98.

SALMON, G., 'Hermas (2)', *DCB* ii (London, 1880), 912–21.
—— 'Miltiades (1)', *DCB* iii (London, 1882), 916–17.
—— 'Muratorian Fragment', ibid. 1000–3.
SANDAY, W., *The Gospels in the Second Century: An Examination of the Critical Part of a Work entitled 'Supernatural Religion'* (London, 1876).
—— 'The Cheltenham List of the Canonical Books, and the Writings of Cyprian', *StudBib* 3 (1891), 217–303.
SANDERS, H. A., *A Third-Century Codex of the Epistles of St Paul* (Ann Arbor, Mich., 1935).
SANDERS, J. A., 'Cave 11 Surprises and the Question of Canon', *McCormick Quarterly* 12 (1968), 84–98.
SANDERS, J. N., *The Fourth Gospel in the Early Church: Its Origin and Influence on Christian Theology up to Irenaeus* (Cambridge, 1943).
—— 'John, Gospel of', *IDB* ii (New York, 1962), 932–46.
SCHAEFER, A. and MEINERTZ, M., *Einleitung in das Neue Testament* (Paderborn, 1949).
SCHÄFER, K. Th., 'Marius Victorinus und die Marcionitischen Prologe zu den Paulusbriefen', *RBén* 80 (1970), 7–16.
SCHAFERDIEK, K., and SCHNEEMELCHER, W., 'Introduction. Second and Third Century Acts of Apostles', trans. G. C. Stead, in Wilhelm Schneemelcher (ed.), *New Testament Apocrypha*, ii (Philadelphia, 1965), 167–88.
SCHMIDT, C., *Die alten Petrusakten* (TU 24/1; Leipzig, 1903).
—— 'Studien zu den alten Petrusakten, II. Die Komposition', *ZKG* 45 (1926), 481–513.
SCHMITHALS, W., 'Zur Abfassung und ältesten Sammlung der Paulinischen Hauptbriefe', *ZNW* 51 (1960), 225–45.
—— 'On the Composition and Earliest Collection of the Major Epistles of Paul', *Paul and the Gnostics*, trans. J. E. Streely (Nashville, 1972), 239–74.
SCHNEEMELCHER, WILHELM (ed.), *New Testament Apocrypha*, trans. R. McL. Wilson, 2 vols. (Philadelphia, 1963, 1965).
SCHODDE, G. H., *Hêrmâ Nabî: The Ethiopic Version of Pastor Hermae Examined* (Leipzig, 1876).
SCHUCHARDT, H., *Der Vokalismus des Vulgärlateins*, 3 vols. (Leipzig, 1866–8).
SCHÜRER, E., *A History of the Jewish People in the Time of Jesus Christ*, rev. G. Vermes, F. Millar, and M. Goodman, trans. S. Taylor and P. Christies (Edinburgh, 1975–87).
SCHWARTZ, E., 'Zwei Predigten Hippolyts', *Sitzungsberichte der Bayerischen Akademie der Wissenschaften*, philos.-philol.-hist. Klasse, 1936, fasc. 3.
SEMLER, J. S., *Abhandlung von freier Untersuchung des Kanons nebst*

*Antwort auf die Tübingische Vertheidigung der Apocalypsis*, 4 vols. (Halle, 1771–6).

Siker, J. S., 'The Canonical Status of the Catholic Epistles in the Syriac New Testament', *JTS*, NS 38 (1987), 311–40.

Smith, A. S., *The Old Syriac Gospels* (London, 1910).

Snyder, G. F., *The Shepherd of Hermas*, in *The Apostolic Fathers*, vi (London, 1968).

Souter, A., 'Reasons for Regarding Hilarius (Ambrosiaster) as the Author of the Mercati–Turner Anecdoton', *JTS* 5 (1903–4), 608–21.

—— 'The Original Home of Codex Claromontanus ($D^{Paul}$)', *JTS* 6 (1904–5), 240–3.

—— *The Text and Canon of the New Testament* (London, 1913).

Stendahl, K., 'The Apocalypse of John and the Epistles of Paul in the Muratorian Fragment', in W. Klassen and G. F. Snyder (eds.), *Current Issues in New Testament Interpretation* (London, 1962), 239–45.

Stevenson, J., *Studies in Eusebius* (*Pamphilus*) (Cambridge, 1929).

Streeter, B. H., *The Primitive Church: Studied with Special Reference to the Origins of the Christian Ministry* (London, 1929).

—— *The Four Gospels: A Study of Origins*, 4th edn. (London, 1930).

Sundberg, A. C., Jr. 'The Old Testament of the Early Church (A Study in Canon)', *HTR* 51 (1958), 205–26.

—— *The Old Testament of the Early Church* (HTSt 20; London, 1964).

—— 'Dependent Canonicity in Irenaeus and Tertullian', *StudEvan* 3/2 (1964), 403–9.

—— 'The Protestant Old Testament Canon: Should It Be Re-examined?', *CBQ* 28 (1966), 194–203.

—— 'The "Old Testament": A Christian Canon', *CBQ* 30 (1968), 143–55.

—— 'Towards a Revised History of the New Testament Canon', *StudEvan* 4/1 (1968), 452–61.

—— 'The Making of the New Testament Canon', *The Interpreter's One-Volume Commentary on the Bible*, ed. C. M. Laymon (Nashville, 1971), 1216–24.

—— 'Canon Muratori: A Fourth-Century List', *HTR* 66 (1973), 1–41.

—— 'The Bible Canon and the Christian Doctrine of Inspiration', *Interpretation*, 29 (1975), 352–71.

—— 'Canon of the New Testament', *IDB*, *Supplement* (Nashville, 1976), 136–40.

Telfer, W., 'Cyril of Jerusalem and Nemesius of Emesa', *LCC* 4 (1955), 30–43.

Thompson, E. M., *Facsimile of the Codex Alexandrinus*, 4 vols. (London, 1879–83).

Tischendorf, C., *Codex Sinaiticus* (London, 1934).

Tregelles, S. P., *Canon Muratorianus* (Oxford, 1867).

Turner, C. H., 'Appendix to W. Sanday's Article: "The Cheltenham List of the Canonical Books, and the Writings of Cyprian"', *StudBib* 3 (1891), 304–25.

—— 'Latin Lists of the Canonical Books: 1. The Roman Council under Damasus, A.D. 382', *JTS* 1 (1899–1900), 554–60.

—— 'Latin Lists of the Canonical Books: 2. An Unpublished Stichometrical List from the Freisingen MS of Canons', *JTS* 2 (1900–1), 236–53.

—— 'An Exegetical Fragment of the Third Century', *JTS* 5 (1903–4), 218–41.

—— 'Latin Lists of the Canonical Books: 3. From Pope Innocent's Epistle to Exsuperius of Toulouse (A.D. 405)', *JTS* 13 (1911–12), 77–82.

—— 'Notes on the Apostolic Constitutions. II. The Apostolic Canons', *JTS* 16 (1914–15), 523–38.

Unnik, W. C. van, 'De la règle *Μήτε προσθεῖναι μήτε ἀφελεῖν* dans l'histoire du Canon', *VC* 3 (1949), 1–36.

—— 'The "Gospel of Truth" and the New Testament', in F. L. Cross (ed.), *The Jung Codex* (London, 1955), 79–129.

—— '*Η καινὴ διαθήκη*: A Problem in the Early History of the Canon', *StudPat* 4 (1961), 212–27.

Violet, B., *Die Esra-Apokalypse* (*IV Esra*), 2 vols. (GCS 18, 32; Leipzig, 1910–24).

Vööbus, A., *Researches on the Circulation of the Peshitta in the Middle of the Fifth Century* (Pinneberg, 1948).

—— *Studies in the History of the Gospel Text in Syriac* (Louvain, 1951).

—— *Early Versions of the New Testament: Manuscript Studies* (Stockholm, 1954).

Vouaux, L., *Les Acts de Pierre, Introduction, Textes, traduction et commentaire* (Paris, 1922).

Waitz, H., *Das pseudotertullianische Gedicht Adversus Marcionem* (Darmstadt, 1900).

Wallace-Hadrill, D. S., *Eusebius of Caesarea* (London, 1960).

Westcott, B. F., *A General Survey of the History of the Canon of the New Testament*, 4th edn. (London, 1875).

—— 'Canon of Scripture, The; IV. The history of the Canon of the New Testament', *Dictionary of the Bible*, ed. H. B. Hackett, i (London, 1860), 368–76.

—— *The Epistle to the Hebrews* (London, 1892).

Whittaker, M., *Der Hirt des Hermas*, rev. edn. (GCS 48; Berlin, 1967).

Wiles, M. F., *The Spiritual Gospel: The Interpretation of the Fourth Gospel in the Early Church* (Cambridge, 1960).

Wilson, W., 'The Career of the Prophet Hermas', *HTR* 20 (1927), 21–62.

Workman, H. B., *Persecution in the Early Church: A Chapter in the History of Renunciation* (London, 1906).

Zahn, T., *Der Hirt des Hermas* (Gotha, 1868).

—— *Geschichte des neutestamentlichen Kanons*, 2 vols. (Leipzig, 1886–92).

—— *Grundriß der Geschichte des neutestamentalichen Kanons* (Leipzig, 1904).

—— 'Ein alter Kommentar zu Matthäus', *NKZ* 16 (1905), 419–27.

—— 'Muratorian Canon', *The New Schaff–Herzog Religious Encyclopedia*, ed. S. M. Jackson, viii (New York, 1910), 53–6.

—— 'Miscellanea: II. Hippolytus, der Verfasser des Muratorischen Kanons', *NKZ* 33 (1922), 417–36.

# GENERAL INDEX